*Herbs for the Kitchen*

*by Irma Goodrich Mazza*

Herbs for the Kitchen
Accent on Seasoning

# HERBS
## FOR THE
## KITCHEN

### by Irma Goodrich Mazza

*Third Edition, Revised*

BOSTON
LITTLE, BROWN AND COMPANY
TORONTO

B

The author is grateful to Little, Brown and Company for permission
to reprint the poem "My Dear, How Did You Think Up This Delicious
Salad?" from *Verses from 1929 On* by Ogden Nash. Copyright 1935
by Ogden Nash, renewed © 1963 by Ogden Nash.

Library of Congress Cataloging in Publication Data
Mazza, Irma Goodrich.
  Herbs for the kitchen.
  Includes index.
  1. Cookery (Herbs) I. Title.
TX819.H4M35    1976        641.6'5'7        75-25639
ISBN 0-316-552151-PBK.

BP

Designed by D. Christine Benders

*Published simultaneously in Canada
by Little, Brown & Company (Canada) Limited*

PRINTED IN THE UNITED STATES OF AMERICA

This book I dedicate to the two persons without whom it could not have been written: *my mother*, who gave me a life to live; and *my husband*, who has helped me to learn how to live it.

Wherefore did Nature pour her bounties forth
With such a full and undrawing hand,
Covering the earth with odours, fruits and flocks,
Thronging the sea with spawn innumerable,
But all to please and sate the curious taste?

— MILTON

# Acknowledgments

For their heartening interest and helpful cooperation during the development and writing of this book, I wish to thank my friends Mr. and Mrs. August Vollmer, Mr. and Mrs. James E. Wales, Mr. and Mrs. John W. Lawton, Mr. and Mrs. G. Giovannini, Mr. and Mrs. U. Giuliano, Mrs. F. P. Walker, Mrs. H. J. Hall, Mrs. J. L. Rogers, Mrs. Helen Lyman, Mrs. Theodore Bernardi, Mrs. Angelo Scampini, and others.

# Contents

# *About the Illustrations*

Each illustration in this book carries a letter from A to I that refers to the original source of the illustration as listed below:

A        From *Hortus Sanitatis* or *Gart Der Gesundheit*, published by Peter Schoeffer. Mainz, 1485.

B        From *Herbarius*, published by Peter Schoeffer. Mainz, 1484.

C        From *The Herball or General Historie of Plantes* by John Gerard. London, 1597.

D        From *The Vegetable Garden* by Mm. Vilmorin-Andrieux. English edition published by John Murray under the direction of W. Robinson. London, 1905.

E        From *Commentarii in Libros Sex Pedacii Dioscoridis* by Petrus Andreas Matthiolus. Venice, 1565

F         From *De Historia Stirpium* by Leonhard Fuchs. Basle, 1542.

G         From *Commentarii in Libros Sex Pedacii Dioscoridis* by Petrus Andreas Matthiolus. Venice, 1554.

H         From *Historia Generalis Plantarum*, edited by J. de Moulins (or Molinaeus) and published by Jacques D'Alechamps. Lyons, 1586–1587.

I          From Handbook of *Plant and Floral Ornament from Early Herbals* by Richard G. Hatton. Dover Publications, Inc. New York, 1960.

# How This Book
# Came to Be Written

ONCE there was a girl who had lived all the years of her life in a real American home, with its many attendant blessings. She took food and its taste for granted, thinking it a subject of little scope which she would master someday, when she had use for the knowledge.

Then she married. Her husband was a Latin. At mealtimes he upset her terribly with his notions about what to eat.

He ate lettuce by the bowlful, with French dressing. He refused boiled vegetables "seasoned" with butter, salt, and pepper, saying they were flat. He adored onions, and averred that garlic was a part of the equipment of all fine cooks.

He clamored for the flavor of herbs in his food, and urged his wife to grow them herself, though the family estate was no more than a narrow box outside the kitchen window. He brought home a gallon of olive oil, when the marriage certificate was only a few days old. When his lavishness was questioned he expressed an opinion that olive oil was the lubricant of the gods.

When she gave him creamed macaroni they had their first quarrel, and he said that presenting him with such a dish was practically equivalent to trying to poison him.

What was a girl to do? Of course it was hard on her, having her complacent notions about food knocked in the head by a husband who yearned after Chicken Hunter Style and *Spaghetti alla marinara,* but she wasn't too old or too stubborn to learn.

She turned over a new leaf. But her husband also made concessions. While she admitted the utter loveliness of onions, garlic, olive oil, and herb seasonings, he conceded that one does not have to eat elaborately to eat well. He even granted that butter has a place in cookery, and that all food should not always be highly seasoned.

Really, the new leaf was theirs, not just hers.

She experimented with food, with flavor, and with simplicity, strong in the belief that the wages of rich eating is indigestion. To make her cooking interesting yet keep it healthful was her aim.

Fourteen years of feeding husband and friends, as well as self, have brought no complaints or damage suits; no ruined dispositions, which doctors say are signs of internal strife.

Somewhere along in those years she began to notice the strange behavior of friends. While no one actually fainted on the doorstep and waited to be carried in, people did drop around suspiciously near eating hours. Invited guests never suggested coming after dinner, but always asked without hesitancy, "What time do you eat?"

Every dinner turned out to be a cooking school, with the feminine contingent in the kitchen, and the male guests leaning in through the door. They watched. They asked questions, just as she had done fourteen years before.

"How do you use garlic? Isn't it heavy on the breath? What are the best ways of using olive oil? Won't salad oil do just as well? What on earth are those funny green and dried leaves you are always throwing into food?" These and like queries they flung at her continuously.

Finally she decided that since she apparently would have to go on and on answering those questions for the rest of her life she might as well do something sensible about it.

So she went to work at those questions. She has answered them all. In short, she has taken that new leaf she and her husband turned over, added all the other leaves into which it developed, and bound them into this book.

We hope it answers all your questions, even those you have never voiced. We hope it helps you to bring the products of an herb garden into your kitchen, mix them with your foods, and learn the variety and romance of simple savor.

*Herbs for the Kitchen*

# ✻ ONE ✻

# *A Parade of Herbs*

"Flavor," a famous gourmet once said, "is the soul of food."

He should have gone one step farther, adding, ". . . and herbs are the soul of flavor."

America is interested in herbs. All over our land nurseries are gathering and offering lists of these sweet revivals of other days. Magazines are publishing hints for the use of herbs in modern life. Up and down the country men and women are wakening to a new-old form of food seasoning that is becoming daily more popular.

There are some to whom herbs and their use will never be more than a passing vogue, followed for a time, then soon forgotten. But to those versatile ones who really learn the secret of cooking with herbs, a fascinating path of culinary discovery and accomplishment will be disclosed.

All the wide world of vegetation blooms and buds for you; the thorn and the thistle which the earth casts forth . . . are to you the kindliest servants; no dying petal nor drooping tendril is so feeble as to have no help for you.

Regardless of whom or what John Ruskin actually had in mind when he wrote those words, he might easily have been speaking of a cook exploring the wealth of culinary herbs, for who else so cunningly turns Nature to his or her good account?

To season with herbs one needs no spices from far lands, no exotic condiments; nothing but a plot of ground or a box in a sunny window, a few seeds, some plants. It is as simple as that, the stocking of your kitchen with herbs, those flavors which are second to none.

Herbs are the seasonings of the people, the seasonings one can always have, no matter what the condition of world commerce or the pocketbook.

Herbs are as old as the first blade of grass on a cooling earth. Man, in his quest for variety in foods, was not slow to discover that some plants have characteristic fragrances that tickled even his green palate. The true story of their first use is not known, nor the land where this occurred, for the story of every country is redolent of herbs, and the world's acquaintance with them is of patently long standing.

Written records of history bear testimony to their use in the earliest known times. Theophrastus, Pliny, Aristophon, Virgil and Horace are only a few of the ancients who wrote of herbs and their place in the life of other times. Such fragrant plants as mint, rue, and cumin are mentioned often in the Bible. Picturing Eden as Milton painted it in *Paradise Lost,* we hear Eve's words with peculiar understanding:

> Adam, well may we labour, still to dress
> This Garden, still to tend plant, herb and flower.

Wherever man went, herbs were there for him, marking their intimate tracery through his history; Mithridates eating each morning his cakes of rue, to counteract poison which might have been in his food; Casanova chewing sweet herbs to perfume his breath; Charlemagne choosing the herbs for his royal gardens; the companions of Columbus sowing borage on Isabella Island; the Pilgrims wearing mugwort leaves in their shoes to relieve fatigue; early San Francisco bearing first the name of "Yerba Buena" (the good herb), for the trailing wild mint that grew so riotously on its hills.

Old maps of London are almost fragrant when one stoops and reads such names as Great Saffron Hill, Camomile Street, Rosemary Lane, Royal Mint Street, and sees the Herb Market that until 1755 stood in Leadenhall.

Many herbs grow wild and native to the soil of the United States. Others, brought by the first comers from Europe, have become naturalized, until this is a richly sweet land of ours. Up to a few generations ago herbs were used in America as freely as in Europe. They were in every household garden, their use a part of every woman's knowledge.

In the light of this, it would seem impossible that they could be forgotten. But Time can so swiftly obliterate even the memory of the thing no longer before one's eyes! Interest in herbs languished, no one understands just why. Kitchen gardens no longer boasted the dainty thyme, the silver marjoram, and the rest of the sweet kitchen aids of other ages. We, whose grandmothers mingled herb scents with food to their undying fame, today find our herbal experience limited to the ubiquitous sage, the monotonous "Poultry Seasoning."

It is sad truth that when we Americans gave up herb culture and herb cookery we relinquished something hard to recover, and lost infinitely by its abandonment; but now at last we are being reintroduced to these magic seasonings, and taking to them like the proverbial duck to the village pond.

Since herbs are such completely forgotten lore, their introduction to the average American will have to be as between total strangers. Each herb must be presented. studied, used, and, if possible, cultivated, so that we will know and appreciate it. They all are worthy of such concentration, and well worth knowing, growing, using, and loving.

My dictionary defines *herb* as:

A seed plant whose stem does not develop woody tissue, as that of a shrub or tree, but persists only long enough for the development of flowers and seeds. Herbs may be annual, biennial or perennial, according to the length of life of their roots.

For practical purposes, however, herbs have come to be understood as those plants whose leaves, stems, or seeds have aromatic or medicinal qualities, so that they may be used as perfume, food, seasoning, or medicine.

Since we in this book are concerned first of all with food and its seasoning, let us consider herbs from that point of view. Most cooks think of *herbs* as little beyond those six primary seasoning plants of which they most often hear — mint, thyme, sage, marjoram, rosemary, and basil. When by chance they are given a glimpse of the further wealth of herbal flavor, which can help make eating and living a daily thrill, they are filled with a sense of luxury. For in addition to those six familiar herbs, there are dozens more that have real value in a home.

Since our crowded lives these days have limits, it would be foolish to insist that every beginning herbal cook equip him or herself with dozens of different herbs. It is wiser to say, "Suit your selection to your needs and your space. You can cook with a wealth of savor from plants of those six basic herbs: mint, thyme, sage, marjoram, rosemary, and basil. You can know luxury with what few you can raise in a window garden, or those you can buy dried from your grocer."

It is safe to prophesy, however, that the cook who becomes interested at first in cooking with these few will shortly become ambitious in an herbal way, and long for space to grow more herbs for the kitchen. For the love of herbs and their use is a love that grows. Experience shows that it soon expands far beyond the scope of a window garden. In this book we must plan for that expansion. First you shall be introduced to the herbs you will want at the beginning of your career, and to those you will want to add to your garden when you have more space. Then, as extra measure, there will be presented for you the other herbs which are, for the true herb gardener, "nice to have."

At least two writers have advanced the premise that "thirty herbs will make an herb garden." Looking over my garden and my menus, and picking out those plants most likely to figure in practical cookery, I amend their statement, and say that "just six herbs will make you a good cook, while twenty-five herbs will bring you culinary fame." In addition, they will make for you an interesting, well-rounded garden.

Here they are, the twenty-five perfumed handmaidens that will make of your dinners family festivals. Know them. Let them work for you.

## ANISE

*Pimpinella anisum,* annual. This herb is one of the most ancient seasonings. Its feathery lengths grew on the shores of Asia Minor, for Theophrastus listed it among the herbs worthy of a second sowing. Charlemagne ordered it for his imperial garden. Pliny urged that it be suspended near the bed, for it assured the sleeper a youthful look when he arose in the morning. It is easy to foresee a good crop of anise next year, when this gets around.

The uses of anise are not numerous, but they are important. The green leaves are refreshing additions to salads, for their delicious, piquant flavor spurs the appetite. The seeds are used in pastry and mixed with cottage or other fresh cheeses.

## BALM

*Melissa officinalis,* perennial. It was once the custom to wear balm among the clothes to "make one beloved when met"; so treasure it, modern woman. Perhaps its charm still

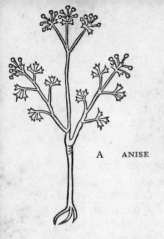

A ANISE

C BALM

holds. A minty, perfumed dark green plant, it yields its scent to the slightest touch. Sprigs newly picked lend personality to salads, and peculiar charm to tea. Its traditional use as flavoring steeped in wine cups might well be revived today.

## BORAGE

> I, Borage
> Bring alwaeis courage.

*Borago officinalis,* annual. The ancients who spun this pretty couplet also thought that borage drunk in wine makes one jolly. Poor Bacchus!

Borage is one of the prettiest of the herbs. Strong and gray-green, with flowers of heavenly blue, it is an addition to any garden. Then too, its tenderest, smallest tops and flowers are welcome in salads. Cool summer drinks are all the more refreshing if borage, flowers and all, is sunk in them and steeped therein.

## BASIL

*Ocimum basilicum,* annual. No Italian garden lacks a green bed of basil from spring till early fall. Perhaps the owners of those gardens lend ear to the East Indian belief that the house surrounded by basil will be blessed. Or they may simply know that this herb blesses the food it touches.

A  BASIL          D  BORAGE

Basil's uses are many and varied. Soups, ragouts, salads, pot cheeses, meats, sauces, and fruit drinks all are more appetizing for a bit of this seasoning. It repays one for the little work involved in growing it each year. The more it is cut the better it grows.

For winter use, dry or freeze it (pages 74 and 26–27), for basil is a warm season plant, and will not live over the winter.

## BAY

*Laurus nobilis* or *Umbellularia californica,* tree. No one who has not space and patience galore should dream of growing bay in the garden. The European bay or laurel is of no small size, while the California bay, or pepperwood, is a large tree with spreading branches. So when you design your herb garden, don't plan a bed of bay!

Dried bay leaves, if renewed each year so that they are fresh, are thoroughly satisfactory for kitchen use. Bay seasons meats, soups, relishes, poultry, and stuffings.

But *be careful.* The best of recipes have a nonchalance about bay leaves that is disarming to the uninitiated, but alarming to the experienced. They say, gaily, "Put in a bay leaf or two," as if one more or less made no difference at all. On the contrary, it makes all the difference in the world. Use bay leaves with a degree of diplomacy worthy of a European envoy, for they are powerful. Use a half leaf, or a third, but never a whole leaf unless you are entertaining an army.

## BURNET

*Sanguisorba minor,* perennial. This pretty, rosetted, bright green plant will add to the salad's savor, if you will grow it in sufficient quantity to be able to pick its tender shoots in abundance. It tastes daintily of cucumber.

Burnet also seasons pot cheeses and cream cheese for sandwiches and hors d'œuvres, but it is in the salad that it shines, and there is where it should be left, for:

> . . . salad is neither good nor fair
> If Pimpinella [burnet] is not there.

## CARAWAY

*Carum carvi,* biennial. Once the seeds of caraway were prescribed for bringing bloom to the cheeks of pale-faced maidens. Today we know that they are for flavoring, not doctoring; but if good food induces good health, then they still fulfill their health-bringing destiny.

Besides their classic use in cookies and coffee cakes, caraway seeds in cream cheese, or strewn over roasting pork, contrive a new flavor. Or perhaps you will care to follow the aged custom of Trinity College, Cambridge, where a saucer of these savory seeds invariably accompanies roasted apples.

Not only caraway's seeds, but its leaves, are piquant in cookery. Pluck the plumy tips and add them to salads, for they are racy and delicious, if used in moderation.

## CELERY

*Apium graveolens,* biennial. America eats its head celery religiously, and likes it. But leaf celery, as seasoning, is almost unknown. Some books give directions for drying celery tops for use in soup. But no one tells the secret of reveling in the spiced pungency that fresh celery leaves give salads and cooked dishes.

In the Italian quarter of any American city that secret is open for all to read. In the tiny kitchen gardens, green plots literally snatched from encroaching pavements, one finds beds of unbanked, leafing celery plants, ready for the knife of the cook. For such a bed celery is sown each spring, and is allowed to grow without hilling or thinning. It will grow about eight or ten inches tall, with tender leaves. Cut it recklessly, for it continues to spring up.

## CHERVIL

*Anthriscus cerefolium*, annual. Chervil is the salad herb *par excellence*. Like a particularly delicate parsley in appearance, it is even more sweet and aromatic. One of the *fines herbes*, it combines well with other herbs, and forms the basis of many mixed herb seasonings. Curled chervil is the most satisfactory type to raise. Salads and soups are better for its presence, as are eggs, cheese, and some meats.

## CHIVES

*Allium schœnoprasum*, perennial. "Little brother to the onion" — that is the chive. Pots of chives appear in grocers' shops and vegetable stores, a dollar's worth of goodness for a few cents.

Europe learned to use chives as early as the sixteenth century. In our own land the Dutch settlers planted them in their pastures so their cows would give chive-flavored milk. I'm telling this, but not recommending it.

Chives are hardy. They like to be cut, springing up abundantly from their shorn stems. As for their uses, they are manifold. Salads, omelettes, sauces, cheese, potatoes, potato salad, all are improved by their addition. Indeed, it was once said that "the chef who makes a potato salad without chives has no soul." "And neither has the salad," might have been added.

## CORIANDER

*Coriandrum sativum*, annual. The origin of this seasoning is lost in antiquity. Athenæus, in his list of seasonings, speaks of "some fennel, anise, assafœtida, mustard and cabbage, some dry coriander." It was one of the bitter herbs ordered to be eaten for the Passover. Coriander was once thought to induce cupidity, and misers were said to have eaten of it. To-day it is a favored ingredient for the making of curry powder. In Mexico it is a frequently used seasoning, and is cooked into Spanish rice, lentils, and meat dishes.

The Chinese consider coriander their own precious green seasoning and call it, unequivocally, "Chinese parsley." Markets in San Francisco's Chinatown sell it in bunches for cooking and garnishing.

But we Americans are chary of fresh coriander, for we fear its breathy strength. The secret of liking these feathery green tips in food is to use them very sparingly, for otherwise their pungency will be too great. A very little bit, sprinkled over a cocktail of avocado topped with seasoned tomato sauce, is delightful; or mixed with finely minced onion blades, salt, pepper, and French dressing and served on sliced tomatoes it is good. But use it always with caution.

The seeds of this herb are more mild, though of the same flavor, and are good additions to meats, sauces, and pickles, if ground in a mortar first.

## CUMIN

*Cuminum cyminum*, annual. This ancient favorite hailed originally from Upper Egypt. Its seeds figure in the Bible, and were mentioned by Pliny. They are another curry ingredient, and supply a Mexican tang to meat dishes, beans, and sauces. The Germans relish them in sauerkraut.

Cumin seeds grown and harvested at home usually possess a fragrant strength greater than those bought in stores, for they are fresher.

## DILL

*Anethum graveolens,* annual. We moderns are prone to think of the juicy dill pickle as a development of our own times. Actually, these tasty morsels were eaten as early as the seventeenth century. Our grandmothers used dill seeds as "meetin' seeds," nibbling them in church to keep their minds off the dullness of long sermons.

Italy uses dill plentifully, calling it *aneto.* Not ony the seeds, but the tender fresh leaves, have a delightfully crisp taste that peps up eggs, cheese, meat, fish, salads, potatoes, avocados, or beans. It is a sort of all-around herb, the tool of the creative cook.

## FENNEL

*Fœniculum officinalis,* annual. Athenæus loved fennel, saying of it:

> Be sure that for the future you remember
> The ever-glorious marathon for good,
> When you do all from time to time add [fennel] to your pickled olives.

Charlemagne included fennel in his list of garden plants to serve his own household, perhaps to be used in turn by each of his nine wives.

Tender fennel leaves mixed with salads are delicious. The seeds cooked with fish, or a very few in fruit pies or in sauces, give them something extra in the way of taste.

Florence fennel, *Fœniculum dulce,* is grown somewhat like celery, and is eaten the same way. Its blades are so crisp and sweet that they rival celery for those who know them as a winter table green. Grated into green salads they prove the delight and bewilderment of guests.

## SWEET MARJORAM

*Origanum majorana,* perennial, except in severe climates, where it is treated as an annual. Sweet marjoram is one of the Big Six — a Kitchen Magician. It is to cookery what a set of accessories is to a costume — the finishing touch. It is a pretty plant, richly fragrant, with fascinating little knots from which the flowers spring. This habit of growth inspired the lyrical early name of "Knotted Marjoram."

The sweeter, more subtle of the two culinary marjorams, it is used for sauces, soups, salads, meats, stuffings, and fish. The Germans use it in sausage, calling it *Wurstkraut* [sausage herb].

Marjoram was one of the old-time strewing herbs, and was also laid by the milk in the dairy, to keep it sweet.

E   BAY

## WILD MARJORAM

*Origanum vulgare,* annual in cold countries, perennial in milder climates. Perhaps you know this herb by the widely used Spanish name of *oregano.* Lucky indeed you are if you rejoice in its old name of "joy of the mountain." But whatever you call it, rest assured that if you grow it and use it it will be for you a "joy of the garden" and "pride of the kitchen." A bold-growing, pretty plant, it is covered in season with small but interesting flowers.

Generally this marjoram is used interchangeably with its sister plant. Frankly, if you have only one of the cooking marjorams you will not miss the other. This statement may call down cries of "Heretic!" on my head, but I still say that the difference in taste, while plainly discernible, is nothing to sit up nights about.

However, if you have the two, and want to understand the differences between them, use this type for practically all Spanish and Mexican dishes, for meats, beans, sauces, soups. Cook it with lamb and fresh mushrooms (see page 99), for the Italians call it *l'erba di funghi,* the mushroom herb. Put the new tips in salads and cream cheeses, and use its dried flowers and leaves in potpourri. This is the one herb I prefer dried rather than fresh, to cook into foods. Its taste is more congenial, friendlier.

## MINT (Spearmint)

*Mentha spicata,* perennial. The sturdy but bland and soft-textured leaves of this mint hold a flavor that actually revives interest in food. Long ago it was said that "the smell of mint does stir up the minde and the taste to a greedy desire of meate," and today we must admit that the claim is just.

Remember the story of Philamon and Baucis offering bread, cheese, and honey to their Olympian guests? Pliny pictured them as scouring their table with fresh mint leaves before spreading it for their guests. The bare thought sends one pining after food.

If you plant mint in your garden, watch it, for it is a bold thing. Unless you keep its straying stolons cut back it will take the garden. Restrain it, keep it well wetted, and revel in its flavor in pot cheeses, salads, salad dressings, pea soup, meat broth, potatoes, tea, ices, and the treacherous mint julep. As seasoning for beef or lamb it is pure poetry.

## NASTURTIUM

*Tropæolum majus* and *minus*, annual. If we take the word *nasturtium* apart we have two Latin words which together mean "to twist the nose." Obviously the nose-twisting quality is that warm, tantalizing pungency which the entire plant possesses, and which it delights to yield. It was always featured in old-time kitchen gardens. Both flowers and leaves were salad fare, and its round green seedpods were pickled to be used as capers.

So let us bring our nasturtiums out of their flower-garden banishment, and promote them into the ranks of the Kitchen Guard. They will work wonders for us.

## PARSLEY

*Petroselinum sativum*, biennial.

**Parsley is the crown of cookery. It once crowned man; it now crowns his food.**

But must we make every meal a perpetual coronation? The world's insistent garnishing with this ubiquitous herb of every dish that leaves the kitchen has vulgarized an otherwise noble plant. Parsley was made to be eaten, not thrust aside with forks and returned to the kitchen, thence to slip into the refuse pail.

We Americans may well reintroduce ourselves to parsley and learn that its delicate savor graces salads, sauces, soups, stews, pot cheeses, meats, and vegetable dishes. Either cooked into food or added the last two minutes of cooking, it

D BURNET

is a distinct addition to flavor. You'll eventually blush that you were ever a parsley garnisher. When you learn to use it in handfuls instead of bits, you will understand its true value in foods.

The fern-leaved or Italian variety is more tender and finer in taste than the common moss-leaved type usually grown. When it is sown in the garden, no amount of prayers will induce it to spring up quickly. In fact, its seeds germinate so slowly that it used to be said, "Parsley goes to the Devil and back again nine times before it comes up."

## ROSEMARY

*Rosmarinus officinalis*, perennial. Rosemary — "dew of the sea." Even if it were not one of my favorite cooking herbs I should still grow it, because of the music of that name.

Tiny pale blue flowers on a proud, Heaven-pointing shrub — blue because the Virgin hung her cerulean cloak on it to dry, and its white blossoms were ever after tinged with that hue in her honor — just one more of the lovely things about Rosemary, that legend.

Ladies, do you desire a "faire face"? Then, as in olden times, boil rosemary leaves in white wine and wash your faces with it. Or, if you fear nightmares, put leaves of the herb under your bed, for they were thought to dispel evil dreams.

Elliot Paul, in his *Life and Death of a Spanish Town,* describes early morning in a town whose fires were daily kindled with fagots of rosemary from the hills. The fragrance of the blue smoke rising from the chimneys is almost noticeable in the leaves of the book, so well does he tell his tale.

Another of the Big Six, rosemary is an indispensable culinary herb if any ever was. Fragrant as a flower, it glorifies meat, poultry, sauces, greens, and stuffings.

SAGE
*Salvia officinalis,* perennial.

> He that would live for aye
> Must eat sage in May.

This much-quoted couplet gives sage its traditional significance of immortality. Also the wise ones ages ago believed that if the household prospers, the sage about it grows strong.

One of the hardiest of perennials, sage starts with alacrity from seeds or cuttings and grows with little care. Perhaps that is why we here in America have elected it almost the sole survivor of a long list of herbs once in use here. If we learn to use it in discreet amounts and with the restraint it demands, it will continue in favor.

Fresh sage is more satisfactory than dried. Its smartly pointed gray leaves can be gingerly and sparingly introduced into beans, pot cheeses, salt fish, stews, duck, or geese. But it is too strong for turkey or chicken. A mixture of savory, thyme, and sweet basil flavors these fowls more subtly.

SUMMER SAVORY
*Satureia hortensis,* annual. This venerable herb is the beloved *Bohnenkraut* of the Germans, so called because it is so delicious as seasoning for beans. Also it is the standard spicing for turkey and chicken in England. Both leaves and flow-

ers are used to flavor, their tang doing wonders with the dishes for which they have real affinity. Such foods as poultry stuffings, salads, peas, pork, green beans, rice, horse-radish sauce are summer savory's real domain.

## WINTER SAVORY

*Satureia montana,* perennial. This one is summer savory's bashful cousin. Though the other herb has a superior flavor, this does nicely in many dishes. Virgil sang impartially of the savories, bowing figuratively to each in turn.

Winter savory can be used in all the foods where summer savory is recommended by increasing the amount slightly Also it is recommended in fish dishes. It will supply fo delight when its summer kin has been killed by winter's cold

## TARRAGON

*Artemisia dracunculus,* perennial. The Society of Gour mets might well erect a memorial to tarragon, the "little dragon," for it has added much glamor to menus, much flavor to food. We in this country have just begun to delve into its potentialities as a seasoning.

Whatever its true origin, Gerarde gives a charming if somewhat fantastic explanation of it:

> . . . the seed of flax put into a radish root or a sea onion,
> and being thus set, doth bring forth this herb tarragon.

Whimsical botany aside, tarragon is a valuable herb, and one to grow for yourself if possible, for it is decidedly at its best when fresh. But remember, real tarragon cannot be raised from seed. It propagates only from cuttings. So if you chance upon a gardener who has a tarragon plant that tastes so hot and racy, so delicious that you know you cannot live without it, grab a root or a slip and run home as fast as you can. Nurture it with care such as no child ever needed, for tarragon is hard to raise. But it is worth the bother.

The leaves and tips introduced sparingly into salads, soups, dressings, fish sauces, stews, meats are welcome seasoning. A little mixed into pot greens before cooking, minced into tartar sauce, or chopped on fish that has been baked, broiled, or fried, is doubly good. Tarragon vinegar, too, is matchless as a cook's assistant, and it is easy to make (page 339).

THYME

*Thymus vulgaris,* perennial. Alexis the Greek playwright, cataloguing the seasonings, bade us:

> . . . first go and take some sesame . . .
> leeks, garlic, thyme, sage, seseli . . .

Thus we know that thyme, the dainty-leaved, aroma-packed little plant, did not burst upon the eating world just yesterday.

There are many of the thymes, all lovely and fragrant. Orange thyme, lemon thyme, caraway-scented thyme are only a few of this sweet family. But one variety, the unassuming common thyme, is the real kitchen herb, and one of the most versatile. Soups, sauces, stuffings, cheeses, salads, meats, hare, fish, pot cheeses, dressings, all respond to the touch of thyme, yielding up more deliciousness than one would dream they possess. As for thyme with tomatoes in salad — there is a dream!

There they are, the twenty-five Kitchen Guardians. Treat them well; use them often. They will reward you a thousand-fold.

No herb can be completely a substitute for another, because they do not taste alike, yet if the cook does not object to a different result as long as it is palatable, then one strong herb can be used in place of another. But the weak herbs, such as parsley, chervil, chives, balm, burnet, borage, celery, and nasturtium, will never replace one of the strong herbs, of which a few are tarragon, rosemary, basil, thyme, and such. In other words, subtract the weak herbs listed above, and the remainder of the so-called "twenty-five herbs that will bring you culinary fame" are strong and can be substituted for each other. Remember, though, that the result will be different, but often will prove as good in taste. Related herbs, such as anise and fennel, are quite similar, particularly the crushed or ground seeds. Sweet and wild marjoram (oregano) can be used interchangeably, as well as summer and winter savory. So, buy or raise what you can, and substitute, if you must, with a clear conscience.

Perhaps some may wish to go even more deeply into herbs, making acquaintance with others not so necessary in a culinary sense, but still useful. Add to your list of twenty-five these others named below, and you will have an herb garden well balanced from the standpoint of beauty, bouquet fragrance, house fragrance, and cookery. You will be a real herb gardener.

Read Helen Morgenthau Fox's *Gardening with Herbs for Flavor and Fragrance,* for it is the Bible of American herb growers. M. Grieve's *Culinary Herbs and Condiments* and *A Modern Herbal* will interest you deeply, for they are admirable in their scholarly thoroughness. Henry Beston's *Herbs and the Earth* is pure poetry in prose form. Of the smaller forms of herbal literature, Helen Lyman's twin books, *Thirty Herbs Will Make an Herb Garden* and *Ten Herbs Will Make an Herb Bouquet* are just the right size for a pocket or a purse, to go with you and fill your idle moments with joy. Of the more modern books, those whose pages contain many notable recipes, my favorites include Helen Evans Brown's *West Coast Cook Book,* Sylvia Vaughn Thompson's *Economy Gastronomy,* Elizabeth David's *Italian Food,* and Robert Farrar Capon's *Supper of the Lamb.* These are very usable, suit-

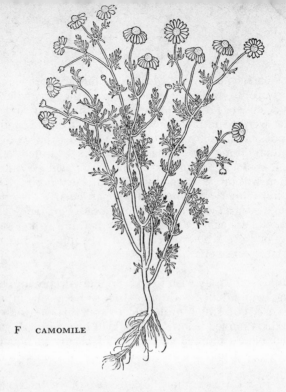

F    CAMOMILE

able for a questing cook's need. For students, looking for a
book that is beautiful, informative, a pleasure to own and
read but not cook from, two possibilities are Alice Cooke
Brown's *Early American Herb Recipes* and *Herbs, Spices and
Flavorings* by Tom Stobart (a publication of the Interna-
tional Wine and Food Society). Of course there are a number
more, written by experienced cooks. (There are also numbers
of the "armchair" variety — too many, unfortunately. When
one becomes experienced in following recipes that give soul-
satisfying results, the armchair cook and writer becomes
easily detectable, merely by reading the recipes without trying them.) These, of course, are only a few of the seriously
written herb books which can give the student so much real
satisfaction.

This is my suggested list of additional herbs:

| | |
|---|---|
| angelica | mignonette |
| camomile | pennyroyal |
| catnip | rampion |
| clary | rue |
| costmary | saffron |
| feverfew | ornamental sage |
| scented geraniums | southernwood |
| horehound | tansy |
| hyssop | other thymes |
| lavender | valerian |
| lemon verbena | sweet woodruff |
| lovage | wormwood |
| pot marigold | yarrow |

If you grow these, you will find yourself using them. Walk into your garden at dinnertime and nip off assorted tips to give pungency to your green salads. Learn to combine herbs with your flowers in bouquets. Make old-fashioned sweet bags for your linen, rose jars for sweet remembrance.

Today, we Americans are learning as never before the twin secrets of good nutrition and good meals temptingly prepared. We are finding that health and zest for living are increased via our kitchens. Meals pleasing in taste are conducive to good health, all other things being equal. How important, then, for the cook to be in some degree an artist. If this becomes so, then the cook attains more honor in the culinary position, is accorded renown in his or her sphere. But a word to the wives, and husbands too, who strive for artistry in the kitchen: leave elaborate, monumental gastronomy to the restaurants and the chefs. Instead, let simple excellence be your goal. It is easier, more satisfying, and often more digestible. Your cooking becomes not only nourishment for the body, but recreation for the spirit. G. K. Chesterton said of such matters:

There is more simplicity in the man who eats caviar on impulse, than in the man who eats Grapenuts on principle.

But no conversion, evangelical or material, is ever all in-clusive. That is too much to hope for. Many eaters and many cooks still are strangers to herbal cookery and its charms and benefits. However, once the cook finds out that here can be the answer to that eternal problem, how to make daily meal planning and preparation less of a grind and more a pleas-ure, his or her conversion has begun. Now it remains only to learn methods that produce tasty and tempting results, and the thing is well-nigh done. Or is it? These delectable cooking secrets, so much better than those of yesterday, may be, and often are, not received so enthusiastically as they are offered. Children in particular are often loath to accept something new in flavor. They hanker after the old dishes, and don't want to try something different. Result, a minor revolution. That something different, especially if they have been ad-vised beforehand of the innovation, is resisted all the way. The cook has slaved in the kitchen for hours and is baffled. What to do? Or maybe what not to do?

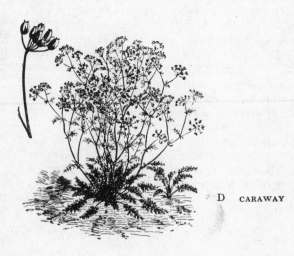

D    CARAWAY

May I offer some advice? First, don't say you are trying herbal cooking tomorrow. *Don't say anything.* Just take a recipe they like and slip in a *little* of one herb, only one herb. They will not notice it, for you have used it in small amount. Next day, another favorite, and in it a different herb, and so on. Unless those children, and the adult eaters as well, represent a new and strange genus, they will severally burst out at the third mouthful, "Say, this is good. What did you do to make it so grand?"

*Even then be careful.* Don't say, medicinally, "It is herbs. Don't you taste them?" Just get a mysterious gleam in your eye and murmur, "Oh, just a little marjoram [or thyme, or basil, or mint, as the case may be]. I'm glad you like it. I'll try to remember to put some in again the next time we have this dish."

Shortly your family will have become botanical sleuths, tasting with knowing mien, asking, "What herb did you use tonight? Marjoram? I thought that was what it was." The conversion will then be complete.

## Green or Dried Herbs?

In the new herb cook's mind there is an eternal question — "Shall I buy dried herbs to cook with, or shall I go to the bother of growing my own herbs that I may use them fresh? Is the pleasure of using fresh herbs great enough to repay me for my extra work?"

The answer is: If you can possibly find a little corner of sunny earth where you can grow herbs, do so. Even if you have to limit your choice and put the plants into flowerpots or window boxes, still grow them. For in crisp, green herbs there is more of fine flavor than in any that were ever dried.

But for those who have no place to grow their herbs: Cook with the best, freshest, and most carefully dried herbs you can find. Your food will still have a flavor that will raise to the nobility your rank as a cook. Cook with these dried herbs and thus live well until you *can* grow your own. That will be a time to look forward to with eagerness.

## Preparing Herbs for Cookery

If green herbs are to be used, pick off the leaves, discarding the stems, which in nearly all plants have a tendency toward bitterness. Either make the leaves into a small bunch and mince them with the kitchen scissors, or mince them on a board with a cleaver, after the European manner.

If dried herbs are to be used, leave them in the leaf until they are to be put into the cookery. Then between the palms of the hands rub them to a dust. Only in this way will they retain their flavor, for herbs that are pulverized and let stand, even in tight jars, soon grow flat. For this reason whole herb leaves or seeds are preferable to those sold ready-powdered in tin spice cans. Several herb-producing firms, including Spice Islands, Schillings, McCormick's, and Wagner's, have good and varied stocks, which are usually to be found in supermarkets and specialty stores.

## Keeping Green Herbs Green

If you have a bunch of green herbs and want to keep them fresh for a few days, put them into a jar with a tight screw top. In the refrigerator they will remain crisp and sweet several days.

## Freezing Herbs

Parsley and other green herbs can easily be frozen for future use. Wash and dry them, then pick the sprigs from the larger stems. Make small packets, wrap them in plastic wrap or plastic bags, seal with freezer tape, and label each. Lay them in a flat foil pan in the freezer until they are hard, then put them into convenient corners of the freezer. I assemble each kind into a plastic bag, so I don't have to go over a lot of packets to find what I want. They freeze well, and stay very green. To use, simply unwrap a packet, cut off what you need, and rewrap the rest.

## Variety in Seasoning

Don't fall victim to the one-herb habit. This may suffice for a time, but eventually those you are cooking for will start grumbling. That is your cue, for that one-herb thing can rob cook and eaters alike of that precious ingredient in foods, variety, and monotony takes its place. If we use thyme here, sweet basil there, or yet tarragon or dill, and go ever back and forth over the sweet array of savors, our fame increases, and those who eat our foods are happy.

## Individual Flavors

At present there is a vogue for buying little packets of "Italian Seasoning" or "Mixed Herbs." They are skillfully blended and undoubtedly good in food. But the clever cook, though he or she may use them, will never come to depend wholly on such ready-made mixtures. The secret of individual cookery lies in learning the uses of each of the various herbs, and using each in its place. Meat pie seasoned with thyme and parsley will be a different dish from the same meat pie savory with rosemary. The difference is so great that it defeats repetition, that Nemesis of the cook.

So season your beans this week with sage and onion, next week with garlic and cumin seed and learn true versatility.

## Herbal Restraint

A good motto for the knowing cook, in dealing with herbs, might be, "Enough is enough." Because we relish the flavor of herbs in our food does not necessarily mean that every dish on our menu must be so seasoned. The temperate and wise cook will agree with Helen Morgenthau Fox, who gives us all our cue for herbal moderation: "But the herbs should not enter into every dish served at a meal. If they flavor two courses, that is sufficient."

Remember, herbs are for the purpose of enhancing the flavor of food, not *disguising* it. A woman once gave me a recipe for heavily seasoned summer squash, saying, "It's wonderful. You would never guess you were eating summer squash." Then why, under such conditions, eat summer squash? If the taste of the food itself is overpowered by the seasoning, that dish is overseasoned and ruined.

## To Fry Herbs or Not to Fry Herbs

Many recipes, in their directions for using parsley and other green herbs, advise cooking them in the oil in which meat or fowl is to be browned. Then, as they say, "Brown the

D   CELERY

meat in the seasoned oil." It does sound wonderful, there is no denying; but in reality it is very bad, for by the time the meat is brown the poor little herbs are hard and bitter and burned to a crisp.

A better way is to brown the meat first, then add the herbs at the same time as the liquid. Herbs are tender ingredients, and must be tenderly handled if they are to behave properly.

## Some Mysteries Cleared Up

The beginner in the study of herb cookery is apt to become confused by the apparently bewildering groups of herbs called for in many books. *Sweet herbs, pot herbs, fine herbs, salad herbs, simpling herbs* — the prospect of ever understanding them all seems remote. Other cabalistic terms, too, are tossed lightly off herbal writers' pens, such as *simple bouquet, soup bouquet, bouquet garni.* The beginner is liable to quit in fatigue and decide to stick to salt, pepper, and poultry seasoning.

Don't be discouraged. It is all so easy that you will shortly laugh at your fright. Here are the answers:

## Sweet Herbs

The plants whose leaves, seeds, or roots have aroma that makes them useful as seasoning, such the thyme, mint, and their kind (pages 7 to 20), are called *sweet herbs.*

## Pot Herbs

*Pot herbs* are plants whose leaves and stems are used for food, as cabbage, spinach, and such. The term applies to food, and not to seasoning, as many suppose.

D  CHIVES

D  CHERVIL

## Salad Herbs

Those plants used to season salads are *salad herbs*. There is great variety in such seasoning, for all of the sweet herbs may be used as flavor pointers for salads.

## Fine Herbs

This term is oftenest met in the French form, as *fines herbes*. Though it sounds cryptic, it means merely a combination of three or four herbs used to flavor certain dishes. There are fixed combinations ordinarily accorded the distinction of the term:

> parsley, chervil, and chives
> parsley, basil, and chives
> burnet, thyme, and parsley

Other combinations often include tarragon, but experiment shows that tarragon, included with other herbs, is liable to dominate the flavor too thoroughly for pleasure. For my taste it is best used alone, when a definite tarragon flavor is desired.

When herbs are used in the accepted fine-herb sense, they are usually mingled, finely chopped, and tossed into food, just before serving. Representative uses are in tartar sauce, cream soups, cream cheeses. When used in omelettes they are mixed with the eggs before cooking.

## Simpling Herbs

Simpling herbs are herbs used medicinally, and have no part in this book.

## Bouquets

Bouquets are bunches of herbs, either tied together or bound into a tiny sack of cheesecloth, and cooked with food. They are so bound that they may be lifted out at the end of the cooking and discarded.

This is neither necessary nor advisable, however. Instead, the herbs called for in the "bouquet" may be minced and put loose into the food. By the time the cooking is finished they will be an integral part of the dish.

A *simple bouquet* is merely a few sprigs of parsley and several blades of chives. Such a bouquet may be minced and added to salads, sauces, or cream cheeses.

A *bouquet garni* is a bunch of assorted herbs such as:

| | |
|---|---|
| 2 *sprigs parsley* | 2 *sprigs thyme* |
| 1 *sprig marjoram* | ½ *bay leaf* |

They may either be minced or tied and put inside a roasting chicken, duck, or pheasant.

A *soup bouquet* is a similar bunch cooked in soup.

So much for the clarification of these strange terms. Let their dictates serve you only until you are an experienced herb cook. Then forget these arbitrary combinations, for you will have developed your own.

Enter this province of cooking with herbs full of the sense of its adventure. Cook with imagination, then make a written record of each recipe you develop. Thus you will be able to repeat the dishes you have liked, and will assure yourself of eternal variety of savor.

Long ago in London herbs were hawked through the streets and sold in fresh bunches, to endow with flavor the Englishman's food. How welcome we could make such vendors today, for there would be a thrill in hearing herbs shouted at the door, in knowing that we could have them fresh-cut, perhaps with the dew still on them:

> Here's fine rosemary, sage and thyme,
> Come, buy my ground ivy;
> Here's featherfew, gillyflowers and rue,
> Come, buy my knotted marjoram, ho!

NOTE: Most of my recipes are based on fresh herbs, and the amounts are calculated on them. However, they may be changed to dried herbs in using by cutting the amounts in half and always measuring the dried herbs after they have been powdered between the palms, as described on page 26. For example, 1 teaspoon of thyme, meaning fresh thyme, would be changed to ½ teaspoon dry, pulverized thyme.

# ❧ TWO ❧

## . . . and Other Seasonings

The use of food does not consist in its rarity, but in its satisfying
the appetite.

CHINESE PROVERB

BASICALLY, foods are the same the world over. Rice, wheat,
potatoes, meats, corn, and all the other sturdy foodstuffs are
cosmopolites which live in all countries and nourish all
people.

Yet regional foods differ, and radically. An Italian dinner
is no more like a Turkish dinner than an Italian is like a
Turk. Fundamentally, their foods are the same, yet the
finished dishes are widely unlike. Consider, for instance, two
dishes such as Italian *risotto alla Milanese* and Turkish
pilau. Both are made from rice, but they are far from the
same dish. Why?

They differ in seasoning.

Rice cooked with certain seasonings becomes a delicious
pilau of the East. Had that same rice been prepared with another set of seasonings, it would have emerged as the beloved
Italian risotto.

Seasonings are the soul of culinary variation. They are not just a row of tin canisters on a shelf, or a border of herbs in a garden, but substances that have intrigued men since cookery began. They are the stuff of romance, the cargoes of storied ships, the preoccupations of the learned. They are the making of inspired foods.

"I like a cook will cleverly season. . . ." So spoke Sophocles, and speaking matched his genius for tragic verse with another, the appreciation for good and abundant living. He was not the first to know the importance of seasoning in the making of meals that entice their eaters. And after him stretches the line of those who shared his feeling, linking the past to the present and pointing far ahead into the future.

The United States, in its development, originally boasted a gastronomic heritage at least as firm and well rounded as that of any other nation. The culinary arts of all countries were our birthright. England, Holland, Italy, France, Spain, Scandinavia, Germany, and other lands, both Occidental and Oriental, merged their kitchen secrets within our borders to give us a richer, fuller food consciousness than any other single people. Surely a legacy to treasure.

But somehow we have dissipated that wealth. We have almost entirely forgotten the fragrance of our ancestral kitchens, lost their countless seasoning secrets. In a world where no two meals need taste alike, we too often cook and eat in the odor of monotony. And since our foods so often lack seasoning, we have developed in defense that time-honored American pre-eating rite, "dusting with salt and pepper." All over our land, before each meal, good citizens swing into the dusting ceremony before they have even paid the cook the compliment of testing the seasoning. O pity of pities! A national admission of culinary carelessness!

In short, we Americans no longer remember the full meaning of the word *seasonings*. Depending too much on salt, pepper, and sugar for variation in taste, we realize little of the further significance of the term. This is needless poverty,

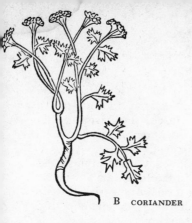

B CORIANDER      C CLARY

for the list of seasoning agents is generous in number and rich in variety.

Let us not, in veering from one seasoning course to another, err in accepting as passable seasoning everything that has a taste, as did the old Greeks. According to Antiphanes, their list included:

> Dried grapes, and salt, and eke new wine
> Newly boiled down, and assafœtida,
> And cheese, and thyme, and sesame,
> And nitre, too, and cummin seed
> And sumac, and honey, and marjoram,
> And herbs, and vinegar, and oil
> And sauce of onions, mustard, and capers mix'd,
> And parsley, capers too, and eggs,
> And lime, and cardamums, and the acid juice
> Which comes from the green fig tree, besides lard
> And eggs and honey and flour wrapped in fig
>     leaves. . . .

Many in that list have true excellence, but others are more astonishing than tempting.

Besides herbs, the other seasonings are no less legion. Let us scan the roll. Acquaintance with its personæ will mean new life for our meals today, new zest for living tomorrow.

## SALT

First appears salt, the patriarch of all seasonings. Old as Time, known even to the ancestors of the ancients as an enhancer of food flavors, salt has fascinating history to its credit. The classics are full of its mention, for people have always valued this most venerable of condiments.

Horace listed the *salinum* or salt cellar among the sacred lares and penates of the Romans. In the Bible, the Divine instructions to Moses regarding sacrificial meats advised: "Neither shall thou suffer the salt of the covenant of thy God to be lacking from the meat offering. . . ."

The blessing and distribution of salt was part of the Russian imperial coronation ceremony. Give salt to one of the Mohammedan faith, and even though he be your enemy, for the twenty-four hours that his body holds it you and your property are sacred in his sight, and entitled to his protection.

Today salt is still the primary seasoning, and when preparing meat or vegetables the cook automatically reaches for it. But this seasoning has other affinities more sub rosa, though fully as effective.

A dash of salt on the dry coffee before brewing is started improves the drink. Likewise, hot chocolate responds to such treatment with all its potentialities.

All sweet desserts are better for the addition of a bit of salt. A little in the sugar to be eaten with fruit is magic.

So use salt carefully but fully. It is a grateful condiment, rewarding with heightened savor those who treat it well.


## PEPPER

If Salt is the patriarch, then Pepper is his wife. Not so old in usefulness, but still no youngster, pepper was one of man's first spices. Through long years of history it has been of curious importance.

In early France church dues and rents, as well as taxes,

could be paid in pepper. The Visigoths, in the fifth century, demanded and received three thousand pounds of pepper as part of a ransom.

Remember the famous sea route to India that we all learned about in grade school? The Portuguese sought and found it that they might have a faster and easier way of bringing pepper to spiceless Europe.

Here in America it is our custom to buy pepper ready-ground, but here and there is a home boasting a pepper mill. That family knows, as no others can, the true flavor of pepper, for in that household it is ground fresh for each using. To compare such freshly ground spices with those bought ready-ground is like comparing a dewy, opulently fragrant rose in the garden with the faded, faintly sweet leaves that have been dried for a rose jar.

A really good pepper mill should be part of every good cook's equipment, every bride's dowry. A handsome one is a double pleasure, for it cuts the kitchen pepper fine and fresh, yet goes to the table without a blush.

Buy a good mill. Don't stint on the price, for it will last generations. Put in some peppercorns, hold it above the dish to be seasoned, turn the little crank, and taste your first real pepper. Fresh-ground pepper will transform a dish, speaking its superiority especially in salads and gravies.

RED PEPPERS

The red pepper (*Capsicum*) family is large and varied, having no relation to the black and white pepper we know so well. Some are used as vegetables, but others are seasoning of a high and virile order. Used knowingly, they are delicious additions to many types of food. Some, such as cayenne, are fiery, so handle with care.

Many of my recipes call for Japanese chile. I was unaware of it when I first wrote this book, but this term became one of the most burning — no pun intended — mysteries of the culinary world. I have received queries from near and far all over the map, all asking, "What is a Japanese chile?" This is an opportunity for me to clear up that mystery.

Briefly, the Japanese chile is a small, pointed, very hot pepper. When ripe and red, it is dried, and sold in Italian and Mexican groceries, and often in supermarkets. (The only other names I know it by are Hontaka chile, which I presume is a Japanese name, and *chile tepin* — plural, *chiles tepines* — its Mexican name, used also in California and the Southwest.) Use in it small amounts, and without its seeds, and *always* wash your hands after handling it. People in the Far East, Mexico, southern Italy, and doubtless in other areas, value its hot breath in their foods. We like it, and I hope you do too.

## SPICES

The spices that stand on our kitchen shelves are commonplace enough to us, for they are easy to get. But there was a time when they were so precious that wars were fought over them. New lands and untried routes were discovered because of them. They were the commodities in which tribute to powerful rulers were paid, the coveted prizes which caused tragic bloodshed. Whole peoples were wiped out by the Dutch and Portuguese in their early attempts to control the spice trade.

Sheba's gift to Solomon was "a hundred and twenty talents of gold, and of spices great store." The literature and history of the world is fragrant with the aroma of spices. Chaucer wrote of cinnamon, cloves, pepper, ginger, and nutmeg. The Song of Solomon is really a song when it invites:

> Awake, O north wind, and come, thou south; blow upon my garden, that the spices thereof may flow out.

Today we know our spices well, and give them honored space in our kitchens, for they are suitable for many dishes.

They can be combined with herbs, used alone, or in spice combinations.

A dash of spice perks up the most modest dish, lending it a bit of Oriental verve that transforms its personality. For instance:

> Spinach responds to mace in a miraculous fashion.
>
> A little cinnamon on sweet potatoes before glazing is excellent.
>
> A pair of whole cloves in the teapot with the tea lends an indefinable something that calls for cups and cups.
>
> A soupçon of allspice enlivens a meat loaf amazingly.
>
> A dash of nutmeg in stuffed eggs is like sweet perfume on a beautiful woman — the touch that achieves perfection.

These are only suggestions. But if they can be the cue to bring spices out of the pastry kitchen, their stature will be heightened.

## OLIVE OIL

We rarely regard olive oil as a seasoning, yet it is one of the best. The fine, delicate flavor does its part, and that no small one, in turning out perfect food.

To be good, olive oil must be pure. And pure oil is *virgin oil*. By *virgin oil* is meant that obtained by the first pressing of the olives. Somewhat thin, sweet, and only faintly green, it is the cream of the olive. Still usable is the second expressing from the olive, though a trifle heavier and a little greener. If you use either of these two grades you will be happy about them. But any further supply of oil obtained from those olives is to be shunned as poor eating and seasoning.

But oils seem to share humans' habits in some part. Many of them pretend to be virgin that have no claim to that virtue. So beware when you select your oil, lest it trick you.

Sometimes, too, olive oil falls in with bad company. Cottonseed oil, rape oil, poppyseed oil, and oil from peanuts, sesame seeds, and soya beans all are adulterants of the precious virgin olive oil. You'll not like the results of the mixing. Still seek the virgin, and her alone.

Whether the oil you choose be Italian, Spanish, or Californian, buy the best. The best, judged according to our standards, always means the costliest. While that does not mean that there are no good oils that are not costly, it is the safest way of judging. Pay a good price for your oil without a qualm, for it goes far and repays you for the expenditure.

The adding of a few drops of olive oil to certain dishes gives a surprising and delightful addition of flavor. If you doubt that such a slight thing can flavor, heat a little oil and notice how your appetite swells as you smell it.

If you have a dish of plain boiled beans, as, for example, pinto or cranberry beans, and haven't time to "Spanish" them, try this instead: Add a teaspoon of minced raw onion and several tablespoons of olive oil to your beans. Salt and pepper them generously. Served with French bread buttered and quickly browned under the broiler, a green salad, and sliced tomatoes, it is a dinner for a king, or for a flavor-wise American.

Olive-oil-seasoned tomatoes are perfect. Slice them in thick slices, salt and pepper them, dot them with minced chives, and sprinkle with olive oil. Serve cold.

Are you boiling globe artichokes? Salt them very generously and add two or three tablespoons of olive oil to the water in which they are to be cooked.

## BUTTER

Butter is the essence of American seasoning, and is not to be sneered at, although margarine has certainly become an acceptable substitute. Used generously either alone or in company with olive oil, it insures tasty richness in food. We season vegetables, meats, and sauces with butter. If we do

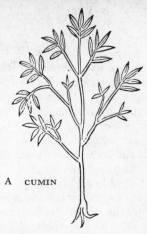

A CUMIN

not make the mistake of depending slavishly on it, rejecting other ingredients which might be better in some dishes, or which could serve to relieve the monotony of stereotyped seasoning, butter will serve us well.

## ONIONS

"Too often the poet sees but the tears that live in an onion, not the smiles." Elizabeth Robins Pennell, a woman with rare feeling for food and its fancies, spoke those words, every one of which is solemn truth.

"Kitchen lilies," someone else feelingly dubs onions, and further says that they are "the wit that enlivens the whole dish."

Yet no more than fifty years ago many Americans accorded the onion nothing more than a mean, back-scullery position. A very wise person once wove words into an immortal truth on this matter:

I doubt not that all . . . love the onion, but few will confess their love. . . . Some people have days on which they eat onions, which you might call retreats. . . . On that day they see no company and deny the kiss of greeting to their dearest friend . . .

That same sage writer it was who said, "Happy is said to be the family that can eat onions together!"

These are happier days, for the onion, green or mature, is an honored seasoning, a delicious vegetable. As example of the magic there is in a bit of onion, the next time you have new, creamy-white *tagliarini*, fresh from the knife of a pasta master, try dressing it, after boiling and draining, with salt, plenty of melted butter, and finely minced new onions. Toss it well, and let no time waste before you enjoy its delicacy.

Onions grace green salads. They need not be used prodigally, but rather with discretion. Green new onions in season are best, and don't let any overcautious ginger-foot tell you that only the white part is fit to eat. The green tops are much more subtle than the bulb. The first whispers its flavor, while the other speaks aloud. So use the green tops as well as the onion itself. But watch your grocer, for he delights to lop off those tops and send you the mutilated remains.

As to mature onions, those with dry, shiny outer skins and juicy interiors, white Bermudas, the yellow and brown skinned as well as the red, sweet ones, are succulent, gentle, and rich, an adorable combination of virtues. They separate into pretty rings, and a few of those nestling among salad greens are prime fare. Lusty appetites will relish an old-fashioned onion sandwich.

But onions will be popping up all over this book, for they are as necessary in a kitchen as either apron or stove. Poor indeed is the family whose onion basket is empty!

## SCALLIONS

These, of course, are the well known and widely used green fresh onions with beautiful green tops and white bulbs. Treasure them and use both tops and bulbs.

## SHALLOTS

A shallot is first cousin to an onion, with perhaps a trace of garlic blood, which shows mainly in its shape. Shallots taste like onions, only not so much so. If you want to go a little mild in your cookery, use them, for they will momentarily satisfy an onion-craving family, and still not keep you from mingling with fastidious friends.

GARLIC

Garlic — there's a man among vegetables. A man who always speaks right out in meeting and makes his presence known. Learn to know this estimable citizen. He is a priceless servant, but a poor master.

You may admit garlic into your kitchen — in truth you dare not exclude him if you would be a really good cook. But keep the rascal under control, for he plays tricks on the unwary.

Since garlic, like onions, will appear so often in this book, it is best here to give you mere hints as to how to use garlic and still remain in society. It can be done.

In garlicking a salad, rub a dry crust of bread with a cut clove of garlic, and put the bread into the salad. Toss it with the salad as you dress it, then remove it. You'll have your desired garlic flavor, and evenly distributed, but no telltale breath.

Garlic actually eaten, if there is much of it, will remain on the breath. So when cooking more than one clove of garlic in food, don't mince it. Instead, split each clove lengthwise, making two flat pieces, and run a toothpick through each. Cook these pieces with your food, but remember to remove them after a half hour's cooking, while they are still intact and on the toothpicks. Cooked longer they go to pieces and are lost. They get eaten and their fragrance lingers on the breath, becoming the cause of much social rancor.

If the flavor of garlic is wished in sauces or salad dressings, cut each clove once and put into the sauce. Leave in the food for fifteen minutes, then remove and discard.

If you will follow these directions you can enjoy the delightsome flavor of garlic in your food, yet live in harmony with all the world.

## VINEGAR

A seasoning of no mean importance is vinegar, but one that must be understood to be well used. To the uninitiated there seems to be a bewildering array of vinegars on the market. Cider, malt, spirit, and red- and white-wine vinegars, all are bottled and waiting. But hold — all are not equally desirable. Good cider vinegar is a choice liquid *if you can find it*. However, most of that on the market is too strong and sharp. As to malt and spirit vinegars, let us ignore them. They merit nothing more.

That leaves virtually one choice to make, between red- and white-wine vinegars. Either is good, when it is good, for with rich, benign wine vinegars your salad relish will increase a thousandfold. But if you can buy only those thin, acid liquids that too often masquerade under the master name, then follow the example of the knowing. Forswear them all, scorning to use them. Instead, make your own vinegar. A recipe that is easy to follow can be found on page 338.

## LEMON

To the most of us, a lemon is a fruit, and nothing more. Yet it is actually a veritable dean of seasoning.

Lemon — delicate tartness within, pungent sharpness and acrid unctuousness without. Its juice is as excellent seasoning acid as you could wish. Its rind, grated, is a bit of dessert spicing as unique as it is good.

The twist of lemon peel that releases its drops of gleaming

A    DILL

oil into an old-fashioned cocktail is the touch that spells *ne plus ultra*.

To drink clear broth without a generous squeeze of lemon juice is never to know what faultless broth is.

Lamb and lemon — there is a marriage made in Heaven. Lamb meat is sweet, and lemon's tangy acid tempers that sweetness into perfect balance. A slice or two of lemon with its peel, cooked into the meat, as well as lemon juice rubbed into it or squeezed over it as it cooks, approaches perfection of taste.

WINE

Wise use of the juice of the grape in cookery gives flavors that are flawless. But the recipes in this book make much use of wines, so the subject need not be elaborated here.

Seasonings — the bloom on the peach, the touch of color on white, the final stroke that completes a perfect picture. He or she who learns to season truly cooks. But to cook without cunning seasoning is to be only a stoker.

## Tasting

> For he who rightly cares for his own eating
> Will not be a bad cook. And if you keep
> Your organs, sense and taste, in proper order
> You will not err. But often taste your dishes
> While you are boiling them. Do they want salt?
> Add some; — is any other seasoning needed?
> Add it, and taste again, till you've arrived
> At harmony of flavor; like a man
> Who tunes a lyre till it rightly sounds.

There, in the words of an ancient Greek who knew food, we have one of the first secrets of good cookery — frequent tasting. For tasting goes hand in hand with seasoning. Only too well do we know the cook ( ? ) who airily dismisses the matter — "Oh, I never taste anything while I am cooking. It spoils my appetite. I have learned to cook without tasting." The food, in too many instances, belies the words.

Too little of any one seasoning, or too much, robs the dish of true savor. Such spoiling is a pity, when a little care would prevent it, and turn out good food instead.

## Smelling

The nose, too, is useful in cookery.

Henry T. Finck said that "with the exception of sweet, sour, salt and bitter, all our countless gastronomic delights come to us through the sense of smell, not taste." That is not hard to believe, remembering how flat the most carefully prepared food seems to one who has a cold.

Webster tells us that originally spices were called *aromas*. We have lost this interesting name, but to this day the Italians refer lovingly to their herb seasonings as *odorini* — literally "little scents." Had we the word artistry of the Latins we might call our seasonings "fragrances."

Since so much of good depends on the nose, why shouldn't we try cooking with it? Can you see a Cyrano de Bergerac, tall chef's cap riding his head at right angles to his famous nose? He is stirring things on a stove. As he bends over the kettle that nose catches every flavor-laden tendril of steam rising from it. Thus he loses no smallest opportunity to judge the perfection or need in the aroma of the dish.

This is only fancy, but fancy by which we may well profit. Heaven forbid we should develop noses as large as Cyrano's (no pun intended). But God grant we may learn to use what noses we have, when we are cooking.

# ❧ THREE ❧

## Herbs in Your Garden

Herbs too she knew, and well of each could speak
That in her garden sipped the silvery dew . . .
                                    WILLIAM SHENSTONE

THERE IS satisfaction in a garden. Balm for wounds, peace
for living, work for restless hands. The French put it well:
"If you want to be happy an hour, get intoxicated. If you
want to be happy three days, get married. If you want to be
happy eight days, kill your pig and eat it. But if you want to
be happy forever, become a gardener."

There are gardens and gardens, to fit every taste, every
ambition, every means. First, there are the great, complete,
compartmented gardens that follow the plan of Seigneur du
Pradel, father of agriculture in the France of Henri IV. *Le
potager, le médecinal, le fruitier, le bouquetier,* he advised,
thus taking care of all that one might want in even a large
garden — vegetables, herbs, fruit, and flowers. Then happily, there are gardens for the rest of us, who have more or
less limited space in city lots, suburban gardens, or country

yards. Since we must suit our wants to our space, willy-nilly we consent to a little mixing. Often we end up with a sort of friendly hotchpotch, carrots hobnobbing with candytuft, and both being pushed out of their bed by a mint with no reservation.

To my mind the best of all gardens is one with an old-fashioned air — hollyhocks along fences, mignonette in masses, jasmine, sweet alyssum, "gillyflowers all in a row," and the rest of those sweet blooms that carry still the dignity of tradition. Boxwood hedges are there, permanent and time-less. A vegetable plot large enough at least for salad things belongs there, and to go with all this, *herbs*. First of all, culinary herbs. For, as an ancient sign in an English inn-garden reads:

> Grow roses that ye may enjoy their perfume and to give;
> Grow cabbages that ye may eat and live;
> For life is strange ye understand
> And that twain must go hand in hand.

Flowers and vegetables and spicing herbs — they all com-plement each other in a garden. Then, as space permits, there may be room and desire for some of the other herbs, those not necessarily adapted to kitchen use but pretty in their gray, modest way and deep with the significance of history. These, with your culinary herbs, will make a well-rounded olitory that will afford you pride and satisfaction. You'll find yourself collecting, bit by bit, the rich lore of those old plants, and like Lelipa you may say:

> A chaplet, me, of herbs I'll make . . .

Soon you'll have a hobby on your hands, one that you cannot but follow with joy and recompense.

How shall your garden grow? Sweeping in spacious dig-nity, laid out knowingly in courtly traditional pattern? Or sweetly small, holding in its embroidered neatness all the charm of antiquity, yet modern enough to be easily cared for, easy to enjoy? Each is equally satisfying for the person whose life it fits.

If your herb garden must be a show place to point to with pride, then you may want an Elizabethan garden of knotted design, a French parterre of the same period, or some other of the striking immemorial forms sanctioned by time. For you, Rosetta Clarkson's scholarly books on historical herb gardens, *Magic Fragrance, Green Enchantment,* and *Herbs, Their Culture and Uses,* go into such matters deeply and ably.

But to be beautiful and useful, an herb garden need not be wide and large. Let it be as small as it will, or perhaps as it must, it still can have beauty if it has order. Design it carefully, plant it prayerfully, care for it lovingly, and you will reap beauty.

## Selecting the Garden Site

Herbs are not hard to raise. They require little in the way of fancy soils. We do find them fussy about one of their garden requirements, however. They must have sun to be really strong and flavorsome, for most of the culinary herbs are native to the sun-drenched shores of the Mediterranean. There they grow hardy and fragrant on hot hillsides. Their American children want that same warming sun to make them truly "sweet herbs." So when you pick your herb garden plot select one that has the maximum of sun the garden affords.

A slight slope, if you have such a place, will be ideal. If not, then good drainage in the place you have is necessary, for the plants then need not stand with wet feet. Almost without exception herbs have the peculiarity of wanting plenty of water, yet resenting too much.

Above all, let your situation be near the kitchen door. This

exerts no magical charm on the herbs, but it will be a big
help to you, the gardener and cook. Even in severe climates
at least some of the herbs are green the year round, and no
matter how far the mercury drops, they will call you from
your warm kitchen at meal-making times. For your own comfort and well-being then, make the journey not too long.

## Herb Garden Design

To be faithfully orthodox an herb garden should be rectangular, enclosed, and laid out in geometrically designed
beds and walks. There is a certain appropriate dignity about
such a garden. Sundials, bee skeps, and turfed seats are its
ordained fittings, their present glamour clouding their practical origins. Today we see them and murmur, "How quaint!"
but formerly bees were in the skep, time was read by the sun-
dial, and the turfed seat, no pretty fancy, was a needed rest-
ing place for the lady "when she did garner her hearbes."
Thus the conveniences of one era become the curiosities of
another.

Without a blush I confess that our own garden has none
of these ornaments. Furthermore, it is not rectangular, but
some sort of a marvel of asymmetry that owes its shape not
to any Mazza design, but only to the fact that the space between the driveway and the house happened to look like that
— and that was where the herb garden had to be. Destiny
shaping our ends, I suppose. Anyway, herbs don't need ornament. They are their own pretty reasons for being. And that
is not whistling in the dark, either.

Some of you, overcome by descriptions of those beautifully designed herb gardens, are saying right now, "Well,
that leaves me out of this whole thing. With my small yard I
can't give up enough space for any decent-sized rectangle.
I only wanted a tiny plot anyway." Don't give up. Shape and
size dictate neither a garden's beauty, its preciousness to the

owner, nor its usefulness. Perhaps you have a sunny border along a walk or the driveway, or a bed under the kitchen window. If this plot fills the other requirements, then its shape, or even its size, is the least part of it. Adapt the above suggestions for herb-garden planning and planting, ignoring what does not fit. You will have that most satisfactory of all possessions, a garden tailored to suit you. Your care and use will make it beautiful.

## Enclosures and Walks

Whatever its shape and scope, an enclosed garden is desirable when that garden holds culinary herbs or salad plants. The reasons are obvious. A wall, a picket fence, or a lattice of wide spaces would be in keeping with the picture. The walks whose crossing forms beds should be easy of width and surfaced with material that affords neat walking in wet weather, such as flagstones, bricks, or small crushed rock. If you want a green walk, then nothing is lovelier than the soft, green, creeping camomile, which "thrives when trod upon" as long as the blossom heads are kept cut off.

## Hedges

Hedges about a garden make green seclusion — box for those with patience, privet for the more headlong are both neat and enduring. Small hedges, no more than a foot high, are often used to outline beds and edge walks. They give a prim charm, an air of other days. English lavender plants, set no more than six inches apart, and kept clipped as they grow, make low hedges that are sweet and unusual. Allow the blooms to develop between clippings and you will have fragrance for your clothespresses and linen closets. Germander makes a good low hedge, or the real dwarf box. In kindly climates rosemary is a fragrant and pretty hedging plant. Santolina trims well and will last for several years. Mrs. Clarkson warns, "do not let the melting snow lie on it," or the branches will rot.

## Edging Plants

Perhaps the man in your house, like the one in ours, votes hedge-cutting as the occupation at which he is least likely to succeed. In such a case you might be wise to skip hedges and compromise on edging plants, which need no regular clipping. Ornamental catnip, with its cloud of blue flowers and dainty gray foliage, is my favorite edging plant. Of course all the cats in the neighborhood will come daily and sit upon it and chew it. That is a drawback, even if you like cats, which, of course, some don't. For anyone who wants cats in manageable numbers, or perhaps no cats at all, common thyme or golden thyme offers no feline temptations and is beautiful and hardy. Moss-curled parsley can be used, if renewed each year, and will serve a double purpose.

## The Tall and Short of It

Herbs, like you and me and our brothers, grow tall and short and in-between sized. It is a happy arrangement, for graduating plant heights in herb beds as well as flower borders make for interesting effects. But investigate plant habits of growth before setting them out, for woe betide him or her who plants without knowing which is tall and which is short. Nothing is so exasperating, not to mention uncomfortable, as winding oneself around, let us say, a tall rosemary bush to pluck a sprig of thyme or parsley hidden behind it. It helps make the matter worse if the gardener and also the picker has no one but himself to blame. For the avoidance of such situations I have provided a chart, on pages 62 to 65, giving approximate heights of plants when full grown.

## Color in the Herb Garden

Few culinary herbs have a great deal to boast of in the way of splendid blooms. It is their pervading fragrance, their quiet, gray greenness, their delicate forms that make them gracious garden inhabitants. But some herbs do flower in arrays of color, and they are worth finding and bringing home to give a spot in the garden plot. The blue of borage, aconite, bugloss, hyssop, and lavender; the pink shades of dittany of crete, valerian, coriander, and anise; the red glow of bergamot, red yarrow, and pineapple sage; and for yellow, rue, yellow yarrow, nasturtium, and pot marigold, that modest ancestor of today's large, showy marigolds, are just a hint of the plants that can give your green herb garden a studding of jewels.

You have it selected, then, the garden for your herbs. A sunny plot, near the kitchen door, perhaps sloping, but surely shaped and sized to your own needs rather than those of the Joneses. The plans for its design, classical or formal, hedged or edged, have all been worked out on paper. You are ready to go.

## Soil Preparation

For good gardening, as for other matters, first things must come first. Soil preparation has proven an important first in an herb garden as well as a flower garden. It is true that herbs are not especially exacting, as plants go, but certain things should be done to keep any plant healthy and growing. Well-prepared soil makes good plants, while hastily and sketchily prepared ground will usually grow unsatisfactory gardens.

Soil for an herb garden should be deeply prepared, as for any other garden use. A large space perhaps should have a plow, but if yours is a spadeable area it can be hand-turned, to a depth of 18 inches or 2 feet. Clay soil will need a liberal addition of ashes to make it into really satisfactory garden soil. A little sand in addition to the ashes will also make it more friable. Ground which is already good loam will need just a few buckets of sand to make it good herb soil. If the spot you have chosen has not good drainage so that there is probability of the water standing, the topsoil should be laid aside when the spading is done, and a layer of coarse gravel put in about 2 feet down, after which the topsoil is returned.

Digging fertilizer into the soil is an exercise one rarely has to endure in an herb garden. Except in a few special cases, normally good but unenriched soil is better, for herbs ordinarily develop their fragrance far better there than in the most carefully and expensively enriched earth. Fertilizer promotes lush growth but little odor in the leaves. They thrive best on a bit of poverty and are the sweeter for it.

## Plant Propagation

There are various ways of producing new herb plants, some herbs doing best with one method, some with another. Growing one's own herb plants doesn't mean just buying numberless little packets of seeds and spending an afternoon casting them about the garden, any more than making any other type of garden allows such carefree and abandoned sowing. Some herbs grow best from seed; others propagate best from root divisions, cuttings, or perhaps layering. Then too, there are annuals, perennials, and biennials in the herb group, all of which must enter into the plan for growing an

herb garden. Last, but certainly not least, there is the matter of what kind of gardener you are.

For instance, there is the gardener de luxe. He yearns to grow herbs, but primarily by proxy. Plants he must have, but he doesn't want to have them the hard way. He learned years ago in this gardening business that nurseries are Heaven's chosen middlemen 'twixt Nature and the finished garden. So he hunts up an herb nursery and orders a ready-made garden. Nearly every metropolis has one such nursery near it. Strong, clean plants, especially perennials with a season's growth behind them, are available. And all scoffing aside, such a way of acquiring your plants has much to be said for it. After all, the main thing is getting them, no matter how.

But perhaps you are one of those people who want to attend personally to the production of the herb plants. For many persons half the fun of a garden is preparing flats or seed beds, planting seeds, and watching them pop out of the ground and develop their personalities. Transplanting, pricking out, thinning have no terrors for them. And as for starting plants from cuttings or root divisions, that is just fun, for them. If you are that sort of gardener, then you can have real joy in your herb plot, from the idea stage through to the finished product.

My own garden is a mixture of methods, including a little larceny of the petty variety. The result is rich in memories: seedlings nursed into maturity; slips given me by herb-growing friends and colleagues, and started in a glass of water on the window ledge of an apartment kitchen; two precious plants, now in their seventh or ninth incarnation via layering, which are the loot of the above-mentioned larcenous expedition; nursery plants; my own layerings, cuttings, and root divisions; plus some wildlings from field and wood. It all makes us a treasured garden, the collection of years of herb growing.

## Plants from Seeds

Let us suppose you are one who likes to grow plants from seed. This method is slow but it has several compensations. You will come to know your herbs literally from the ground up. Then too, suppose you plant a package of savory seed or basil seed and find yourself in possession of more flourishing seedlings than you can possibly use. You are now able to call your friends and offer them some. Either they will be thrilled to get them because they are new (all gardeners love something new) or they will shout into the telephone, "Savory? God love you! I've been wanting some for ages." Either way you'll be ahead of the game.

All of the annual herbs (see chart, pages 62 to 65) can be grown successfully from seed. Many of the perennials, though they require more time and patience, are gratifying in results from seed, especially if you have use for many plants.

While herb seeds may be sown indoors or under glass, there is really little gain, even in severe climates. For perennials, sowing out of doors in well-prepared soil in September and not disturbing the soil until spring is best. Some of the plants, in mild climates, will come up before winter and be well established by spring. Others will not germinate until spring and will get a strong start. Plants so sown are stronger and quicker than those sown indoors and transplanted in the spring. Annuals can be sown in the spring after the danger of frost is well over. In dry climates cover the seed beds with burlap and keep wet until germination starts.

Thin the plants when they are 2 or 3 inches high, and those of varieties that will stand transplanting (see chart, pages 62 to 65) may be set out elsewhere. Some gardeners find it interesting to set out the thinees in the main flower garden, a few here and there among the other plants. If you are not depending on these émigrés for flavor, you will be delighted with the new growth habits the fertilizer in the enriched beds gives them. And after all, they add variety, and that is never to be sneezed at, in a garden.

Individual hints for growing, thinning, transplanting, etc. according to the nature of each herb will be found in the chart on pages 62 to 65, and under the heading of individual herbs farther on in this chapter..

## *Propagation Methods*

Now, making little ones out of big ones. Herb gardeners all want to be perpetually making new plants — it is a mark of the breed. First, we do it so we can have strong new specimens true to type when we make over the perennial beds or replace plants that have grown too woody to keep. Then, all gardeners are givers, otherwise plants won't grow for them. We herb gardeners grow extras to offer seasoned fanciers or budding enthusiasts. The love of herbs is contagious, and often a handful of slips or a few plants awaken a latent interest in spice-gardening. Then too, herbs are ideal hospitality gifts. Hostesses enthuse sincerely over a potted thyme or rosemary, or a sweet-scented geranium.

1. LAYERING

Layering is a simple process, requiring no mumbo jumbo, and is one of the best ways of producing healthy new plants

quickly. All of the common perennials layer well and produce stronger specimens than those seed-grown. To layer a
plant pick out a branch lying close to the earth. Loosen the
earth under it, pin the branch down with a bent wire or long
hairpin, and cover the pinned-down portion with a layer of
earth. If this is kept moist, in about a month roots will have
formed on the underside, making a new plant. Cut it away
from the parent, for it is ready to plant. This is an easy
method of obtaining new plants to replace the old perennial
herbs, which grow woody and straggly after a few years'
growth.

## 2. CUTTINGS OR "SLIPS"

There is something fraternal about "getting a slip" from
someone's garden that is bound to endear the plant to the
new owner. In former times when nurseries were not so
numerous, slips of prized plants passed from friend to
friend, leaving the glow of giving with the donor, bringing
the joy of beauty to the new garden. Now nurseries supply
us with the plant wealth of the hemispheres. So we buy what
we want and bear it home in a flush of ownership. Making
a garden that way is undoubtedly effective, but to a certain
degree the personal warmth is lacking.

Something of the old, friendly spirit remains in herb gardening, for herbs are not so easily obtained as other plants.
My herb garden, and those of the other herb growers I know,
scatter slips all over the San Francisco Bay area. Herb fanciers are born slippers. Truly, to show a guest my garden
without stooping to pluck a sprig here, another there, of all
its fragrant plants, would be a failure in hospitality. In fact,
such a tour usually starts frankly, on my part, with clippers,
a basket, and paper and pencil for labeling. Maybe it is su-
perstition, but I almost believe my garden would wither if I
did not so share it. However, I hope this confession does not
start an avalanche of callers. There is a limit to the number
of slips a plant may yield and still be useful to its owner.

Cuttings, often known also as slips, can be made of most perennial herbs, especially where there is no opportunity for layering. New end growth, hard enough to snap when bent, may be cut with clippers or a sharp knife, or pulled from the parent stem in such a way as to leave a "heel" on the slip — a little bit of the parent stem skin. Rosemary and the scented geraniums must be slipped with heels. Moist river sand or water are the best materials to start slips; hormone powder hastens the rooting process, but constant moisture is more important.

## 3. ROOT DIVISION

This method means just what it says — division of roots. All the perennial herbs can be so propagated; for certain ones this is the only effective way. In the spring (in the fall in mild climates) the entire plant is dug up, and the tangle of roots is untangled so that the clump can be cut into smaller clumps with a sharp utensil. Each clump can be replanted and will be a new, fresh plant. Balm, the marjorams, sage, the thymes, winter savory, the mints, horseradish, hyssop, all do well in root division. True tarragon, which throws no seeds, must be thus increased. Sweet woodruff, the zest of may wine, should be so divided.

## Self-Seeding

Some herbs self-seed so industriously that it is wise for your own peace of mind never to allow the seeds of these to scatter. The mints are such prolific characters and sweet fennel is another. Dill, too, has such habits, but for the sake of my boiled potatoes, fish, and pickles, I let them come up where they will, the better to eat them, my dears!

Certain other herbs may well be allowed to self-seed, as a painless way of securing new plants. Marjorams, thymes, sages, rue, and borages are notable successes. When the seeds are ripe shake the bush, then do not disturb the ground around the plant too much until late spring. Result, fine new plants.

## Pests?

In respect to possible plant pests, herbs are the delight of the gardener. With few exceptions they are not bothered with those bugbears that make flower and vegetable gardeners' lives so miserable. Perhaps beetles, bugs, and their ilk don't care for seasoned food. Whatever the reason, herb gardens do enjoy comparative freedom from pests.

But I mentioned exceptions, for what good is a rule without them? Aphids have a real liking for chives, garlic, shallots, nasturtiums, parsley, borage, and dill. But plant cloves of garlic among these plants, and when they grow, a lot of those aphids will quit in disgust. Snails will nestle in parsley, basil, and celery. Since these are edible plants they cannot well be sprayed. Ant control stakes set near them will control the ants which bring the aphids, and soaking instead of overhead watering also helps. For snails, the same effective brands of pellets in use elsewhere in the garden will solve the problem.

## Two Herb-Gardening Hints

### 1. SETTING OUT PLANTS

When planning the herb garden it is best to plant the annuals together and the perennials in a company by themselves. Thus, at the end of the annuals' year the ground can be worked and prepared for another year without disturbing established perennial plants, which are only reset every three or four years.

## 2. FOR FELINES ONLY

If you and your family are "cat people," please give the king of the household a break by planting some true catnip. If you do, and you will not regret it when you see your cat reveling in good, green branches of it, heed one warning. Plant seeds rather than purchasing plants, and sow the seeds where they are to stand. Else your catnip bed will be an infant casualty and never get high enough to harvest. This is the reason: the odor of catnip will call a cat from an astonishing distance, and if he once finds out where it is growing, he goes right to work on it, with disastrous results. When seeds are planted the catnip sneaks out of the ground and is knee high to Pussy before he discovers it. Then, chew as he will, he can't wear it completely down. But if the young plants are transplanted, the odor will be disseminated and the plants are doomed. For once an old proverb holds true:

If you set it, the cats will eat it;
If you sow it, the cats won't know it.

Since each herb, as each human being, is a personality and should be so considered, a glance at the principal herbs with an eye to their differences makes their acquaintance easier to cultivate. In the main they are grown similarly, but idiosyncrasies do exist.

| Herb | Part Used | Height | Annual or Perennial | Plants Needed | Distance Apart | Notes |
|---|---|---|---|---|---|---|
| ANISE | Fresh leaves, seeds | 18" | Annual | 3 or 4 | 8" | Will not transplant |
| BALM | Fresh leaves | 15" | Perennial | 2 to 4 | 8" | Will spread |
| SWEET BASIL | Leaves and flowers | 8" to 10" | Annual | 12 | 7" | Pinch back center |
| BORAGE | Tender leaves and flowers | 12" to 15" | Annual | 4 to 6 | 10" | Will self-seed<br>Will not transplant |
| BURNET | Tender, young shoots | 15" | Perennial | 2 to 3 | 15" | Self-seeds<br>Will not transplant<br>Cut back often |
| CARAWAY | Dried seeds | 15" | Biennial | 2 to 4 | 10" | Use stakes<br>Will not transplant |

| Herb | Part Used | Height | Annual or Perennial | Plants Needed | Distance Apart | Notes |
|---|---|---|---|---|---|---|
| CELERY | Leaves, dried seeds | 18″ | Biennial | 2 to 4 | 8″ | Cut back often<br>Let 1 plant grow for seed |
| CHERVIL | Fresh leaves | 8″ | Annual | 8 to 10 | 6″ | Sow successive crops<br>Will not transplant |
| CHIVES | Fresh tops | 8″ | Perennial | 12 to 18 | 2½″ | Cut back often<br>Fertilize<br>Do not let bloom |
| CORIANDER | Fresh tips, dried seeds | 24″ | Annual | 2 to 3 | 8″ | Use stakes<br>Will not transplant |
| CUMIN | Dried seeds | 8″ | Annual | 3 | 6″ | Will not transplant |
| DILL | Fresh seed heads and dried seeds | 24″ | Annual | 6 to 10 | 10″ | Use stakes<br>Will self-seed |

| Herb | Part Used | Height | Annual or Perennial | Plants Needed | Distance Apart | Notes |
|---|---|---|---|---|---|---|
| FENNEL | Fresh leaves and dried seeds | 4' to 6' | Annual | 1 to 2 | 3' | Do not let seed, as will scatter plants over yard |
| SWEET MARJORAM | Leaves and blossoms | 12" | Depends on climate | 4 | 10" | Shade new plants till started |
| WILD MARJORAM (oregano) | Leaves and blossoms | 18" | Depends on climate | 2 | 18" | Self-seeds freely Sprawls |
| MINT | Leaves | 10" to 12" | Perennial | 3 | 8" | Plant by itself Will spread Do not let seed |
| NASTURTIUM | Blossoms and seed pods | 6" to 12" | Annual | 2 to 4 | Depends on species | Will self-seed |
| PARSLEY | Leaves | 12" | Biennial | 6 to 12 | 6" | Cut down frequently Plant new each year |

| Herb | Part Used | Height | Annual or Perennial | Plants Needed | Distance Apart | Notes |
|------|-----------|--------|---------------------|---------------|----------------|-------|
| ROSEMARY | Leaves | 36" | Perennial | 1 | | A large bush Do not cut down when it blooms |
| SAGE | Leaves | 12" | Perennial | 2 | 10" | |
| SUMMER SAVORY | Leaves | 12" | Annual | 3 to 5 | 6" | |
| WINTER SAVORY | Leaves | 12" | Perennial | 2 | 14" | Sprawls |
| TARRAGON | Leaves | 10" | Perennial | 3 | 12" | |
| COMMON THYME | Leaves | 8" | Perennial | 4 | 8" | Will spread Will self-seed |

## ANISE

This annual will grow profusely from seed if that seed be fresh. For this reason it is best to buy the seed from a reputable house and plant it early. Sow it where it is to stand, for it does not transplant successfully. A slow grower, it must be kept free of weeds, for they will spring up and outdistance the anise, choking it out. Stakes are advisable, for the plants have a tendency to sprawl. Full sun is best for this herb.

## BALM

A perennial which comes up strong and green each year from the same roots, this plant does not grow readily from seed, since it is very slow to germinate and mature. Root division or slips are better ways of making new plants. Curb its growth from year to year by cutting away the outer growth, or it will preempt too great a space in your garden. Full sun or partial sun are acceptable.

## BASIL

This plant may be grown from seed where it is to stand, or plants may be purchased from a nursery, since it transplants very well. Grow at least a dozen plants, for this, an annual, must be dried for winter use or frozen green (pages 26–27). Since it is so delicious you'll need plenty. When it is growing well and is about 6 inches high, pinch out the tops of the plants to make them branch. When the blossoms appear and the basil is in full bloom, cut it only half the way down, so that a second crop will form. Full sun will make this herb doubly fragrant.

## BORAGE

This annual dislikes transplanting, so it must be sown where it is to grow. One sowing will do for several years, for it self-sows if the seed is allowed to fall. These second-year plants are more beautiful and stronger than their parents. Since it is one of the really beautiful color plants of the herb garden, sow it generously. You will enjoy it.

# BURNET

This faithful perennial, if not allowed to go to seed, will go on for you year after year. An old clump will grow wider (you know how middle age is) but behaves itself well in the garden. If it is to be used for salads, keep cutting it back and do not let it get above 6 inches tall. Thus the new shoots are always tender. Root division is very effective, or letting one shoot grow tall and go to seed will produce good new plants. Burnet likes full sun.

# CARAWAY

Caraway is best started from seed, for it germinates freely. But plant it in the place where you want it, because it does not transplant well. A biennial, for its seed does not ordinarily set the first year of growth. But if seeds are planted in the early fall, those plants will have seeds the next summer. When harvesting the seed crop, let some fall and dig them in for the next year's crop. If the ground is not disturbed too early in the spring, the new plants will soon appear. If one follows this procedure, a caraway crop each year is assured. As for most seed-bearing plants where the seeds are the part harvested, full sun is best.

# CELERY

Our celery is a domesticated refinement of smallage, that bitter and perhaps poisonous wilding of the roadside. Today, instead of hunting the original herb, we plant seed of our ordinary cultivated celery, cut it often so that it stays only 5 or 6 inches tall, and use it leaves for seasoning. A small pocket handkerchief plot or a short row, thinned to 4 inches, will supply the tang of celery all season long. In the fall let it go to seed and harvest those seeds. They will help you season cleverly. If you can buy the seeds of "spice celery," it can be used green as directed above, and its seeds will be more fragrant than the ordinary table celery. An annual, celery must be sown anew each year, in the sun.

CHERVIL

This annual does not transplant, so it must be sown in the plot or row where you wish it to stay. Light shade, such as that of taller plants, shelters its tender growth. This herb matures rapidly, and since, like parsley, it is used in the young and tender stage, successive sowings every few weeks are necessary to insure a season's supply.

CHIVES

Though these seasoning gems can be grown from seed, it is a slow process. A clump from the grocer's shop, or witched from a kind friend, can be divided into individual bulblets, planted 5 inches apart, and if the soil is rich, will provide you with beautiful little chives to cut for the whole season. Fertilize them lightly when you cut them, and never let them bloom. Divide again every third year, making over your entire setting. Full sun makes rich fragrance in chives.

CORIANDER

This, to my mind, is one of the most beautiful of the herbs when in flower. It grows full and branches into feathery umbels of rosy lavender. Such beauty surely is sufficient to redeem it from the disgrace some heap upon it for what they consider the unpleasant odor of its foliage. To me it is not unpleasant, perhaps because I find that its leaves, used charily, are a good seasoning. Sow the seeds in the ground where they are to stay, in the sun, thinning to 8 inches when they are well out of the ground. Stake the plants when they begin to grow tall, for they will lop over.

CUMIN

An annual, this seed plant is best started from seed sown quite thickly in a sunny place. Germination is not likely to be generous, for it is somewhat tricky to raise. But any crop at all will be reward enough, for this dainty little foot-high plant has rosy blooms for the garden, and fragrant, spicy seeds for the kitchen. Do not try to transplant.

## DILL

Virgil called this a "pleasant and fragrant plant" and today we still think so. An annual that courts the sun, it should be sown in the open ground where it is to stand, for it resents transplantation. Since it grows tall and produces heavy seed heads, staking is necessary when the plants are 12 inches tall. The tender young flower heads can be used for seasoning, but be sure to cut some when they are full of seeds and dry them for pickles. Other flower heads should be let to grow brown so that the seeds themselves can be harvested. Also let some drop on the ground, for new plants next year.

## SWEET FENNEL

This herb is an annual if it is allowed to seed, but otherwise behaves as a perennial, coming up year after year if it is cut down before the seed matures. If plants are to be started from seed, they should be thinned to 12 inches. A sunny spot is best for them. My own fennel, the wild variety, was brought as a small plant from a California roadside. In my garden corner it has lasted for over 10 years, growing 7 feet tall and supplying me with enough green seasoning to cook all the fish in Steinhart Aquarium. Since I do not let it go to seed it has never reseeded itself in parts of the garden where it is not wanted, but through the years has stayed put, acquiring a comfortable, middle-aged spread, befitting a plant of its years.

## MARJORAM

Wild marjoram (oregano) is always a perennial, but sweet marjoram is perennial only in mild climates. In severe regions it behaves like an annual and must be renewed each year. It comes well from seeds, but root divisions or slips are equally successful. This is a sun-loving herb and needs no sheltering. Wild marjoram, a large plant, should be spaced at 18 inches, while sweet marjoram needs only 10 inches elbow room.

## THE MINTS

These errant herbs need special placing and handling if they are to be a credit to your garden. Pick a spot near a drippy faucet, if you can bear to be that type of gardener. In this damp spot plant your mints, for they must wade a bit to grow brightly green and crisply sweet. Select a bed where they have physical barriers from the rest of the garden, such as a walk, a wall, or even metal plates (old license plates are good) set down into the earth between them and the rest of the plants. For mints travel far and fast, being active members of the Underground Movement. They send out runners under the earth, rooting at intervals, and unless you are vigilant you will have, not a sweet little mint bed, but a great big mint pasture.

To Rosetta Clarkson's *Herbs, Their Culture and Uses*, I am indebted for the thickness and delicacy of the mints in my mint bed. She advises, after the fall cutting down has been done, that the bed should be cut down into with a sharp spade, in checkerboard fashion, to cut the underground runners into segments. Then, she says, soak the bed, and cover with a layer of enriched topsoil. At each place where a segment of root has been cut a new plant will spring up, tender and green. I have followed this advice several seasons, and my mint bed, instead of the hit or miss affair that an old mint bed usually becomes, is a miracle of beauty and kitchen usefulness.

While on the subject of the necessary, delightful, but wayward mints, do not let them go to seed. The seed blows about, and someday you will find mint in the lily bed, or rubbing elbows with your darling plant exotics in the front garden.

## NASTURTIUM

Of course these are annuals and must be sown from seed. Dwarf, standing, or climbing, any variety will do, for they all look beautiful and taste exquisite. Sun, of course, makes them grow fragrant and flower lavishly. Thinned to 8 inches, given abundant water, they will provide spice and color for salads and sandwiches.

## PARSLEY

Though a biennial, this is best treated as an annual, for its second-year growth is not lush and full enough for the uses to which we put it in the kitchen. A new parsley bed sown each fall will repay for the effort. Sow seeds in rows or in a small plot in soil that has been lightly fertilized. Mine grows in the shade of a hedge that protects it part of the day, and it grows graciously and well. On the other hand, I have had it in full sun with equally good results. Plants should be thinned to 5 or 6 inches. In using parsley make your cuttings gradually down the entire row or across the entire bed, so that each plant gets several cuttings during the year. This keeps it young and tender. Parsley will transplant, but doesn't highly approve of the practice.

## ROSEMARY

Never underestimate the size of a full-grown rosemary bush when you plan your herb garden. That modest little plant you have started from a slip or bought in a small can from a nursery will grow, and grow, and grow. Allow a space of several feet, preferably against a sunny wall or fence. This herb, though hardy, needs a good shelter in winter, and if given this will live in a severe climate a number of years. Propagation is by slips, and care should be taken that each slip is pulled with a heel of the parent stem skin hanging to it. Starts slips in sand or in a glass of water. Layering is successful with rosemary, too.

## SAGE

Sage is an amenable herb in the matter of propagation. Plant seeds, and they all come up twice. Put slips in sand, they start roots before your back is turned. Layer branches from a parent plant, and you have new plants in nothing

flat. And root division? It works like a charm. No wonder
sage has stayed on in American gardens when the other
herbs have been lost. It defies extinction. Plant your sage in a
sunny spot, and renew the plant every third year by starting
a new one by one of the above methods, and you are set for
life.

## SUMMER SAVORY

This is the annual savory, so of course it must be planted
each year and dried or frozen in the fall for winter seasoning.
But it springs easily from seed planted in the open ground.
When large enough to thin, thin to 6 inches apart, and plant
the thinees in another place, as they thrive on such moves.
This is an erect little plant, with rather spare growth habits,
but full of vigor and flavor.

## WINTER SAVORY

This savory is the perennial, first cousin to the annual, and
an acceptable substitute for it. While this variety will start
from seed, patience is necessary, for it is slow to germinate.
New plants should be thinned to 12 inches, transplanting the
surplus elsewhere. Also, cuttings grow readily, or the old
plant can be layered to make new ones. Savory wants plenty
of sun.

## TARRAGON

In a news column the other day I read that, "in California
tarragon does not set seed." To be entirely true and at all
valuable to the culinary herbalist, the statement should have
read, "True tarragon does not set seed either in California,
Timbuktu, or anywhere else." Never let anyone talk you into
sowing tarragon seed, if you want the flavorful variety. New
plants must be made either by slipping or root division, with
the latter more likely to succeed. Frankly, for me tarragon is
elusive. Today I have it, but tomorrow I may not. Yet in the

yard of friends a few blocks away, tarragon is given the same sort of care that I give it, and yields abundant growth. I can only believe it a prima donna among herbs. Plants should be set 18 inches apart, in the partial shade of taller plants, and in a deep, loose soil. Each year start new plants, otherwise you will find yours have all disappeared, and you will have to start all over again. In severe climates a winter mulch will carry the plants over to spring.

THYME
Of course there are many varieties of thyme, but that most commonly grown in culinary gardens is common or garden thyme. This is another amenable plant. Seeds come up quickly and freely, though other varieties are hard to grow that way. All varieties are easily layered or slipped, and root divisions are equally successful. Set new plants in a sunny location, 6 to 9 inches apart, and clip severely when they flower. I cut mine to within 2 inches of the ground, and find that they do not develop wood quickly. In cold regions mulch in winter, for thyme is a hardy perennial. If plants are renewed every 3 years a thyme border will remain full and leafy.

## Harvesting Herbs

If you live where the winters are cold and most of the herbs are not green all year round, prepare to dry or freeze them in the fall for your winter cookery. Annuals, of course, are always dried or frozen for winter, in any part of the country. Or if you are interested in the various forms of house fragrance such as herb sachets, herb pillows, bath herbs, or potpourri, dry herbs and flowers for that purpose.

Allow the plants to blossom; then on a warm, sunny day, after the morning dew is gone, cut them down. Tie them in small, loose fagots, or spread them in large, shallow box tops (suit boxes are good). Dry them either in a warm room or in a very slow oven. When fully dry pick off the leaves and blossoms and store them in jars with tight covers, to preserve the flavor and fragrance. We all know the charming traditions of the attics and kitchens "hung with store of fragrant herbs." Romantic to be sure, but how dusty! Furthermore, such herbs, along about Christmas time, would taste like nothing but a bale of last year's hay. Be on the safe side and store yours in jars. Hang up some "prop" fagots if your soul demands them, but don't try to season with them after they've been there awhile. Or you may prefer to freeze your herb harvest (pages 26–27).

If you are harvesting cumin, caraway, anise, dill, fennel, or coriander seeds, leave them on the plants until they are fully ripe and the foliage is brown. Then pull up the plants on a warm day, excepting, of course, the fennel, which should be cut and the root left. Garner the seeds, sift out the chaff, and store the clean, spicy seeds in tight jars.

Now, a solemn warning to both cooks and gardeners. The oldsters, hundreds of years back, looked upon these fragrant plants with awe, endowing them with magic powers. If you follow their advice in harvesting your herbs you will soon realize that it is serious business.

According to an old herbal one should gather herbs *at sunrise, in silence, without the use of iron implements, and looking toward the East during the entire proceedings. After they are picked, walk straight away and don't look behind you.*

After all, it is best to be careful. Life *is* sweet.

A garden with the herbs for cookery may well contain also the scented plants so desirable for potpourri and rose jars. Plant a few cabbage roses, ideal for such use. Include clove pinks, lemon verbena, costmary, southernwood, and always plenty of lavender. Rose and lemon geraniums are sweet additions.

Thus you may bring your summer garden indoors, fill your jars with it, pack it in linen sachets for your chests, bureaus, and clothespresses. All winter long the spirit of your garden will give you benison.

# ❧ FOUR ❧

## Cockle Warmers

It was, you remember, the Mock Turtle who sang:

> "Who would not give all else for two p
> ennyworth only of beautiful soup?"

Any soup enthusiast knows the emotion of the Mock Turtle, understands his devotion to this dish of dishes. For man, from Esau down, has had his soup and relished it.

There are two distinct schools of soup eating: one which takes soup seriously, as something of sufficient substance to preclude trifling; the other, a lighter school, conceiving of soup as a prelude to a meal, a teaser rather than any real satisfaction.

There is something to be said on both sides. If one wants something that will snuggle up to the ribs and stick, there is the kind of soup called by the French "Family Soup" (*potage de ménage*) or by the Italians "Big Soup" (*minestrone*) — bean soup, vegetable soup, and all the rest of that fine com-

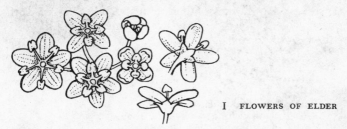

I    FLOWERS OF ELDER

pany of lusty fellows, fit companions for an open fire when wind and rain make the outer air poor invitation.

But if one wishes only a palate tickler to usher in a meal of varied courses, then those honest pottages are not to be sought. Choose instead a light soup with pretty *juliennes* floating therein — a clam broth with its crown of cream — a bouillon bold in flavor but with little substance to rob the appetite.

Pottages, those soups thick with the goodness of their ingredients, were originally the soups of the people, made to sate hunger roused by toil. They were of everyday materials, whatever was in the garden or the larder. The thin soups, on the other hand, were the conceits of aristocrats. Fine with flavor, but blessed of no power to stay hunger, they were designed by gifted cooks for masters whose appetites were stunted by too much leisure.

So if you are of proletarian turn of mind today, and of a sophisticated one tomorrow, let pottage be your fare today, a consommé tomorrow. You'll be the richer for liking both kinds, for variety in one's taste for soups forecasts delights to come, year after year.

Whichever sort you choose for the day's menu, herbs may thrust delicate fingers into its depths to lend just that one finishing touch that brings perfection of flavor. It will be marjoram for some, thyme for others, and so on through the fragrant roll, each bringing in turn its own peculiar contribution to savor.

Tastes in soups, as in other things, have changed with the years. Listen for a moment, tasting mentally this dainty credited by Athenæus to Axionicus:

> I am making soup,
> Putting in well-warmed fish, and adding to them
> Some scarce half-eaten fragments; the which I sprinkle
> With savory assafœtida; and then
> I make the whole into a well-flavored sausage,
> A meat most saleable. Then I do add a slice
> Of tender tripe; and a snout soaked in vinegar.
> So that the guests do all confess, the second day
> Has beaten o'er the wedding day itself.

Think of our own excellent broths, and thank Fortune for the passage of time.

# POTTAGES

There is something about the unsophisticated honesty of soups thick with meat and vegetable goodness that warms the heart as well as the stomach. Like friends untaught, they give of their best without restraint. Such food is easy on the palate, on the cook, and on the pocketbook.

## Minestrone

Closest to the heart of our household is the Italian "Big Soup" or *minestrone*. A plate of this pottage topped with grated Romano cheese, served with crisped and garlicked French bread, a salad, and a glass of wine, and *we have dined*. Though there are many versions of this soup, all follow a more or less faithful pattern. No meat, but dry beans boiled until mealy and then pureed, form the base on which to build the savor. Onions, garlic, potatoes, leeks, savoy or "curly" cabbage, and tomatoes are an accepted and fairly constant part, while other vegetables are used in their seasons. The result is a thick soup into which small pasta, like broken spaghetti, has been added last. Dished piping hot, it melts the shower of grated Romano cheese into just one more bit of assembled deliciousness to make a superlative meal. This is the way it is done:

First, the assembling of the vegetables, which is an important and tricky bit of procedure. No mere and haphazard ordering of a "soup bunch" and letting an uninformed vegetable man dictate the flavor of that soup. Instead, those vegetables must be personally ordered, one by one, and insisted on. If in your market you can find an Italian employee, he will know the requisites for a kettle of *minestrone* as well as the inside of his mother's kitchen. Lacking such a paragon, and just to be safe, make your own choice and tell your salesman you want in your basket:

| | |
|---|---|
| *1 green onion with tops* | *2 large, ripe tomatoes* |
| *1 leek with tops* | *2 Italian squash* (zucchini) |
| *2 large leaves curly cabbage* | *or 2 summer squash* |
| *10 or 12 green beans* | *1 carrot* |
| | *1 handful green peas shelled* |

With these fresh vegetables and the following ingredients you can make a large pot of excellent soup:

| | |
|---|---|
| *2 cups dried cranberry beans* | *1 tablespoon olive oil* |
| *water* | *2 large dry onions* |
| *salt* | *1 clove garlic* |
| *piece of lean salt pork 2 inches square* | *1 teaspoon fresh sweet basil or 1 tablespoon dried* |

| black pepper | 1 cup dry pasta about size |
| 1 large potato | of broken spaghetti |
| 2 tablespoons parsley | 1 cup grated Romano cheese |

Soak dried beans overnight in 2 quarts water. In the morning add 1 teaspoon salt and boil about 2 hours, or until very tender. Drain half the beans out of their liquor and put them through a colander, puree sieve, or blender; then return the resultant puree to the remaining beans and the liquor. Set this aside.

Dice salt pork into small pieces. Heat oil in a soup kettle, add pork, and slowly fry until the fat has cooked out and the pork pieces are dry. Remove them and discard, leaving oil and liquid fat in kettle. Into this put finely minced dry onions and garlic, stir well, and cook slowly 10 minutes without browning. Peel tomatoes and add them. Add parsley and basil and cook 10 minutes more. Put in bean puree and liquor, and black pepper. Stir well. Mince all green vegetables, mince squash and carrots, peel and dice potato, shell peas, and add all these to the kettle. Put in enough cold water to cover the vegetables amply (from 2 to 3 quarts at least). Cover, bring slowly to a boil, then add salt to suit taste. Simmer until vegetables are very tender, which will take about 2 hours. When three quarters done add more salt if needed.

Cook pasta in boiling salted water until tender. Drain and add to soup just before serving. Top each plate of soup with a heaping teaspoon of cheese sprinkled over the surface. *8 servings.*

Traditionally and deliciously, this soup usually has Crushed Basil Sauce (*Pesto di basilico,* page oo) stirred into it just before serving. Then, with its topping of grated Romano cheese, it is a dish to console *maigre* diners and other hungry souls.

This soup will be at its best cooked one day and eaten the next, in which case do not add the pasta until ready to serve. It keeps well in a refrigerator, so one can safely make twice as much as is needed for one meal, put away what remains, and serve it several days later. Thus food costs and time are reduced.

## Meat and Vegetable Soup

Another Big Soup, though not the traditional minestrone, this is rich with meat flavor, and swimming with vegetables and herbs.

3 *pounds lean cross ribs of beef cracked*
1 *pound veal shank cracked*
1 *lamb shank cut in half*
1½ *gallons of water*
2 *tablespoons salt*
½ *pound boneless beef stewing meat*
2 *tablespoons olive oil*
3 *dry onions*
1 *clove garlic*
3 *tablespoons tomato paste*
2 *slices lemon with peel diced*
2 *tablespoons dry white wine*
*grated Romano cheese*

HERBS:
1 *teaspoon chervil*
½ *teaspoon sweet marjoram*
1 *teaspoon savory*
½ *teaspoon thyme or basil*
1 *leaf costmary*
6 *peppercorns*

VEGETABLES:
½ *pound green peas shelled*
2 *leaves curly cabbage*
10 *string beans*
1 *carrot*
1 *turnip*
1 *parsnip*
1 *leek with tops*
4 *sprigs parsley*
1 *Italian squash*
1 *potato*

Into a large soup kettle put cross ribs, veal and lamb shanks, water, and salt. Set over a low fire. Brown stew meat in olive oil in a frying pan, then add to kettle with other meats. Boil the broth up and skim. Add ¼ cup cold water to settle, boil, and skim again.

Meanwhile mince onions and garlic and cook slowly until yellow in pan where stew meat was browned. Add tomato paste, lemon, herbs, and peppercorns. Mix well, cook slowly 5 minutes, then add this mixture to the meat in the kettle. Cover and cook slowly at simmering heat for 4 hours. Then take off cover, fasten a thin cloth, or plastic wrap over the kettle, and refrigerate overnight.

In the morning skim off the fat. Lift out the meat and set aside for other uses (pages 169–171). Into the broth put the shelled peas and all the other vegetables, which should be minced. Cook slowly 2 hours, tasting for salt seasoning at the end of the first hour, and adding more if needed. Add wine just before serving, and serve hot with a teaspoon of grated Romano cheese over each plate. *6 to 8 generous servings.*

# BROTHS

Broths, delicate temptations — pools of rich meat juices in company with enlivening seasonings. They should be clear and sparkling; their cooking long and gentle to take their store of goodness from the meats that make them; they must be seasoned *just so.* If the liquids you are surveying meet all these requirements they are broths. If not, they are poor substitutes.

To make good broth, buy good meat. The old habit of frugally collecting odd bones and bits of inferior meat that could not be used elsewhere has proved false economy. Good meat will give you broth that is nectar, and in addition will furnish you boiled meat that is tasty and usable. For boiled meat of a desirable cut, allowed to cool in broth before removing, can be enjoyed either in salads or served hot or cold with horseradish, mustard, or Spanish sauce.

Meat for broth should be started to cook in either hot or cold water, according to your intentions, and should be started to cook with or without salt, also according to those same intentions. That is: If you are to make a broth or soup whose meat is to be shredded and left in the liquid to be eaten as part of the soup, then put the meat to cook in cold, well-salted water. Thus you will draw from the meat every bit of its flavor and goodness. But if the meat is to be served separately from the soup, then start the broth with boiling, unsalted water, in order to leave the meat tasty and firm. This latter method takes longer in cooking to make a broth full of flavor, but it is well worth the extra time.

An important point in broth making is religious skimming. When the kettle first comes to a boil skim off the foam that has gathered, then add a half cup of cold water to stop the boiling. Boil up again and skim. If you have time do this the third time. Then your broth will be as clear as amber wine. Unskimmed broth may be as good, but it is not so pretty.

## Broth No. 1

Follow the directions in the recipe for Meat and Vegetable Soup (page 81) to the point where the vegetables are to be added. This makes a fine, clear broth, excellent for either clear soups or for cookery that calls for broth as an ingredient.

## Broth No. 2

| | |
|---|---|
| 2 *pounds veal or lamb* | *(see comments on broth,* |
| 2 *pounds lean beef in one* | *above)* |
| *piece* | ½ *tablespoon salt* |
| 2 *tablespoons olive oil* | 1 *scant teaspoon minced* |
| 3 *quarts cold or hot water* | *marjoram* |

| | |
|---|---|
| 1 heaping teaspoon minced thyme | 4 cloves |
| 2 tablespoons minced parsley | 1 clove garlic minced |
| | ¼ cup diced carrots |
| ½ bay leaf | ¼ cup minced celery leaves |
| ½ teaspoon peppercorns | 1 onion minced |

Cut one-third of the meat into 2-inch cubes and brown in olive oil in the kettle. Add rest of meat and water, then salt. Put over slow fire, bring to boil, skim, and add ¼ cup cold water. Boil up again and skim. Add herbs, seasonings, and vegetables and simmer for 5 hours. Strain and let stand overnight in the refrigerator. In morning remove fat from top of liquid. This is now a finished broth, ready to serve as it is or to use in any of the following recipes for broth.

## Chicken Broth

In the preceding recipe substitute for the meats a 4-pound hen and a small knuckle of veal. Otherwise follow the recipe. This makes a broth to serve hot or jellied, for it will jell if left overnight in the refrigerator. Remember, however, that any broth which you wish to jell must always be *simmered,* never *boiled.*

There are numberless tricks with broth, each serving to vary either slightly or greatly that versatile liquid. If you try these and decide that you care to start more meals with clear soups, graduate to combinations of these ingredients in the following list, and see what charming innovations can be poured into the soup plates each day.

Here is a list of herbs, condiments, and other broth season-ings that will help in your experiments:

## Herbs for Soups

bay leaves
thyme
savory (winter or summer)
sweet marjoram
wild marjoram (oregano)
spearmint
sage
sweet basil

chervil
sorrel
tarragon
chives
rosemary
costmary
saffron (powdered)
parsley

## Condiments for Soups

curry powder
horseradish
celery salt
onion salt
garlic salt
allspice berries
mace

whole cloves
paprika
peppercorns
nutmeg
ground mustard
cayenne
cumin seeds

## Other Seasonings for Soups

lemon juice
sherry wine
grated Romano cheese
grated Parmesan cheese

Worcestershire sauce
herb brandies
dry white wine

Here is food for thought and a field for adventure. But just

as a starter in taking advantage of the vast matter of seasonings for soups, why not add:

1. Savory to black bean soup?
2. Thyme and wild marjoram (oregano) to beef broth?
3. Just a tiny bit of ground mustard to bean soup?
4. Celery salt and onion salt to potato soup, or a dash of
   nutmeg?
5. Sherry wine to vegetable soup?
6. Lemon juice to consommé?
7. Curry powder, just a little, to lentil soup?
8. Worcestershire sauce to split pea soup?
9. Thyme to clear tomato soup?

Can't you see how much fun you could have, with a list of
seasonings to consult, and soups or broths to vary for your
own and an admiring family's delight?

## Soups Based on Broth

Now that we have made the broths, let us see what can be
done with them. Of course they are a good ingredient for
general cookery, and many dishes in other sections of this
book call for broth or bouillon in their making. A large pot
of broth, made at the beginning of the week and kept in the
refrigerator, allows one to cook with it during the week, and
also to add dash to an otherwise simple meal by serving thin
soup as a first course. You've no idea how it helps, unless you
too use broth in these ways.

## Broth with Cheese

It was Alphonse Daudet who said, "*Ah! la bonne odeur de
soupe au fromage!*" He spoke truly, for the odor of hot, savory

soup rising through melting particles of fine imported cheese is inspiration. And now, to make this dish:

To each person serve one portion of either Broth No. 1 or No. 2, or Chicken Broth (pages 83–84). To each serving add ½ teaspoon lemon juice or a fine grating of lemon peel, and sprinkle the top with a teaspoon of either Romano or Parmesan cheese just before serving.

## Julienne with Herbs

Measure a cup of broth, either No. 1 or No. 2 (pages 83–84), for each serving, and one for the pot. Bring to the boiling point and to it add a few fine slivers of raw carrots, onions, turnips, and celery. Have enough to give each person a fair representation of vegetables, but not enough to make it a thick soup. Boil covered until vegetables are tender but not soggy. Portion out in dishes, and over the tops sprinkle ½ teaspoon minced parsley, tarragon, and chives, mixed.

## Variations of the Preceding Recipe

Choose any three herbs in the list on page 85, preferably selecting one of strong flavor and two of less pronounced taste. Let either parsley or chervil predominate in any mixture you may choose to use. Chop and mix, then sprinkle on the soup ½ teaspoon of each to each serving.

If desired, the vegetables may be omitted, and a plain broth served with the herbs.

## Broth with Pasta and Cheese

Bring either Broth No. 1 or No. 2 (pages 83–84) to a boil. For each quart of liquid have already boiled, rinsed, and drained ½ cupful (measured after cooking) of small semolina pasta (see page 000) such as *orzi*, *ditalini,* or spaghetti finely broken, or any pasta about the size of our familiar "alphabets." Add this cooked pasta to hot broth. Portion into dishes, top each portion with 1 teaspoonful of grated Romano or Parmesan cheese, and serve at once.

## Broth with Vegetables

By introducing into broth single types of vegetables, an even larger variety of thin soups may be served. Either cut the vegetables into thin strips about 1½ inches long (as carrots, potatoes, turnips, beets, onions, and such), cut them into paper-thin rounds (Italian squash, leeks, green onions, asparagus, mushrooms), or add them after shelling out of their pods (peas and mature beans). Add them when the broth is boiling and cook until tender but not soggy. Serve hot with either a sprinkling of herbs or grated cheese.

## Broth with Meat

Into the broth measured out to heat for the meal shred very fine some of the meat used in making the broth. Serve as soon as hot, with herbs or cheese.

## Broth with Garlic Croutons

Into one tablespoon of melted butter for each person to be served, grate finely ¼ of a medium-sized garlic clove. Cook very slowly 5 minutes, but do not brown. Then add small cubes of French or Italian bread, 10 or 12 for each serving, a few at a time. Turn the heat up slightly and brown the bread, stirring gently but often so as not to scorch. Throw these croutons into the broth just before sending to the table.

## Broth with Wine

Either dry or sweet sherry, haut Sauterne, Marsala, or Burgundy may be added to hot broth just before serving, in the proportion of a tablespoon to each serving of broth. Serve at once with grated Italian cheese.

## Broth with Herb Brandy

Flavor hot broth barely to taste with Herb Brandy (page 338) and serve with grated cheese. Be careful to add the brandy in drops rather than in quantity, for it is very strong. Taste after each drop, to judge amounts. Do not boil after adding brandy, as that removes the alcohol.

## Spinach Soup Made with Broth

This delightful soup tastes like a spring garden. Green as a leaf, thick with fragrant goodness, it is a spring tonic that is pleasing to take.

| | |
|---|---|
| *1  tablespoon butter* | *marjoram, thyme, and* |
| *1  tablespoon olive oil* | *sweet basil minced* |
| *½  clove garlic* | *3  cups broth (pages 83–* |
| *1  green onion with tops* | *84)* |
| *1  tablespoon minced pars-* | *salt* |
| *ley* | *⅔  pound raw spinach* |
| *1  teaspoon each of sweet* | *½  cup thin cream* |

Melt butter and mix with oil. Mince garlic very fine, add to oil and butter, and cook slowly 5 minutes without browning. Mince onions with tops, mix with herbs, and add. Cook slowly 5 minutes. Add broth, salt to taste, and bring gently to a boil. Simmer 10 minutes.

Meanwhile cook spinach with only such moisture as clings to its leaves, until well wilted but not too soft. Run through puree sieve or blender, retaining not only the pulp but any water that has cooked off the leaves. Add both to the broth and herb mixture. Add more salt if needed, mix well, and simmer 5 more minutes.

Heat the cream, but do not allow to boil. Divide it equally among 4 soup dishes, then into it pour equal portions of soup. Mix very lightly, just enough to give a marbled surface effect, and serve at once with Melba toast. *4 servings.*

## Herb Soup with Cheese

1 tablespoon butter
2 tablespoons each minced chives, chervil, and sorrel
1 cup finely shredded celery
½ teaspoon minced tarragon
1 tablespoon minced parsley

1 quart broth (pages 83–84)
salt
black pepper
nutmeg
⅓ cup dry white wine
6 scant teaspoons grated Italian cheese

Melt butter and into it put the minced chives, chervil, and sorrel. Cook very slowly 5 minutes, then add celery, tarragon, and parsley. Stir well, then add broth. Cover, bring slowly to boil, and let cook until all green things are tender (about 20 minutes). Rectify salt seasoning, add a dash of black pepper and nutmeg. Last of all add the wine. Put a piece of toast in each dish, portion out the soup over the toast, and top each dish with a teaspoon of cheese. Serve at once. *6 generous servings.*

## Tomato Soup with Basil

| | |
|---|---|
| 3 cups tomato juice | salt |
| ½ teaspoon celery salt | 6 peppercorns |
| 4 cloves | 2 cups broth (pages 83–84) |
| 1 teaspoon minced sweet basil | |

Add all seasonings to tomato juice and simmer 15 minutes. Strain, add to broth, heat to boiling point, and serve. *6 servings.*

So much for the thin soups made with broth. To originate others, all one needs to do is to "season with imagination." Now we come to some isolated soups that do not seem to fall naturally under any of the preceding classifications. But they are too good to leave out entirely.

Antiphanes, the comic poet who amused Greece so long ago, was not joking when he sighed after "a little lentil soup, a slice of sausage." So must we not joke with this great dish, one of the best. It dances down the gullet, warming every inch, making the diner happy with its goodness.

## Lentil Soup

| | |
|---|---|
| 1 cup brown lentils | 1 onion |
| 1½ quarts water | 1 clove garlic |
| 1 scant teaspoon salt | 2 tablespoons parsley |
| 2 slices bacon | 2 teaspoons winter savory |
| 2 tablespoons butter | 1 carrot |
| 1 tablespoon olive oil | 2 stalks celery with leaves |

*Worcestershire sauce*                    *salt*
*half a lemon*                            *black pepper*

Pick lentils over carefully and wash. Cover them with water and soak overnight or use 1 can cooked lentils. In the morning drain them, put them into the 1½ quarts cold water with a scant teaspoon salt and the bacon cut up fine. Simmer for 3 hours. At end of first hour melt butter in frying pan, add oil, and in this mixture fry minced onion and garlic, cooking slowly for 10 minutes. Add herbs and vegetables chopped, cook 10 minutes more, then add to lentils. Cook for the rest of the 3 hours. Drain lentils and vegetables from the liquor, run them through a puree sieve or blender, and turn again into the liquor. Add a small amount of Worcestershire sauce to suit taste. Mix well. Slice lemon in paper-thin slices, put one into each soup dish and pour soup over it. Serve at once.

If you, like Antiphanes, think this soup calls for sausage, serve garlic sausages or frankfurters boiled 20 minutes in a little broth as a side dish. They are easy to handle if sliced before serving. *6 servings.*

## Cranberry-Bean Soup

| | |
|---|---|
| 2 cups cranberry beans | 1 small carrot |
| 1½ quarts water | 1 teaspoon sweet basil |
| 1 teaspoon salt | ½ teaspoon thyme |
| ⅛ teaspoon black pepper | 1 teaspoon summer savory |
| 1 tablespoon butter | ⅛ teaspoon dry mustard |
| 2 tablespoons olive oil | Worcestershire sauce |
| 2 onions | 2 tablespoons dry sherry |
| 1 clove garlic | wine |

Soak beans overnight in clear water. In the morning drain them, add the 1½ quarts water, the salt and pepper. Set over

A FENNEL

a slow fire. In a frying pan melt butter and blend oil with it. Add onions and garlic finely minced. Cook 10 minutes, then add carrot shredded and herbs minced. Cook 5 minutes, then add this mixture to the beans. Cover and simmer slowly 3 hours. Remove beans from liquor, puree them, and return pulp to the liquor. Add mustard, Worcestershire sauce to taste, and heat again. Last of all add wine, and do not let boil at all after this is added. Serve at once. *6 to 8 generous servings.*

Once upon a time there was an editor, W. A. Croffut by name, who lived an important life, to others as well as to himself. Aside from his editorial gifts, and more to our concern in these pages, was his passion for food in general, and for clam soup in particular. One day he fell into verse on the subject, bringing forth a rhymed recipe for this delicious nectar, sweeping to triumphant finish in this pæan:

> Fruit of the wave! O, dainty and delicious!
> Food for the gods! Ambrosia for Apicius!
> Worthy to thrill the soul of sea-born Venus,
> Or titillate the palate of Silenus!

There is praise — even an overstatement at first glance. But think of what he was praising, before you accuse him of over-enthusiasm. For clam soup is, after all, quite special.

## Clam Soup

| | |
|---|---|
| 1½ quarts water | salt |
| 1 quart clams and their liquor | black pepper |
| | 1 cup cream |
| 1 teaspoon butter | 1 teaspoon minced thyme |
| ½ bay leaf | 1 cup toast cubes |
| 1 good dash mace | paprika |
| 1 stalk celery | parsley |
| 1 leek | |

Bring water to a boil, add clams and their liquor. Boil 10 minutes, then add all other ingredients except cream, thyme, toast cubes, and paprika. Boil gently 20 minutes, then remove clams and chop them, continuing the boiling of the broth meanwhile to finish cooking the vegetables. The clams themselves must not be cooked long, for in Mr. Croffut's words, "If much boiled they will suffer — you'll find that Indian rubber isn't tougher."

Return chopped clams to broth, along with cream and thyme. Pour over toast cubes in a tureen, and sprinkle all over with paprika. A sprinkling of minced parsley adds a pretty touch. *4 servings.*

## 🌿 *FIVE* 🌿

# *A Dish of Meat*

Some hae meat and canna eat,
And some wad eat that want it;
But we hae meat and we can eat;
Sae let the Lord be thankit.

BURNS doubtless intended embracing all forms of food in this fervent thanks. But let us put in an extra word for meat itself as such, for it is a princely food. Meat that cooks with such a heart-touching odor, meat from which we get a sense of satisfaction that has no parallel. Little wonder that man's devotion to this food has been so deep.

Examination of dinner menus of other days shows an astonishing preponderance of meats. Lady Mary Wortley Montagu wrote from Vienna in 1716: "I have been more than once entertained with fifty dishes of meat." The incomparable Pepys in 1658 detailed a Christmas dinner that pleased him as being "a dish of marrow bones, a leg of mutton and a loin of veal; three pullets and a dozen larks, all in a great dish. Also a great tart, a neat's tongue, a dish of anchovies and prawns, and cheese."

As time passed meat has been forced more and more to share its prominence with other foods. But still it is held in great affection by those who value taste. Of what do we dream when we are really hungry? Of meat — a steak, a browning roast, perhaps a bubbling stew. But surely of meat.

Since this food is still foremost in favor, it deserves interesting treatment, that it may realize its utmost destiny as fine fare. The basic rules for its cookery are neither many nor involved. But they must be followed. The results will be their own justification.

# *BROILING*

Once men ran green spits through their meat and cooked it over the fires that guarded their dwellings. The juices dripped upon the embers and rose again in incense-breathing smoke that perfumed Heaven.

Today we still broil our meats, but no longer in such wasteful fashion. Our beautiful stoves house gleaming broilers, where steaks and chops are cooked to perfection, retaining all the delicious juices that once were lavished on the Olympian deities.

Broiling is a comparatively simple process of cookery, if one follows the rules. There are many who believe that the unalloyed flavor of broiled meat, with a bit of salt, is pure delight that needs no addition. But others of us hold that, delightful as simply broiled meat may be, it might in time grow monotonous, if never varied. We therefore practice, for variety's sake, more elaborate modes of seasoning. Here herbs enter into the story, for they can touch foods and put into their flavor something irresistible. Sometimes the herbs are cooked into the meat, then again they are scattered green and fresh upon the already cooked surface.

## Broiled Steaks

Agamemnon feasted Ajax, after that famous Hectorian combat, on rump steak. But that was long ago. Now we buy T-bones, fillets, porterhouse cuts, New York cuts, and rib steaks, and think them better fare than Ajax got.

The herbal way with steaks is varied, and easy. For instance:

## Steaks with Bay Leaf

FOR EACH STEAK:

*1 tablespoon red-wine vine-*
    *gar*
*1 bay leaf*
*salt*

*black pepper*
*oil*
*butter*

Put the bay leaf into the vinegar and let soak for 1 hour. When ready to cook the steak, wipe it with a cloth wrung from cold water. Then with the bay leaf slap vinegar over the entire surface of the meat, wetting both sides. Place steak on broiler, break bay leaf into small bits, and strew over surface of meat. Broil in the usual way. Salt and pepper when done, drip a little oil and butter that has been heated and blended over each steak. Serve at once.

Then do as Thackeray's hero did: "put bits of bread into the [silver] dish and wistfully sop[péd] up the gravy." Maybe the Country Club set doesn't do it, but *it's good*.

## Steaks with Marjoram

New York cuts, or fillets, respond with a full quota of delightful taste to this prolonged marinating with seasoned oil.

FOR EACH STEAK:

| 2 | tablespoons olive oil | 2 to 4 crushed cloves garlic |
| 1 | teaspoon wild marjoram | salt |
|   | (oregano) | black pepper |

Let garlic soak in oil for 1 hour, then remove garlic. Brush both sides of steak with this oil, and over one side sprinkle wild marjoram (oregano). Roll steak up in oiled paper and leave in refrigerator overnight. The next day brush off the herbs and broil steak. Serve with salt and pepper.

## Steaks Basted with Herbs

Preheat this basting liquor,

| 1 | tablespoon olive oil | salt |
| 1 | teaspoon red-wine vinegar | black pepper |
|   | gar | butter |
| ½ | teaspoon minced thyme | |
| ¼ | teaspoon minced rosemary | |

Broil porterhouse steaks, basting them with this liquor. Keep the liquor hot during the basting process, but do not let it boil away. Spread steaks with butter and serve at once. If cooking steaks in multiples of 2 or 3, double or triple the ingredients in the basting liquor, and follow directions.

## Broiled Chops

Lamb chops, if cut thick and seasoned with herbs, present reason enough by themselves for maintaining an herb garden.

But don't let your butcher talk you into buying chops less than 1½ inches thick, for thinner ones dry out under even the lightest broiling. Large chops called round-bone chops, *cut from spring lamb,* are noble tidbits, each being a firm, united piece of meat that broils to perfection. An older animal, however, produces undesirable cuts of this type, the meat being too separated by membranes to be really good.

## Chops with Herbs

For each chop take:

¼ bay leaf
¼ teaspoon chopped thyme
¼ teaspoon chopped sweet basil
½ teaspoon chopped parsley

¼ teaspoon chopped sweet marjoram
salt
black pepper
olive oil

One hour before the meat is to be cooked mix the finely minced green herbs and pulverized bay leaves together, salt and pepper them, and mix with enough olive oil to make them stick together. Set aside.

Broil the chops until they are done to your taste. Salt them on both sides, transfer to serving platter, and over each chop scatter some of the herb mixture. Serve very hot. *1 thick lamb chop for each serving.*

## Broiled Lamb Chops with Mushrooms and Marjoram

6 round-bone lamb chops 1½ inches thick
½ pound fresh medium-sized mushrooms
4 tablespoons olive oil

fresh leaves of wild marjoram (oregano)
garlic, peeled and halved
salt
black pepper

Cut chops into pieces about 2 inches square. Peel mushrooms, using only the caps and saving the stems for some other purpose. Dip mushroom caps into oil so they are coated, then lay on a paper towel to drip. Pick the marjoram (oregano) leaves from their stems, using all but the tiny ones.

Thread the ingredients on 12 metal skewers in this order: first a mushroom, then a couple of marjoram (oregano) leaves, a slice of garlic, a piece of meat — then begin all over again. Fill skewers to within an inch of their points, and lay them on the broiler. Broil on one side, then turn and broil on the other. Salt and pepper after taking from the fire, and serve at once while very hot. Serve on the skewers, letting the diners remove the morsels from them. Only the meat and mushrooms are eaten, while the seasonings are left on the plates. *4 servings*.

## Sauce for Chops

Broiled chops or steaks are often anointed with a sauce after they are taken from the fire. Sauces for this use are many, but our favorite is one that combines herbs with its other contents:

| | |
|---|---|
| 1  *small onion* | 4  *tablespoons chopped* |
| *small grating garlic* | *parsley* |
| 2  *teaspoons Worcester-* | ¼  *teaspoon rosemary* |
| *shire sauce* | ¼  *teaspoon savory* |
| ½  *teaspoon salt* | 5  *tablespoons butter* |
| *dash cayenne pepper* | |

Grate onion and garlic on a flat plate and add seasonings and herbs that have been finely minced. Work to a smooth paste, cream with the butter, and spread over the surface of the piping hot broiled meat. Serve very hot. The quantity of salt makes it unnecessary to salt the meat itself.

You will doubtless discover herb combinations different from these of ours. After all, with the many herbs suitable for seasoning, their use becomes to a certain degree a matter of personal taste. But you will find that when you serve green herbs on broiled meat, the heat of the meat rising through the green particles will produce an aroma that will make you throw all diets to the winds.

# ROASTING

One of the trickiest of all the tricks in the cook's bag is this business of roasting. Brillat-Savarin, writing in his usual reverent vein about food, insisted that "a cook may be taught, but a man who can roast is born with the faculty." However, he was doubtless being positive, for roasting *can* be learned, if one follows the rules.

## Rules for Roasting

These are the roasting rules that never vary, for they are basic. Follow them, adding your own ruffles in the form of seasonings, and you will have invariably good roasts:

1. Wipe meat with cloth wrung from cold water
2. Place in roasting pan fat side up, or bone down
3. Sprinkle with a very little salted flour
4. Roast in an open pan in oven preheated to 325°:
   Beef — rare — 18 to 20 minutes to the pound

> medium — 22 to 25 minutes to the pound
> well done — 27 to 30 minutes to the
> pound
> Pork — must be well done — 30 to 35 minutes to
> the pound
> Lamb — 30 to 35 minutes to the pound
> Veal — 25 to 30 minutes to the pound
> 5. Take up meat on a hot platter

Roasting at these temperatures cuts down shrinkage and makes the meat juicier than if cooked at a high heat. Remember that small roasts take longer to the pound than larger ones, and rolled roasts longer than those with the bone left in. Basting can be done if some special flavor is desired that can only be achieved with a seasoned basting liquor, but ordinarily basting is not necessary. If no basting is done sprinkle on a little salt several times during the roasting.

## Garlic in Roasts

The addition of garlic to roasting meat assures heightened savor if correctly done. Many rules suggest slitting the meat and inserting whole cloves of garlic. Actually this method has drawbacks; it localizes the garlic flavor instead of sending it through the entire roast; it necessitates puncturing the meat, a poor practice; and it makes eaters liable to biting into whole cloves of garlic.

A more practicable way of bestowing garlic flavor on roasts is to grate a clove of garlic into 2 tablespoons of olive oil or melted butter, and paint the meat's surface with the mixture. Then sprinkle the salt, pepper, and flour on the oiled meat. Thus the garlic is evenly distributed and will not be disagreeably obvious. Also the flour and seasonings will adhere better to an oiled surface and will stay on throughout the cooking process.

## Basting Roasts

While no basting is necessary if you are cooking at 325° and if you wish the flavor of your roast to be just that of roasted meat, there are other occasions when basting is called for. If you wish to enjoy a roast with some special seasoning other than just the meat, then make a basting liquor which partakes of that seasoning, and with it baste faithfully every 15 minutes during roasting.

Suppose, for instance, that you are fond of a special combination of herbs, and wish your Sunday roast to have this flavor. Make a basting liquor, cook those herbs in it for a few minutes, then baste the meat with the unstrained liquor. This allows the flavor of herbs to permeate the meat as it could in no other way.

There are many bases for basting liquors — wine, either white or red; broth; a combination of wine and broth; any one of these three with a bit of tomato juice added, or catsup, chili sauce, or tomato sauce. Garlic, herbs, onion, spices, and pepper may be added as desired. A few minutes of gentle simmering serves to combine the flavors into one, making a tasty sauce for basting. It should be kept hot while being used. For recipes see pages 98, 104, and 105.

## Salting Roasts

Many roasts are flat for lack of sufficient salt, in spite of the salt rubbed over them before their cooking was begun. This is particularly true of roasts that are basted, for each time the meat is basted some of the salt on the outside of the meat

is washed off. If no more is ever added, the roast will taste un-
dersalted when it is served.

After each basting a little more salt should be sprinkled
over the surface of the meat. This small but consistent effort
will make a more tasty roast at the end of the cooking.

Those are all general pointers in the business of roasting.
Now for some recipes.

## Lamb with Mint

Rub a roast of lamb with butter, then with salt and pepper.
Dredge with flour. Place in a hot oven to brown, then reduce
heat to 325°. Baste every 15 minutes with this liquor, which
has been mixed and simmered 5 minutes:

| | |
|---|---|
| ½  cup broth (*pages 83–84*) | 2  tablespoons minced spearmint |
| ½  cup dry white wine | ½  onion minced or shredded |
| ½  clove garlic minced | |

After each basting sprinkle a very little bit of salt over the
meat. When the liquor is exhausted start basting from that
in the bottom of the pan. Cook until tender (*pages 101–102*).

## Lamb with Rosemary

Follow preceding recipe for Lamb with Mint, substituting
for the mint 1 teaspoon fresh or dried rosemary, minced.

## Beef Roast with Herbs

Rub roast with butter, then with salt and pepper, dredge

with flour, and brown in a very hot oven. Reduce heat to 325°
and cook, basting every fifteen minutes with the following
basting liquor, until tender (pages 101–102). When basting
liquor is exhausted use that in the bottom of the pan.

| | |
|---|---|
| *1 cup broth (pages 83–84)* | *1 teaspoon thyme* |
| | *1 teaspoon savory* |
| *½ cup red wine* | *black pepper* |

## Roast Pork with Herbs

Rub the meat with oil or butter, salt and pepper it, and
dredge with flour. Put into an oven preheated to 325°, and
after 30 minutes of cooking start basting with this liquor:

| | |
|---|---|
| *1 cup broth (pages 83–84)* | *1 clove garlic minced* |
| | *½ teaspoon rosemary* |
| *½ cup white wine* | *½ teaspoon fennel or anise* |
| *⅛ teaspoon nutmeg* | |

Cook liquor 5 minutes before using, then keep it hot. When
it is exhausted use liquor from bottom of the pan. Cook this
meat 40 minutes to the pound.

Perhaps you are a small family and prefer to roast small
pieces of meat, just enough for one meal. It is possible to
have good roasted meats without cooking a large cut. One of
our favorites is:

## Lamb Blocks with Potatoes (Agnello al forno)

First, in case your butcher does not know lamb blocks,
they are cuts from the shoulder just above the shank. Cut

from yearling lambs, they are about 3 inches thick, 6 inches long, and 4 inches wide at the widest point. Since they weigh about a pound apiece, each will amply feed a person.

5  *lamb blocks*
*oil or butter*
*salt*
*black pepper*

*flour*
5  *medium-sized potatoes, peeled and halved length-wise*

BASTING LIQUOR:
½  *cup red wine*
⅛  *cup olive oil*
 1  *cup broth (pages 83–84)*
½  *can tomato sauce*
 1  *teaspoon minced fresh rosemary*

 1  *clove garlic minced*
⅓  *small onion minced*
 1  *teaspoon salt*
⅛  *teaspoon black pepper*
½  *Japanese chile with seeds*

Rub meat with oil or butter, salt and pepper, and flour. Put into roasting pan and put into very hot oven until brown. Then reduce heat to 325° and lay potatoes around the meat. Salt and pepper potatoes.

Mix the basting liquor ingredients, bring to a boil and cook 5 minutes. Keep hot.

Roast the meat and potatoes at 325° for 1 hour, basting every 10 minutes with the basting liquor. *5 servings.*

These recipes will show you how you can introduce herbs into any of your roast recipes, when the flavor of plain roast meats palls on you, and thus vary your menus.

## STEWS

The combining of various meats, seasonings, and other ingredients into savory stews is as old as cookery itself. There was a long period in the development of the art of preparing food when any dish that did not bristle with an unrelated assortment of birds, beasts, and fishes was not considered worth bothering with. But as the art of cooking advanced it was found that too many ingredients make nothing but a conglomeration. So the damper was put on cooks who mixed with too enthusiastic an imagination, and food gradually became less bewildering and more eatable.

All this time that cooking history was being made, the prevalent habit was to "cook in a gravy." That custom had largely been lost in this country until revived by cosmopolitan food interest. But it still persists to this day in Europe, where cooking meats *en ragoût, all'intingolo, al sugo*, and the rest is high in favor. Meat so cooked is, like the veal and ham pie in *Our Mutual Friend*, "mellering to the organ . . . wery mellering to the organ."

If you like stews and such dishes "in a gravy," and want to make the acquaintance of one that has had its face lifted, try one with herbs in it. It may be your own family stew recipe, with a few snippets of herbs added, but you'll never know the old dish. Its verve will astonish you, its flavor delight you, for herbs in stews are touches of genius.

### Brown Stew with Herbs

suet
  2 *pounds boneless beef stew meat*
flour
salt

black pepper
  1 *clove garlic minced*
  1 *large onion sliced*
  ½ *teaspoon marjoram*

½ teaspoon thyme
2 tablespoons chopped
   parsley
1½ cups dry red wine

hot water
1 carrot
3 medium potatoes peeled
   and quartered

Preheat oven to 350°. Cut suet in small pieces and fry in an iron Dutch oven until fat is cooked out of it. Discard suet and leave fat in vessel. Roll meat in salted and peppered flour, cook slowly in fat until well browned, then add garlic and onion and cook slowly 10 minutes without browning them. Add herbs, wine, and 1 cup hot water. Cover Dutch oven, place in oven, and allow to cook for 3 hours, renewing water as liquid cooks away and stirring from time to time to prevent sticking. Last hour of cooking add carrot and potatoes and salt to taste. Ten minutes before serving taste for salt seasoning, adding more if necessary. *6 to 8 servings*.

## Swiss Steak with Herbs and Wine

3 pounds Swiss steak 2½
   inches thick
⅔ cup flour
½ teaspoon salt
⅛ teaspoon black pepper
suet
dash cayenne pepper

1 teaspoon marjoram
½ teaspoon summer savory
1 clove garlic
1 onion
½ cup dry white wine
½ cup water

Wipe meat with damp cloth, and into it pound the flour mixed with salt and pepper. Putting this much flour into the meat is a gradual process. Rub and pound as much into each side as it will take, set it aside a half hour, then repeat the process — and so on until flour is absorbed. Only with this much flour in it will the meat be tender and the gravy of the right consistency.

Cook suet slowly in a skillet, discard the dried-out pieces, and leave the hot fat in the pan. In it brown the floured steak quickly on both sides. Transfer to a Dutch oven (unless the browning was done in one), sprinkle lightly with cayenne, strew over it the herbs and minced garlic. Slice over them the onion. Pour on the wine and water mixed and heated to boiling point, pouring carefully so the vegetables and seasonings will not be washed off. Cover closely and simmer 2 hours, basting frequently with the liquor in the bottom. Baste even if you have a "self-basting" Dutch oven. After 1½ hours of cooking taste for salt seasoning, adding more if necessary. Cut into serving pieces when done, put on platter, and spoon gravy over top. *6 servings.*

## Tender Round Steak

This top round steak, cut into strips, marinated, and simmered, attains a tender succulence that makes it a true company dish. Allow 3 hours in all, for the meat must marinate for 2 hours and cook for 1. But the process need not be continuous, and the time is well spent.

2 *tablespoons soy sauce*
1 *teaspoon wild marjoram (oregano)*
½ *Japanese chile without seeds, cut fine*
3 *cloves garlic, 2 of them halved and slightly crushed, the other cut into 4 or 5 pieces*
1 *tablespoon liquid or ½ teaspoon powdered unseasoned meat tenderizer*

*flour*
4 *tablespoons oil*
12 *fresh mushrooms sliced*
1 *cup hot water*
½ *cup chopped parsley*
1 *level teaspoon salt*
¼ *teaspoon black pepper*
3 *pounds round steak, cut into 1-inch strips*

First, make marinade by mixing soy sauce, wild marjoram

(oregano), and chile. Pour over meat strips in a flat-bottomed receptacle and lay the garlic pieces among the strips. Be sure that all the meat is covered with the marinade, and let it stand 2 hours, preferably in the refrigerator. Then add tenderizer.

TO COOK: lift the meat strips from the marinade and roll lightly in a little flour. Heat oil to bubbling in a skillet and brown, stirring often, until lightly colored. Mince 1 clove of garlic, stir into the meat, and let cook gently about 5 minutes. Strew mushrooms over meat, stir in, and cook 5 minutes.

Add the hot water to the marinade, discard the garlic, and pour the well-mixed marinade and water over the meat. Stir in parsley, cover skillet, and simmer for 1 hour, adding salt and pepper after 30 minutes.

Serve with baked potatoes. The sauce on the meat will have cooked down so it may be used as gravy for potatoes. *8 servings*.

## Marrow Bones (Osso buco)

Have you cooked marrow bones? Don't envision a dish of bare, yawning bones, with no meat to solace the tired cook. These are meaty morsels, the more flavorful for being left on the bones. They are delicate and unusual.

| | |
|---|---|
| 4 *meaty pieces of veal shank sawed, not chopped, 2 inches thick, with marrow inside* | 1 *clove garlic* |
| | 1 *carrot* |
| | 1 *stalk celery* |
| | 2 *tablespoons butter* |
| *salt* | 1 *large tomato* |
| *black pepper* | 1 *cup dry white wine* |
| 4 *tablespoons flour* | 1 *teaspoon rosemary* |
| 2 *tablespoons olive oil or butter* | ½ *Japanese chile without seeds* |
| 1 *large onion* | *boiling water* |

1 tablespoon minced pars-    1 teaspoon grated
  ley                          lemon peel

Salt and pepper meat and roll in half the flour. Brown in olive oil or butter in a terra-cotta cooking dish or a Dutch oven. Remove meat, and to the oil add chopped onion, garlic, shredded carrot, and celery. Cook slowly 10 minutes. Cream butter and remaining flour together, and add to onion and vegetable mixture in kettle. Cook 5 minutes slowly. Peel tomato, cut up in mixture. Add wine, rosemary, and chile. Cook 5 minutes, then salt and pepper to taste. Put meat into this sauce, add enough boiling water to cover meat, put on lid and cook slowly 3 hours. Take from fire, scatter parsley and grated lemon peel over top. Cover kettle and let stand on back of stove 5 minutes before serving. *4 servings.*

## Veal Steak Strips with Herbs (Scaloppine)

1 pound veal steak from leg,    ½ small onion
  cut thin                      ⅔ cup broth (pages 83–
salt                              84)
black pepper                    ⅓ cup dry white wine
flour                           ⅔ cup tomato juice
1 tablespoon butter             ½ teaspoon chopped rose-
3 tablespoons olive oil           mary
1 clove garlic                  1 tablespoon parsley

Cut veal into small serving pieces, discarding bones. With a wooden mallet or potato masher pound out each piece to half its original thickness. Salt, pepper, and roll lightly in flour.

Heat butter and oil in skillet and brown meat slowly on both sides. Remove meat, to the fat in skillet add garlic and onion, minced, and cook slowly 10 minutes. Add broth and wine mixed with tomato juice, cook 10 minutes, add rosemary. Then return meat to skillet, spoon liquid over it, cover, and cook slowly 1 hour. Meat should be turned several times so it will be moist on both sides. If sauce cooks down too much add a little more broth, for sauce should never become really thick. However, it should barely cover the meat.

Before serving, sprinkle finely chopped parsley over the top. 2 *servings*.

## Bean-Pot Casserole of Beef with Rice

| | |
|---|---|
| 2 *pounds shin spur of beef* | 1 *teaspoon rosemary* |
| *salt* | ½ *Japanese chile* |
| *black pepper* | ½ *cup dry white wine* |
| *flour* | 1 *cup tomato juice* |
| 4 *tablespoons olive oil* | *boiling water* |
| 1 *clove garlic* | ½ *cup raw rice* |
| 1 *small onion* | |

Cut meat into pieces about 4 inches square. Salt, pepper, and flour them, and brown in the oil. Remove meat, and in oil cook slowly for 10 minutes minced garlic, onion, rosemary, and chile. Add wine, tomato juice, and salt to taste. Bring to a boil.

Preheat the oven to 300°. Into an earthenware bean pot put meat, pour over it the sauce, and add enough boiling water to two-thirds cover it. Put on the lid and cook in the oven for 2 hours. The last half hour add the rice and enough more boiling water to cover it. Stir well once, return to oven, and cook until rice is tender. Do not stir again after rice starts to cook, or it will be soggy.

Place meat on platter, and serve with the rice around it. 4 *servings*.

## Kidney and Mushroom Sauté

| | |
|---|---|
| 1 tablespoon butter | salt |
| ½ small onion | black pepper |
| 4 lamb kidneys, skinned, sliced, and blanched by boiling up once in clear water | 1 teaspoon summer savory |
| | 6 large fresh mushrooms |
| | ⅓ cup broth (pages 83–84) |
| 1 level tablespoon flour | 1 level tablespoon parsley |

Melt butter in a skillet and in it brown finely chopped onion. Add prepared kidneys and toss in the fat. Then sprinkle with the flour, add about ¼ teaspoon salt, a little black pepper, and the savory. Cook 10 minutes slowly, turning at the end of 5 minutes. Add mushrooms and hot broth. Cook 5 minutes more, and serve at once with parsley sprinkled over the top. *4 servings.*

## Porcupine Meatballs

MEATBALLS:

⅔ pound ground beef
⅓ pound pork sausage
¼ cup raw rice
½ onion minced
1 teaspoon minced bell pepper
½ teaspoon salt
⅛ teaspoon black pepper

SAUCE:

½ onion minced
1 clove garlic minced
1 teaspoon marjoram and thyme mixed
2 cups tomato juice
½ cup dry white wine
⅛ teaspoon mace
salt
black pepper to taste

Mix meatball ingredients well and form into 8 balls. Flour and brown in 3 tablespoons olive oil. Remove from pan. In the oil make the sauce: Put minced onion and garlic into oil and fry slowly 10 minutes. Add herbs and cook 5 minutes more. Then add liquids, mace, and salt and pepper to taste. Bring to a boil. Put meatballs into a terra-cotta pot or heavy saucepan, pour over them the boiling sauce. Cover and cook slowly for ½ hour. Serve with rice. *4 servings*.


# PORK


Long ago gentlemen chased the wild boar and brought him home to fill their trenchers. He was supposed to have a superlative flavor. Today, with the supply of wild boars not what it once was, we are content to get along with the domestic porker, knowing him for royal food.

While roast of pork is many persons' choice of the best cut of this meat, smaller bits for smaller families may be prepared to make them fully as desirable. With herbs scenting one's dooryard, the potentialities of pork are endless.


## Pork Chops with Rapini

Rapini, in case you do not know, are those tender turnip tops which the Italians eat. They are not raspy and horny like those we cut from our full-grown turnips. Since they are raised for the tops and not for the roots, they are pulled while the turnips are still little larger than marbles, and the green parts are still young and tender. Mustard greens also may be used for this dish, and even spinach is acceptable.

Cut rapini tops from the tiny turnips, wash, and cut up. Wash the turnips also and cut them up without peeling. Into a kettle put a layer of rapini, a pinch of salt, another layer of greens, and so on until all greens are salted and in. The turnips themselves are mixed in with the greens. Cover and cook slowly for about 20 minutes or until greens are well

D  FLORENCE FENNEL

wilted. Drain them of the water which has cooked from them. You should have a good pint of greens after they are cooked. To complete the recipe take:

salt
2 tablespoons olive oil
2 large loin pork chops 2
  inches thick
2 large cloves garlic

2 sprigs rosemary
½ cup dry white wine
1 cup tomato juice
black pepper

Heat oil in a large iron skillet or terra-cotta cooking dish and lay chops in it. On each chop place 1 clove garlic halved lengthwise and run through with toothpick, and a sprig of rosemary. Let chops brown on one side. Remove herb and garlic, turn chops, and return herb and garlic. Brown chops on that side. Add wine, cook 10 minutes, then add tomato juice, and salt and pepper to taste. Cover and cook 45 minutes, or until chops are tender. Then put drained rapini in liquor around chops, spoon sauce over them, and cook covered for 10 minutes more. Serve at once, after discarding garlic.

And please, don't turn up your nose at the lowly turnip top until you have tasted this dish. It will be *Sir Turnip Top* to you, forever after. 2 *servings*.

## Double Pork Chops Stuffed

salt
½ pound spinach
1 clove garlic
1 tablespoon olive oil
½ cup chopped parsley
½ teaspoon thyme
1 teaspoon summer savory
pinch sweet basil
½ cup dry bread crumbs

black pepper
4 double pork chops at least 3 inches thick, cut with "pocket" on the meat side
⅓ cup hot water
2 tablespoons dry white wine

Preheat the oven to 350°. Wash spinach, salt it, and cook without water for 10 minutes. Drain and chop. Mince garlic and fry in oil for 5 minutes. Add parsley and herbs chopped fine, stir well, and add crumbs and spinach. Mix well, salt and pepper to taste, and cook 5 minutes. Let cool, then stuff pockets of chops with this mixture. Bake chops for 1 hour and 15 minutes, basting every 15 minutes with a basting liquor of the hot water, wine, and salt to taste. *4 servings*.

## Pork Chops with Cumin Seed

2 pork chops 1½ inches thick
flour
2 tablespoons olive oil
½ cup tomato juice
¼ teaspoon cumin seed

1 tablespoon parsley minced
boiling water
salt
black pepper

Roll chops in flour and brown in oil. Remove them, add tomato juice, cumin seed, and parsley to oil. Stir well and cook 5 minutes. Return chops, add enough boiling water so the liquid in the pan will just cover chops. Stir, salt and pepper to taste. Simmer 1 hour, covered, renewing water when necessary to keep sauce from cooking away. *2 servings*.

G HOREHOUND

With these recipes for savory pork to add to your own tried favorites, you will never have to fall back on the concoction that Athenæus described:

>. . . a slice of boiled pig's paunch,
>Dipping it in a bitter sauce of rue.

If this description does not startle you, go into your herb garden and bite into a leaf of rue. Then you will see what it means.


## LIVER

"Doctor's orders" in recent years have lifted one type of meat far above its traditional station. Once liver was a lowly dish, bought because it was inexpensive, and eaten in humility. Now it is less soothing in price, and eaten proudly, because it is "good for us."

Like most of the foods of the people, liver has a quality that is full of delicious homeliness. Even without the health-giving properties credited to it, it still would be good food.

Herbs combine gratefully with this meat, and the partnership is a notably tasty one. A good piece of liver, seasoned with skill and prepared with care, can become a dish that no one should fear to serve.

Calves' liver is the preference of many. Other types, how-ever, acquit themselves so well in cookery that we may buy them without qualms. For instance, lambs' liver is tender and full of flavor. Young pork liver is delicious. Even the liver of young beef is not to be despised.

These meats should never be cooked so long that they be-come tough and desiccated. If a recipe calls for long cooking, see to it that the meat has sufficient moisture around it to keep it from drying out. Liver should never be salted before browning it, but always after, to keep it from being hard.

## Baked Liver

½  teaspoon salt
1  Japanese chile without seeds
1½  pounds liver in one piece, larded with fat
2  tablespoons olive oil
1  clove garlic minced
1  onion minced
2  stalks celery diced
1  tablespoon bacon drip-pings
2  cloves

1  slice salt pork cut in strips
2  tablespoons flour
⅛  teaspoon pepper
1  small carrot shredded
½  bay leaf
6  peppercorns
1  teaspoon thyme
2  tablespoons dry sherry
1  teaspoon tomato catsup
1½  cups hot water

Use for this dish a Dutch oven or any heavy roasting pot with a tight lid. Sprinkle ¼ teaspoon salt on the bottom of the pot, then over it strew the chile in small pieces. Over that lay the piece of larded liver, and on it the strips of salt pork. Fasten pork on with skewers. Sift flour and rest of salt and the pepper evenly over the whole. Put into a 450° oven until meat is richly browned.

Meanwhile heat oil in a frying pan, add garlic and onion, and cook slowly 10 minutes. Then add vegetables, herbs, and cloves, and cook slowly 10 minutes more. Pile this mixture around the liver.

Melt drippings, add sherry, catsup, and water, and bring to a boil. Keep liquid warm on back of stove.

Reduce oven temperature to 325° and bake liver covered for 1 hour, basting every 15 minutes with the hot basting liquor. After each basting sprinkle a little salt over the meat. When done, the vegetables should be cooked to pieces and moist enough to form a sauce. If they are too dry, remove liver, keeping it warm, and add a little hot water to the vegetables. Stir well, cook 5 minutes. To serve, slice liver and cover with sauce. *4 servings.*

## Liver in White Wine

| | |
|---|---|
| *1 pound lambs' liver sliced* | *salt* |
| *flour* | *black pepper* |
| *4 tablespoons olive oil* | *1 teaspoon sweet basil* |
| *2 cloves garlic* | *½ cup white wine* |
| *1 small onion minced* | |

Scald liver in boiling water, drain, and wipe dry. Dredge with flour and brown slowly in hot oil. Remove and keep warm while browning garlic (which has been split in half length-wise and run through with toothpicks) in the oil. When garlic is brown on both sides add onion, stir well, and cook 5 minutes. Return liver to pan, spoon garlic and onion over it, and salt and pepper. Mince basil over it, and over this pour the wine. Cover, and cook slowly ½ hour, basting every 10 minutes with the liquid in the pan. Discard garlic before serving. *3 servings.*

## Liver Strips Anchovied

| | |
|---|---|
| 6 slices calves' or lambs' liver, cut into 1-inch strips | ½ laurel leaf or ¼ California bay leaf |
| 4 tablespoons butter black pepper | ⅓ cup dry white wine |
| 1 2-ounce can anchovy flat fillets, drained and chopped | 2 tablespoons finely minced parsley |

Toss the liver strips in the butter heated to bubbling for 2 or 3 minutes, until slightly browned but still soft. Then add a good sprinkling of black pepper, the anchovies, laurel or bay leaf, and wine. Turn up heat, stir meat well, and let bubble furiously for about 1 minute. Stir in parsley and serve at once over a bed of spinach sautéed in olive oil, as directed on page 264.

If you don't fancy spinach, you may serve it with hot buttered French bread and a serving of broccoli and Hollandaise sauce. *4 servings.*

## Sweetbreads Piccanti

If you are so lucky as to hanker after sweetbreads, this is one more way you may enjoy them. And just in case you are not enthusiastic about this delicacy, if you will give these a try, you may change your mind. Others have. Sweetbreads must be very fresh to be good. As soon as you get them from the store trim them, remove connective tissues and tubes, and wash them. Put them into cold water with the juice of a medium-sized lemon. Bring to a boil and plunge into cold water to cool. Drain until ready to use.

3 tablespoons butter
2 tablespoons olive oil
3 tablespoons flour
1 medium onion chopped
  coarsely

1 clove garlic minced
1 medium carrot sliced
  thinly
10 fresh mushrooms sliced

A SEASONING MIX OF:

3 tablespoons parsley
  minced
½ laurel leaf or ¼ Cali-
  fornia bay leaf minced
⅛ teaspoon nutmeg

1 teaspoon wild marjoram
  (oregano)
1 teaspoon thyme
¼ teaspoon black pepper

4 pairs veal sweetbreads
2 thin slices lemon with
  peel, quartered and
  crushed

A LIQUID MIX OF:

½ cup hot chicken broth
  (page 84)
½ cup dry sherry wine

Preheat the oven to 450°. In a covered, flame-proof cooking receptacle such as a French terra-cotta terrine or a casserole dish, melt butter, mix in oil, and add flour, stir, and cook slowly for 5 minutes. Add onion, garlic, carrot, mushrooms, and the dry seasoning mix. Stir well, put into the oven and cook, stirring often, until the vegetables begin to brown. Add sweetbreads, lemon bits, and the liquid mix. Stir well, then cover, bake at 450° for 20 minutes, then uncover and cook at the same temperature until the liquid is almost gone and the contents are pleasantly tanned.

Serve with buttered rice. *4 servings.*

No catalogue of meat dishes is complete without that good old standby, *meat loaf.* So many families serve it once a week that no one will resent having its familiar face changed by the addition of some new seasonings. For herbs in a meat loaf do make a difference, and a desirable one, too.

## Herbal Meat Loaf

1 pound ground beef
½ pound ground pork
⅓ cup toast crumbs
2 onions minced
1 clove garlic minced
1 tablespoon olive oil
½ teaspoon minced marjoram
½ teaspoon minced savory
1 Japanese chile without seeds

½ teaspoon salt
black pepper

BASTING LIQUOR:
1 tablespoon bacon drippings
1 tablespoon olive oil
1 teaspoon dry red wine
1 tablespoon tomato catsup
salt
black pepper

Put all meat loaf ingredients into a bowl and mix well. Shape into a loaf, put into an oiled pan, and brown in a very hot oven. Reduce the heat to 325° and bake 45 minutes to 1 hour, depending on the thickness of the loaf. Baste every 10 minutes with the basting liquor, which should be kept hot on the back of the stove.

When the loaf is done, slice and serve. *4 servings.*

## Fresh Beef Tongue Savory

Tongue is one of those articles of food which is the essence of iffiness. Some like it. Many love it. But there are those who avoid it in any guise. That is truly sad, because tongue, well cooked and knowingly served, is a delicate and beautiful food. Let's try it this way.

1 fresh beef tongue about 2½ pounds
2 cloves garlic minced
1 laurel leaf, or ½ bay leaf, crumbled

½ teaspoon thyme
½ Japanese chile without seeds
6 whole peppercorns
3 allspice berries crushed

2 *whole cloves*
½ *tablespoon soy sauce*
½ *teaspoon salt*
 1 *slice lemon with peel*
*cold water*

6 *raw, peeled potatoes*
6 *raw, peeled onions*
*butter*
*cream horseradish sauce*
*prepared mustard*

Wash tongue, lay it in kettle wide and deep enough to accommodate it generously, and add all other ingredients except the potatoes, onions, and prepared cream horseradish sauce and prepared mustard. The cold water should entirely cover the tongue. Bring slowly to a boil, add ½ cup more cold water to arrest the boiling, and skim off any foam from the top. Reduce to a bare simmering heat, cover and let simmer for about 2½ hours until fork-tender. Take from heat and let cool somewhat, until the tongue is cool enough to handle. Removing from liquid, drain, then skin it, removing the bones and cords at the base. Return it to the liquid, add potatoes and onions, and simmer until they are tender.

To serve, remove tongue from liquid and drain well. Slice it in about ¾-inch slices and cut each potato and onion in half. Dot them with butter and dust with black pepper. Accompany this with a bowl of cream horseradish sauce, the mustard of your choice, and salt and pepper shakers for the vegetables.

If from somewhere some miscreant surfaces, demanding catsup or chili sauce, give him some, for he won't be happy without it. But he will never know how good tongue can taste.

Leftover tongue makes superb sandwiches. Or slice it fairly thin and marinate it in your favorite vinaigrette sauce, or even mine (page 329) for an hour. Serve on a bed of escarole or curly endive, and spoon the sauce over the whole. With hot French bread slices, it makes luncheons come alive. *6 servings.*

To all of you I dedicate these dishes of meat, knowing that you will come within the limits set by Izaak Walton. For he dedicated his recommended recipe thus:

This dish of meat is too good for any but anglers or very honest men.

## ❧ SIX ❧

# Chicken in the Pot

A cook they hadde with hem for the nones,
To boille the chicknes with the mary-bones . . .
He coude roste, and sethe, and broille, and frye. . . .

So EVEN in Chaucer's day "chiknes" were delectable fare! Surely, though, they could not have been more appreciated then than today. For we Americans have always placed chicken, as a delicacy, on an especially built and exclusively dedicated pedestal. It is our Number One treat, our company dish *par excellence*.

Fryers, broilers, roasters, fricassee-ers, or boilers; White Leghorn, Plymouth Rock, Rhode Island Red; stuffed, fried, or stewed — all are good cooking and eating. And how they do ally themselves with a bit of garlic and a soupçon of herbs. In such company the creatures surpass themselves.

First, a glance at the family tree of the chicken tribe. Its members have titles which it is best to know, much as one should know the orders of nobility when visiting in style abroad — so that one may know how to address them, how to treat them, what special courtesies to show them. The noble hen and her offspring will reward you richly for such small study, yielding every bit of good their personalities hold, if you understand a few simple rules of etiquette on "the entertainment of chicken."

## Broilers

When a chicken first becomes old enough for gastronomical consideration (that is, from six weeks to two months) and weighs from 1 to 2 pounds, it is called a *broiler*. So, of course, it is broiled, and makes very fine eating indeed. To cook it thus split the bird down the center and flatten out the two halves. Brush them with oil, put them under a quick broiler flame, and brown them, skin side up. Turn them, and finish cooking under a lowered flame. The entire process takes from 20 to 25 minutes. If you want the meat to have not one jot of resistance to your fork, but only tender fineness, cover the broiling pan the last 10 minutes of cooking with a roaster cover, so the chicken may steam. Remove the cover at the end of the 10 minutes, let the chicken re-crisp under the flame for a minute, and serve.

## Fryers

A chicken that escapes the broiling pan and gambols in happy adolescence yet a little while becomes a *fryer*. It is larger and heavier, and has a more meaty makeup. From 4 to 6 months old, it weighs from 2½ to 3½ pounds. This meat takes longer to cook, but still may be classed as a quick-cooking bird, which does not need tenderizing. As the name implies, this young fellow is fried, thus becoming the idol of Southerners, to say nothing of Northerners, Easterners, and Westerners.

Fried chicken is easily prepared. The secret is to brown the floured and seasoned meat richly and slowly, so that at the end of the browning process it is tender — so tender that a fork, inserted in the flesh and twisted, makes a clean break in it. Butter and olive oil are the best frying agents, and a mixture of half and half is better than either alone.

## Roasters

If a fryer is left unmolested until he gains the fine size of 3½ to 6 pounds without getting elderly, he is dubbed Sir *Roaster*. A capon is also in this class, and weighs about 5 pounds. He may be stuffed with any of a multiplicity of stuffings, and roasted in an open pan in a 300° oven. He is then a subject for action, and for conversation of the finest and most laudatory quality.

## Fricassee-ers

A roaster which lingers on in the social whirl without being snatched off by a questing cook shortly becomes worthy of fricasseeing. Still young, still tender, but mature and at his zenith of plumpness, he will grace the fricassee pot with aplomb and elegance. He is cut up, salted, peppered, and floured, then browned in half butter and half olive oil. An added allotment of boiling water, and what seasonings are desired, and he cooks until the fork test reveals his tenderness as complete. That is a real "fricassee."

## Boilers

Now the lady enters the picture. For a *boiler* is a hen. Not a young hen that has not been around. Nor yet an old hen that has become suspicious and hard to get along with, so that she is no longer adaptable and ready to yield her all in cooking. The ideal hen for the role of boiler is a middle-aged matron, mother or grandmother, but not withered in age. Cut her up, place her in enough boiling water to cover her, and boil her for 2 or 3 hours. Salt added after the first hour will be the best courtesy you can afford her. When tender, thicken her gravy, and you have something — a delectable chicken stew.

But suppose you prefer chicken broth or soup? The same lady will lend her support to producing a full-bodied soup that makes lips smack in defiance of the etiquette-mentors. Simply put the cut-up chicken into salted cold water, season as you wish, and after bringing slowly to a boil, simmer until done — about 3 hours.

Meet them then, the Peerage of the Poultry Run. Learn their titles and their deserts, and act accordingly.

Besides all these ways of dressing this amenable bird, Europeans have another, which in its many variations opens to Americans a whole new list of dishes in which chicken figures with notable charm. This is the practice of cooking it in a "gravy."

By this "gravy" I do not mean the flour-thickened milky liquid we pass in a boat, nor yet the rich, delicious juices that drop from a roast or steak. This gravy is a sauce, especially concocted, in which the fowl is cooked, so that the flavor of the sauce and that of the bird blend by reason of long and happy association into an exquisite whole. The result is what the Italians call *pollo in umido*, literally "chicken in dampness." But it is a most benign and soothing dampness, of which one could never complain.

These sauces for the cooking of *pollo in umido* are as full of variety as could be wished. One Italian housewife fixes her sauce this way, another that. One district excels in such and such a chicken sauce, while that just over the mountain makes it differently. So with these dishes we could never be bored.

Of course you all have your pet ways of preparing chicken. But the pet ways of another may surely be accepted as just that much more equipment for the gaining of that coveted title of Perfect Host or Hostess.


# BROILERS


## Spring Chicken Rosemary

2  small broilers
oil
salt
black pepper
2  cloves garlic

2  1-inch sprigs fresh or 20 leaves dried rosemary

BASTING MIXTURE:
½  cup olive oil
½  cup hot water
salt

Preheat oven to 500°. Split broilers down the backs, press them out flat, and rub them with oil, salt, and fresh black pepper. Oil the floor of a heavy basting pan and lay the chickens on it, skin side up. On each chicken lay 2 halves of a clove of garlic and a small sprig or 5 leaves rosemary.

Put chickens in the preheated oven and brown on the skin side under the flame. Remove seasonings, turn chickens, and return seasonings. When this side is brown lower oven to 300° and continue cooking at this heat for about 30 minutes more, basting every 10 minutes with the basting mixture. 2 *servings.*

## Whole Spring Chickens with Herbs

2 *spring chickens left whole*
salt
black pepper
oil

SEASONING PASTE:
1 *clove garlic minced fine*
2 *tablespoons parsley*
   *minced*
2 *shallots minced*

*chicken gizzard and liver*
   *minced*
½ *teaspoon minced rose-*
   *mary*
½ *teaspoon summer savory*

BASTING MIXTURE:
½ *cup olive oil*
½ *cup white wine*

Preheat the oven to 500°. Mix the seasoning ingredients together, salt and pepper generously, moisten with a little olive oil to bind together.

Divide the paste into two portions. Rub the chickens inside with oil, then put half the seasoning paste into each. Tie the legs to the body, oil or butter the outsides of the chickens, rub them with salt and pepper, and brown all over in an oiled pan, uncovered, in the oven. Reduce to 300° and bake until a fork inserted in the breast and twisted makes a clean break. This takes at least 30 minutes. During that cooking time baste every 10 minutes with the basting mixture, kept hot. At each basting sprinkle chickens lightly with salt.

It is possible to make this a complete dinner by laying small peeled onions and quartered raw, peeled potatoes by the chickens, salting and peppering them, and basting them each time the meat is basted. 2 *servings*.

If rosemary and summer savory pall on you, try some new herb combinations. Thyme and savory, basil and parsley, marjoram and thyme. And so on, down the green lanes of your herbs. There is no end to the combinations which may lend piquancy and novelty to your broiled chickens.

But mind you, I am not denying the deliciousness of plain-cooked chicken. Eat it now and then, to remind you that chicken is a food that can stand alone. Then turn again to herbs and seasoning, that patrician simplicity need never become tiresome through excessive use.

For half the fun of eating is in savoring differing tastes.

# FRYERS

## Chicken in Special Seasoning (Pollo in battuto)

First of all, to dispel any mystery about this special seasoning, a *battuto* is a seasoning paste mixed in a mortar and pestle. There are many of these magic seasoning pastes, prepared before the cooking of the dish begins so that it will be ready to use at the proper time. Its making is simple, and if you don't have a mortar and pestle use a small deep bowl and a muddler, such as is used to make certain cocktails. Keep this muddler for this use alone, for it takes in the *battuto* ingredients' taste permanently.

| | |
|---|---|
| breasts, legs, and thighs of 1 fryer | 1 small carrot |
| flour | 1 stick celery |
| 4 tablespoons olive oil | 2 medium-sized tomatoes peeled and minced |
| 5 mushrooms sliced | ½ cup minced parsley |
| | ½ teaspoon thyme |
| BATTUTO: | ½ teaspoon rosemary |
| 2 tablespoons butter | ½ cup dry white wine |
| 1 tablespoon olive oil | salt |
| 1 small clove garlic minced | black pepper |
| 1 small onion | |

To make the *battuto*, melt the butter in a small skillet and mix in the oil. Add the finely minced garlic, onion, carrot, and celery and cook slowly for 10 minutes. Add tomatoes, herbs, and wine, mix well, season and set aside. Preheat the oven to 325°.

To prepare the chicken and assemble the dish, first cut the chicken breasts in two crosswise, cutting across the rib section. Dip the chicken pieces in the flour and fry them in the oil until golden. Then drain them and lay them in a casserole and spoon all the *battuto* over and around them. Bake ½ hour, basting a few times with the liquid that forms in the bottom of the casserole. Then scatter the mushroom slices over the chicken and continue baking ½ hour longer. Serve with baked potatoes, spooning some of the *battuto* from the casserole bottom over them. *4 servings*.

Now the flavor of chicken that has been fried with no other seasoning than fat, salt, and pepper is an unforgettable one. But if that chicken has chummed with a bit of garlic during its sojourn in the pan, it achieves another peak in flavor.

## Chicken Fried with Garlic

| | |
|---|---|
| 1　3½-pound fryer | black pepper |
| 1　lemon | 3　tablespoons each of but- |
| flour | 　　ter and olive oil |
| salt | 1　clove garlic |

Disjoint the dressed chicken, and after drying it thoroughly, rub each piece with the cut surface of a lemon. Roll in seasoned flour. Mix the butter and oil in a heavy frying pan, and in it slowly fry the chicken, turning often until it is richly browned. Introduce the garlic, halved, at the same time as the chicken, and leave in until the meat is tender. Then lift out and discard garlic before serving meat. *4 servings*.

## *Chicken and Potatoes*

Chicken and Potatoes, cooked with the delicate aroma of rosemary, has the twin charm of novelty and tastiness. Serve it with a green vegetable and a salad, or just with an extra large green salad, and you will need nothing more.

| | |
|---|---|
| 1  3½-pound fryer, dis-<br>    jointed<br>olive oil<br>3  potatoes<br>salt<br>black pepper | 2  cloves garlic minced<br>3  tablespoons minced<br>    parsley<br>½  teaspoon minced rose-<br>    mary |

Have the chicken disjointed, and dry each piece well. Heat olive oil in a heavy frying pan, putting in enough to barely cover the bottom. When hot lay in chicken and the potatoes, which have been peeled and cut into 2-inch cubes. Add salt and pepper, and fry slowly until brown, stirring often. This cooking may be done on the stove top or in the oven. When richly browned and nearly tender, throw in the garlic, parsley, and rosemary mixed, stir well, cover, and cook 10 minutes more. By this time, if the browning process has been sufficiently slow, the chicken and potatoes both will be very tender, and the garlic cooked. *4 servings.*

## *ROASTERS*

There is something noble about a roasted chicken or turkey, lying on its back, legs and wings folded peacefully against its sides, which are bulging with savory stuffing. If that stuffing has been seasoned with herbs in magic propor-

**H** HORSERADISH

tions, if the bird's skin has been rubbed with glistening olive oil or golden butter, and if the roasting has gone forward in an uncovered pan at slow heat, that bird will be truly imperial.

## Poultry Seasoning

Many people buy mixed "poultry seasoning" already pulverized and cherish it in a paper carton or tin canister until it is used up. If their households do not boast frequent poultry feasts, it takes long months to exhaust that supply of seasoning. Often, long before its substance is gone, the flavor has departed, leaving only dust.

Could we but make a small effort, and just once mix our own poultry seasoning, we would never again buy it ready mixed. For we would mix it without sage, which has no place in the flavoring for chicken or turkey. Summer savory would predominate, accompanied by sweet basil and thyme. These herbs are fit company for the delicacy of poultry, and none better.

Mixed and left in the leaf until used, these herbs can be pulverized between the palms of the hands to a powder, and be as full of flavor and fragrance as the day they were picked. Of course that means that they must be stored in tightly closed jars in the meantime.

## Roast Chicken

Of course a roast chicken must be stuffed, and of course nothing is better in the way of stuffing than fine old American celery and onion stuffing.

## Stuffing for Chicken

| | |
|---|---|
| 1 4- to 5-pound roaster | 1 teaspoon thyme |
| 2 medium onions | ¼ teaspoon black pepper |
| 1 clove garlic | ½ cup hot water |
| 3 tablespoons butter | 3 cups dried bread grated |
| ½ cup celery, both leaves and stalks, minced | 3 tablespoons pine nuts, or 10 peeled chestnuts, or 10 walnuts |
| 1 tablespoon summer savory | salt |
| 1 teaspoon sweet basil | |

Fry finely minced onion and garlic in butter slowly for 10 minutes, then add celery, stir, and add herbs and pepper. Fry 5 minutes, pour in hot water, and cook 10 minutes. Put crumbs into a bowl, add vegetable and herb mixture and the coarsely chopped nuts, and mix well. Season with salt, and stuff chicken with it.

## Roasting the Chicken

| | |
|---|---|
| 1 roaster | 1 tablespoon butter |
| olive oil or butter | 1 teaspoon salt |
| salt | 1 tablespoon catsup |
| black pepper | ½ cup dry white wine |
| BASTING LIQUOR: | 1 tablespoon olive oil |
| ¼ cup water | ¼ teaspoon black pepper |

Rub the stuffed chicken with oil or butter, then with salt and pepper. Lay it in an open roaster with legs and wings trussed. Put into an oven preheated to 325° and roast until tender. After first half hour baste every 15 minutes with liquor. Keep liquor hot while basting with it. When it is exhausted use that in the bottom of the roaster. The very frequent basting may seem a bore, but it is necessary to produce a chicken that is flavorsome with the herbs and wine flavor of the liquor. *5 to 6 servings*.

## Pollo in Umido

Now for the "Chicken in Dampness." I can give you only a few varieties of the dampnesses which distinguish this dish's variety. But all are worthy of your notice and adoption.

Fryers are the best to cook in this way, as they cook quickly while the sauce is making, yet give the sauce long enough cooking so it will not be unblended.

The recipes that go to make up this *pollo in umido* group are from the kitchens of the best Italian cooks I know.

## Gemma's Chicken in Umido

| | |
|---|---|
| 1 3- to 3½-pound fryer | ½ cup minced parsley |
| 4 tablespoons olive oil | ⅓ teaspoon rosemary |
| salt | ¼ teaspoon each basil and |
| black pepper |   thyme |
| cinnamon | 1 large, well-ripened to- |
| allspice |   mato |
| 1 clove garlic minced | ½ cup dry white wine |

Cut up fryer, wash and dry the pieces well. Heat olive oil in a frying pan, add chicken, dust with salt, pepper, and a dash of cinnamon and allspice. Let fry slowly until brown all over. Add garlic, parsley, rosemary, basil, and thyme. Stir well. Scald and peel tomato, cut up small, and add. Pour in the wine, mix well, cook slowly until tender. If more salt is needed, add it the last 15 minutes of cooking.

When serving, put the chicken on a platter and serve as meat course, while the "gravy" is used to dress pasta such as ravioli or spaghetti, or polenta. *4 servings.*

## Chicken Hunter Style (*Pollo alla cacciatora*)

Another grand dish on this list — the famous "chicken hunter style" which is so delicious and so costly in the finer restaurants. Its preparation is relatively simple, and it is very popular with guests.

| | |
|---|---|
| 1 *4-pound chicken* | 1 *leaf costmary* |
| 4 *tablespoons olive oil* | 4 *large tomatoes* |
| 1 *small onion* | *handful dried mushrooms* |
| 1 *stalk celery* | ½ *cup hot water* |
| 1 *clove garlic* | 2 *tablespoons parsley* |
| *pinch allspice* | ½ *cup red wine* |
| ¼ *teaspoon black pepper* | *salt* |
| ½ *teaspoon fresh rosemary* | |

Cut up chicken, wash and dry thoroughly. Heat oil in a kettle with a heavy bottom. Brown chicken in it until a rich brown all over. Remove chicken and keep warm. In oil cook slowly the minced onion, celery, and garlic for 10 minutes, adding allspice, pepper, and minced rosemary and costmary at the end of first 5 minutes. Then scald and peel tomatoes, cut them up and add, stirring well. Cook the mixture for 5 minutes, meanwhile washing the mushrooms and soaking them in the hot water. After 5 minutes drain the mushrooms and cut them up. Save the water in which they were soaked, adding it to the sauce together with mushrooms, minced parsley, and red wine. Season to taste with salt, add chicken, cover, and cook slowly until tender. Serve very hot, with boiled potatoes flecked here and there with butter. *5 or 6 servings.*

## FRICASSEE-ERS

### Chicken Fricassee

| | |
|---|---|
| 1  tender 4- to 5-pound hen | ⅓  cup chopped parsley |
| flour | 2  shallots with tops |
| 3  tablespoons olive oil | salt |
| boiling water | 4  tablespoons butter |
| ½  bay leaf | 4  tablespoons flour |
| 5  peppercorns ground | 2  egg yolks |
| 1  teaspoon summer savory | 1  cup hot cream |

Cut up the chicken, wash and dry it. Roll in salted and peppered flour and brown in the olive oil in a deep pot. When richly brown cover with boiling water. Add bay, pepper, savory, parsley, and minced shallots. Add ⅓ teaspoon salt, cover the pot, and simmer until chicken is tender, 60 to 90 minutes. Add more salt if needed at end of first half hour. Remove chicken from stock, placing it where it will keep warm. There should be three cups stock. If not, add boiling water to make this much, and test salt seasoning again.

In a small saucepan melt the butter, stir in the flour, and smooth to a paste. Let this cook slowly several minutes, stirring to keep from burning, then pour over it gradually a cupful of the stock, stirring constantly. Simmer a minute, then add to rest of stock and simmer 10 minutes. Beat egg yolks well, and pour over them in a bowl the hot cream, adding it gradually and stirring all the time. Then remove gravy from the fire, stir into it this cream mixture slowly, stirring constantly. Return chicken to gravy and very slowly reheat, but take care not to let it boil after eggs are added. *5 or 6 servings*.

This is excellent served with hot biscuits or boiled potatoes.

# HARE

The modest hare has been overlooked by many who may, in its use, find yet one more kind of meat worthy of gastronomic praise. Next to chicken, there is no more delicate eating than this.

Hares have the same delightful versatility as chickens, and may be cooked in almost every way that has been described for them. Fried, roasted, fricasseed, *in umido*, they are to many people as good as the more aristocratic chicken itself.

However, there are subtle tricks in their cookery which can well be learned. First, if they are soaked in salt and water with 2 tablespoons of vinegar added, for an hour before cooking, their taste is finer. Also, if cooked with a small piece of fat pork, either salt or fresh, the meat will have a richness that will otherwise be lacking.

C    LAVENDER

## Fried Hare

Follow the recipe for fried chicken on page 131, using instead a good-sized hare, and cooking with a small piece of fresh fat pork.

## Jugged Hare with Herbs

"Jugged hare" — such a pictorial name! It calls up a sturdy brown jug whose top is off. From its depths curls in tantalizing tendrils a steam so laden with savor as to drive a hungry person mad.

Of course jugged hare is no longer cooked in a jug in the good old style. Such cookery was once a process of seething the meat in a sealed jug placed in a receptacle of hot water. Today we merrily dispense with this paraphernalia, cooking it instead in an honest brown beanpot on the stove top. It is so good this way that we may fearlessly challenge the spirits of Mrs. Hannah Glasse and her culinary sisterhood to rise and produce a better feast.

| | |
|---|---|
| 1  2-pound hare | black pepper |
| 1  quart water | 2  tablespoons flour |
| 2  tablespoons vinegar | 2  tablespoons olive oil |
| 1  teaspoon salt | 1  thin slice salt pork |

SAUCE:

| | |
|---|---|
| 1  onion | |
| 1  clove garlic | 1  teaspoon minced mixed |
| 1  tablespoon lard | herbs: basil, marjoram, |
| 1  tablespoon butter | and rosemary |
| 2  tablespoons chopped parsley | pinch ground cloves |
| | 2  cups dry white wine |
| | salt |

Wash hare, cut into serving pieces, and soak in water, vinegar, and salt for several hours. Then drain, discarding the liquid. Wash hare again, dry thoroughly, and roll in salted and peppered flour. Brown in olive oil, together with the salt pork cut into squares.

Meanwhile, in another pan fry onion and garlic minced in lard and butter. Add herbs, cloves, wine, and salt, and bring slowly to a boil. Put meat into this sauce, cover, and cook on stove top for 2 hours, stirring often to prevent sticking.

Serve with hot boiled rice that has been mixed with 1 tablespoon chopped parsley and 1 teaspoon chopped chives, and moistened with 2 tablespoons melted butter.

## Stewed Hare

| | |
|---|---|
| *1  2-pound hare* | *1  strip bacon cut up* |
| *flour* | *1  cup sherry wine* |
| *2  tablespoons olive oil* | *½  cup broth (pages 83–84)* |
| *1  small onion minced* | *½  cup tomato juice* |
| *1  clove garlic minced* | *¼  cup dried mushrooms* |
| *⅓  teaspoon rosemary* | *salt* |
| *1  tablespoon minced celery* | *black pepper* |
| *1  tablespoon minced celery leaves* | |

Wash hare, cut up, dry well, and roll in seasoned flour. Brown in olive oil, then remove from pan. In the oil cook slowly onion and garlic for 10 minutes. Add rosemary, celery, leaves, and bacon, and cook 5 minutes more. Add wine, broth, and tomato juice. Wash mushrooms, cut up, and soak 5 minutes in just enough hot water to cover. Add mushrooms and water to sauce. Cook 5 minutes, then put hare into it. Cover, and cook over slow fire until meat is tender.

## ❧ SEVEN ❧

# *Herbal Salads*

Salad . . . has an undoubted preference over every other product of culinary art, to wit: it is suitable to all seasons, as well as all sorts of persons, being a delectable conglomerate of good things.
— FREDERICK SAUNDERS

WHAT is a meal without the green succulence of salad? Salad, pointed with fragrant vinegar, crowned with shining oil, emerald-jeweled with fresh plants and herbs. Heaped-up goodness to whet a lagging appetite.

Elizabeth Robins Pennell goes us one better in praise of salads, actually finding fault with Heaven on their account. She says, "There has always seemed one thing lacking in Omar's Paradise; a salad." Whether or not she is just in mentioning this lack is a question, for no one knows whether such a thing as a salad existed in those days.

Just how old is the custom of lightening meals with green salads is not known. Nebuchadnezzar may have begun it, when he "did eat grass like oxen." Athenæus, ancient scribe of the gourmets, described an Attic banquet in part:

D   SWEET MARJORAM

Large in the middle lay a vacant space,
Which herbs and salads did with verdue grace.

John Evelyn in 1699 praised the French and Italians who "gather anything almost that is tender . . . so as every hedge affords a sallet, and seasoned with vinegar, salt and oil, which gives it both the relish and name of Salad." But in England in 1509 Queen Catherine could not procure a salad until her royal lord sent to the Netherlands and engaged a gardener to come over and raise the proper plants.

So on and on we might go gathering salad-mots from the literature and history of all ages and all lands. The peoples of the earth have not only realized the healthfulness of green plants, but have felt pleasure in their delicacy and savor, finding them delicious food.

Yet we Americans have overworked and misused the name of *salad*. What sweet, cloying mixtures we have passed off under the term, a weary succession of bastard foods. *Desserts*, many of them might be called, or compotes, but certainly not salads. If we can only return to the real spirit of salads, forgetting all sweet nonsense, and reawaken our appetites with freshness of the fields, seasoned with cunning simplicity, we shall have regained something of value.

There is a time to weep and a time to laugh — a time also for sweet food and a time for sour. Blessed be the cook who gives you a salad when salad is the thing, and sweets in their proper place. But for the cook who mixes the sequences, may special punishment be devised to fit the crime. Disgust trails in his or her wake, and indigestion.

Evidently there are others roused to the printed word on the subject of sweet salads. Hear what Ogden Nash has to say:

#### My Dear, However Did You Think Up
#### This Delicious Salad?

This is a very sad ballad
Because it's about the way too many people make a salad.
Generally they start with bananas,
And they might just as well use gila monsters or iguanas.
Pineapples are another popular ingredient,
Although there is one school that holds preserved pears or peaches
  more expedient,
And you occasionally meet your fate
In the form of a prune or a date.
Rarely you may chance to discover a soggy piece of tomato looking
  very forlorn and Cinderella-ry,
But for the most part you are confronted by apples and celery,
And it's not a bit of use at this point to turn pale or break out in a cold
  perspiration,
Because all this is only the foundation,
And the further we go into the subject the quicker you will grow
  prematurely old along with me,
Because the worst is yet to be,
Because if you think the foundation sounds unenticing
Just wait till we get to the dressing, or rather, the icing.
There are various methods of covering up the body, and to some,
  marshmallows are the pall supreme,
And others prefer whipped cream,
And then they deck the grave with ground-up peanuts and maraschinos
And you get the effect of a funeral like Valentino's
And about the only thing that in this kind of salad is never seen
Is any kind of green,
And oil and vinegar and salt and pepper are at a minimum,
But there is a maximum of sugar and syrup and ginger and nutmeg
  and cinnamum,
And my thoughts about this kind of salad are just as unutterable

As parsnips are unbutterable,
And indeed I am surprised that the perpetrators haven't got around to
   putting buttered parsnips in these salmagundis,
And the salad course nowadays seems to be
A month of sundaes.

Now, having discoursed at length on what a salad is not, perhaps it would be fitting to say just what a salad is. A mixture of salad greens, salad herbs, salad fruits, salad trimmings, any or all, and seasonings — of these a salad consists. In explanation of those terms:

## Salad Greens

The greens for salads are a fascinating company, varied, colorful, and delicious. With such materials at our command there seems to be no excuse for dreary salad monotony. While each locality does not offer all varieties of salad greens, each can have several, allowing for seasons. The difficulty in the matter lies with those cooks who for so long have accepted head lettuce as their only green, and who thus have moved gardeners and grocers to offer nothing else. Lettuce, lettuce, and more lettuce. Delicious in its place, it does pall in time.

Examine with me a list of additional salad greens. Its mere perusal will help you relegate head lettuce to its proper place, one of relative importance.

C   WILD MARJORAM

## LOCAL LETTUCE

First, there is local lettuce, otherwise called leaf lettuce, creamy heart, or butterhead lettuce. Only partly headed, it still has its own green hue, and its leaves are oily to the touch, rich and tender.

## CORN SALAD

Corn salad, also called lamb's lettuce, fetticus, or leaf lettuce, does not head, but grows in single leaves about 2 inches long. It makes delicate salads.

## ROMAINE

Romaine, Roman lettuce, or cos lettuce, growing in long, loose heads, is sturdily dark green. Each leaf may be eaten, for they are crisp to perfection.

## ENDIVE

Curly endive, or chicory, is one of the slightly bitter salad greens. Crisp, shading from white to green, all parts are edible.

## BLANCHED CHICORY

Blanched chicory, also called French endive or witloof, is in small, narrow white heads. It is a costly delicacy obtainable only in quality markets in large centers.

## ESCAROLE

Escarole, or Batavian endive, is not bitter like curly endive, though it is the same white and green, and in the same flat heads.

## SPINACH

The fresh, green leaves of spinach, well washed, de-stemmed, and well dried, are most valuable and flavorful. Dressed with oil and lemon juice they are full of taste.

## SMALL ROOTED CHICORY

This green is an Italian salad, called by them *radicetta,* and is the foundation for their appetite-provoking *insalata amara* or bitter salad.

## WATERCRESS

Most of us know watercress, fringing the banks of remembered streams. Its peppery stems and leaves blend well with other salad greens, supplying zest for the whole.

## DANDELION

Dandelion is another of the beloved bitter salads of the Latin races. Slender, dark green leaves of soft texture, they marry oil and vinegar in happy, harmonious union. The bitterness whets the appetite.

The greens listed above are good used alone in salads, or in company with salad fruits such as tomatoes, cucumbers, or avocados. In addition there are some salad greens which are better in company with others. They are full of flavor, but used alone are too strong to be comfortable eating. Mix any of this second list with any of the first, in the proportion of five of the first to one of the second, and see how the whole salad will be pepped up.

## SORREL

Sorrel, an acid herb, needs other greens to tone it down. Mixed with lettuce, escarole, or any other of the first list, its sourness is welcome to the palate. It is used also as a pot herb.

## LOVAGE

Lovage, with its hot pungency, seasons salads appetizingly. Sow it near streams or water, and pluck the tender leaves.

## NASTURTIUM

If you have never known the lifting spice of nasturtium tips and flowers in salads, you have not tasted perfection.

## ROCKET

Salad rocket has a succulent leaf that tastes surprisingly like fresh mushrooms. Mix the leaves with your salad for a new and luring flavor.

## RAMPION

Rampion is an old-fashioned plant whose leaves and roots are used in salads. I have not tasted it, but the French people value it highly.

## PURSLANE

Purslane also has a succulent leaf whose pleasant taste mixes well with salads. Our grandams plucked it from fields and called it "pussley."

# Salad Roots

The edible roots suitable for salads are easily presented, for we are all familiar with them. That familiarity only serves to make them more valuable.

## RADISHES

The flowery red of young radishes, served *au naturelle* with the smallest green leaf left intact, or sliced into your salad, is precious color and flavoring. The long white variety is equally fine for eating.

## BEETS

Boiled and sliced beets marinated in seasoned oil and vinegar complete some salads, while shredded uncooked beets are welcome in others.

## ONION

Onion — there's a salad root. Whether dry, or new and green-topped, onions are salads' first aids. Just a hint of juicy Bermuda, rosy Italian torpedo, or shreds of green tops and bulbs if new onions are used, will be full sufficiency. As Sydney Smith expressed it:

> Let onion atoms lurk within the bowl,
> And scarce suspected, animate the whole.

## LEEKS

We are too ready to confine leeks to the soup pot, never knowing their uncooked fineness of flavor. But there was a time while England was still peopled with Angles and Saxons when leeks were important food. In fact, a garden was known then as a *leac-ton*, and a gardener was a *leac-ward*. The wise men of early times said:

> Eat leeks in oile, and ramsines in May,
> And all the year after physicians may play.

In case you were wondering, ramsines were old-fashioned broad-leafed leeks.

So copy the Angles and Saxons — eat leeks in your salad, cutting the bulbs into fine rounds, thinly sliced.

## FLORENCE FENNEL

Though Florence fennel is not a root, but a growth above the ground, it is put here for want of a better place. White and blanched, known also as "Italian celery," it may be eaten *en branche,* or grated into green salads to their vast improvement.

## OTHER ROOTS

Potatoes, celery root, and carrots are all time-honored salad components, the first always cooked, the latter two either raw or cooked.

## Salad Vegetables and Fruits

The familiar roster of salad fruits is soon scanned. Old friends, all of them — cucumbers, tomatoes, green beans and peas, green peppers, avocados, and young artichokes tenderly cooked. Seasoned with various versions of French dressing, they are fitting proems to good meals.

## Salad Herbs

Since so many herbs have a definite affinity for green salads, it is difficult to name a cut and dried list of "salad herbs." Some, of course, lend themselves better than others to this use, but almost all, used with discretion, will blend with the salad bowl's leafy contents. The seasoning of salads with herbs is in part a matter of knowledge of herbs, in part a matter of whim and fancy. Sometimes you will want to pluck and add to your greens some one distinct herb flavor. But at other times you will roam the garden, garner tips from many fragrant plants, mix them, and toss them into the bowl.

For the beginner it is wise first to learn the best and the most frequently used salad herbs, leaving the whimsical experiments to a later time.

For a beginning there are eleven well-known herbs which are easily grown and are well worth your consideration as salad necessities.

### PARSLEY
While few cooks use parsley in salads except in the useless role of a garnish, the tender fern-leafed Italian parsley is a delicious salad seasoning, for its delicate flavor blends well with any green. The tightly curled variety usually found in markets, however, is a trifle too tough when raw for comfortable eating unless very finely minced.

D    NASTURTIUM

## CHERVIL

Chervil, like parsley, improves any green salad, for it has a flavor that adds cautious zest.

## TARRAGON

Tender tarragon sprigs enliven every type of green salad, but should not be used too constantly, for the dominating tang of this herb will pall if encountered too frequently.

## CHIVES

Chives you may add to salads without stint. They adapt themselves to any surrounding, and never fight with their associates.

## DILL

Finely minced green dill leaves or blossom umbels are seductive additions to a green salad. Lacking the green herb, which is hard to get unless one raises one's own, dried "Dill Weed," so titled by herb packers, is a satisfactory substitute.

## SWEET BASIL

Use sweet basil with discretion but with enthusiasm, for it has a liveliness that increases appetite wondrously.

## MINT

How cool green mint insinuates itself into our favor! To him who mixes a little green spearmint with his salad, this herb will teach the secret of true indispensability.

## BURNET

The small, inside leaves of burnet have a delicate cucumber taste that is delightful in company with crisp greens.

## THYME

Thyme with fresh tomatoes — a culinary idyll. Sink these two in a bed of lettuce, cover them with olive oil and vinegar, starred with salt and pepper — the result is too delicious to describe.

## MARJORAM

Go gently with marjoram. It has a strong flavor, and only if used in small amounts will it aid salads. But introduce it charily and you will like it.

## ANISE AND FENNEL

Sprigs of anise and fennel, if young and tender, may be minced over a green salad with heartening results.

# Salad Trimmings

Salad trimmings — truly an unprofessional term. But what else can one call them to properly suggest their use? Let the name stand, for they are just that, accessories used to complete salad ensembles.

## ANCHOVIES

Anchovies deserve a poem at the very least. But being no poet, nor even poetaster, I shall begin and end by calling them *inspired fishlets*. Salted or in oil, alone or with capers in their embrace, they have IT — that *je ne sais quoi* that sets one dreaming greedy dreams at the bare mention of their name. A few anchovies on a salad's top give rare fullness of flavor.

## EGGS

Slice hard-boiled eggs for your salad trim. They are circlets of gold and white, gastronomical daisies. Soak them in beet liquor before slicing and you have exotic flowers, pink edged.

## CAPERS

Don't put capers into your salad too often, for they pall. But used now and then they are added piquancy. Pickled nasturtium pods also may be used in the same way.

## OLIVES

Words of mine cannot increase the value of these salad jewels, so why repeat what we already know of the olive's excellence? Those known to the trade as "green-ripe olives," half-ripened on the tree, then home-cured, full of oil, achieve a new high in richness of taste.

## TUNA

Tuna tops salads gracefully and tastefully. Either the imported Italian brands or America's own packs are equally good, provided they are packed in olive oil and not some inferior substitute.

So, as Peter said to Parson Adams, "An excellent salad is to be found in every field — health in the hedgerows." And, we might add, "Salad sophistication in vegetable stands, in grocery stores, in herb gardens."

## Making Salads

You may say, after all this fuss about what to put into salads, "Yes, but how does one make a *green salad*?"

Listen carefully, follow directions meticulously, for once you learn you will never forget.

## SALAD BOWL

First, have you an adequate salad bowl? Or have you fallen a victim of your own trusting nature, and bought the bowl advised by the department-store salesperson — a bowl 8 inches in diameter and 2 inches deep —"just the thing to mix salads in!"

Of course, if you have a real salad bowl you are all right. But if yours is a pygmy such as that just described, go out and begin to hunt for a young bathtub. Don't be too quickly satisfied, or you'll be sorry. When at last you find a hardwood or pottery bowl that has mammoth proportions, 14 to 16 inches in diameter, and 5 to 7 inches deep, *buy it at once,* before someone else gets it. The salesperson no doubt will ask if you run a boardinghouse, but don't let that bother you. Hurry home with thanksgiving in your heart, for you have a real salad bowl.

If you have ever known the utter hopelessness of trying to mix a salad in a too-small bowl, you won't think this is a joke. If you are a novice, then heed the voice of experience, and *don't buy a small salad bowl.*

## SALAD FORK AND SPOON

Maybe it's just an old wives' tale that a wooden fork and spoon mix a salad better than any other kind. But the rough surface of the wood seems to take hold of the greens better than glass, china, or metal. Then too, wooden utensils are usually of generous size, and in their grasp the salad has no choice but to go where it is pushed.

And now, the salad:

## DRY THE GREENS

Wash the salad greens and dry them thoroughly with a towel. If any moisture clings to them it will dilute the salad dressing.

DIVIDE LEAVES

Divide each leaf into several parts, either with the fingers or the kitchen scissors, and heap in the big salad bowl.

GARLIC

A little garlic is a gracious accent for green salads. But mind that the accent is slight, for a salad reeking of garlic disgusts. On the other hand, one that is delicately garlic-flavored pleases and refreshes. So, to introduce this subtle bit of seasoning (for garlic can be subtle): Take a dry heel of bread, such as the French call a *chapon*. Rub it all over with a cut piece of garlic, so it will be wet with juice. Toss it into the bowl with the greens, and dress it with them.

HERBS, ROOTS, AND TRIMMINGS

On top of the greens lay the other salad ingredients, such as beets, artichoke hearts, onion slices, herb tips, olives, or whatever you have chosen.

## Dressing the Salad

*The dressing of a salad will make or mar it.* No matter how fine the greens and other materials in it, it will fail to please unless the dressing of it is rightly done.

OIL

First, with a careful hand *sprinkle*, don't pour, olive oil over the salad. Do this by holding the bottle cork half in, half out of the bottle opening, and dribbling the oil. No one can tell you how much, for it depends on your taste and the size of the salad. Perhaps two tablespoons, perhaps more or less. You will soon learn to judge. An approximate guide will be given in the first recipe in this chapter (page 159).

A   PARSLEY

Next, with wooden fork and spoon lift greens and toss gently. "What!" you say, "toss when oil is added, and before the vinegar and seasonings are in?" Indeed yes. Oil first of all, then a tossing until each leaf is coated with the shining drops. Thus the leaves are sealed so the salt and vinegar will not wilt them quickly, as they would if added first.

### SEASONINGS

Grind over the salad a generous sprinkling of black pepper. Add a little salt — not too much, for later you will taste — and if need be add some more. This salting, like the rest of the salad seasoning, is all a matter of taste and habitude.

### VINEGAR

Dot the surface generously with good wine vinegar, using the same method as for the oil. The amount of this too is determined by the palate, so go slowly in putting it on.

Carefully toss the whole salad again until the seasonings and the vinegar are well mixed with the greens.

### TASTE

Taste now, and judge for yourself whether the salad's sourness, saltiness, and oiliness suit you. If not, rectify the fault, toss again, and confirm your amended judgment by retasting. It is good? Then remove the garlicked *chapon*, discard it, and serve the salad at once.

SERVE

Just a warning — but heed it, for it means for you a reputation as a good salad maker, or the reverse. Never dress the salad until the diners are ready and waiting. If dressed and left to stand for even ten minutes, it will become wilted and weary, wholly unfit to eat. For what is so dejected as a salad worn with waiting?

Some know-it-all said:

It takes four people to make a salad — a miser for the vinegar, a prodigal for the oil, a lawyer for the salt and spices, a madman for the mixing.

This pretty bit of foolishness, if anyone has ever taken it seriously, must have ruined many a salad. "A madman for the mixing" indeed! A diplomat is needed for that. A diplomat so gentle in approach that he or she can turn that salad over and over softly, never bruising a leaf. True, the French call mixing a salad "fatiguing" it (*fatiguer une salade*), but don't take that too seriously. No true artist tires out a salad, but rather massages it tenderly to make it sit up and feel fine.

MAYONNAISE

As to mayonnaise dressing for salads, it belongs to the desserty type, or is very good as a sauce. But for green salads it is not suitable. A bit of mayonnaise mixed into some of the more elaborate dressings, to lend richness and body, is permissible. But a green salad with a blob of mayonnaise sitting on top, like a bug on a tomato vine, is horrible.

BOTTLED DRESSINGS

Don't buy bottled dressings if you value true excellence of taste. Most of them are like canned music — loud, sharp, and disturbing.

DRESSING BOTTLES

The so-called "dressing bottle" is the bane of real salad makers. Very pretty, it is true. A crystal bottle, sweetly shaped, with a mark part way up for "vinegar" and still farther up another for "oil" — a sterling stopper — it makes a fine wedding present, until the bride finds out that it isn't good for anything.

Such a bottle couldn't possibly be any good for the purpose of mixing salad dressing, which is what it was intended for. For how can a manufacturer of crystal bottles know how much oil and vinegar you are going to want in your French dressing tonight? One learns that from experience, not from a bottle.

If we Americans could form the large salad habit, eating more salad and less bread and starch, we should be happier people. But how could we have formed this habit, reared as we have been on polite dabs of cottage cheese on pineapple, smug scoops of "macaroni salad" — God save the mark! — and such heresies? A real serving of honest green salad would discourage all but the initiated.

If we can forget those salads of other days, and work up on our salad servings, increasing them day by day until everyone in the family is eating lavish servings, we shall be the better for it.


## SIMPLE SALADS


To learn the art of making a good, simple green salad is a commendable achievement. That cool, crisp, uncomplicated green mixture, either at the beginning of the meal or revivifying the appetite after the meat course, is a godsend to the wise diner. And the variety one can achieve is never-ending.

In the following recipes, the method of dressing the salads is that outlined in detail in the preceding pages.


## Mixed Green Salad with Herbs

This salad is like a plain dress with numerous sets of accessories. Each set makes of the whole a different costume, and just so each combination of herbs makes a different salad.

Choosing the greens for this salad is a matter of personal taste and seasonal offerings in the markets. Use either one kind of green alone, or combine two or three. Lettuce, endive, romaine, blanched chicory, escarole, spinach, dandelion, cress — take your choice and fill your bowl. Add a *chapon* of bread rubbed with garlic. Mix in at least a teaspoon of minced chives.

Then the fun begins. Pick fresh tips of herbs: rocket, nasturtium, rosemary, chervil, tarragon, basil, spearmint, burnet, thyme, marjoram, anise, or fennel. Do not use more than three different kinds. About 6 sprigs in all for a salad for four will do. Bruise them with the fingers, discard all large stems, and toss into the salad. Dress with oil, salt and pepper, and vinegar. For a salad for four the proportions would be approximately:

| | |
|---|---|
| 6 *tablespoons olive oil* | *salt* |
| 2 *tablespoons wine vinegar* | *black pepper* |


## Green Salad with Anchovies

| | |
|---|---|
| *curly endive* | 1 *tomato* |
| *romaine* | 4 *radishes* |
| 1 *garlicked* chapon (*page 155*) | 1 *cucumber* |

6 anchovies washed and
  boned, or 12 anchovy fillets cut up
1 teaspoon thyme

oil
salt
black pepper
vinegar

Fill salad bowl with equal parts curly endive and romaine. Add *chapon* of garlic-rubbed bread, and slice in the tomato, radishes, and cucumber. Strew over this the anchovies or anchovy fillets. Top with thyme. Dress with oil, salt and pepper, and vinegar. Remove the *chapon*.

## Green Salad with Cheese Bits

escarole
romaine
tiny spinach leaves
1 garlicked chapon (page
  155)
radishes
1 teaspoon each chervil and
  chives

2 slices French bread
  spread with nippy cheese
  spread
olive oil
salt
black pepper
vinegar

Heap a bowl with escarole, romaine, and spinach leaves. Add *chapon* of bread. Over the top slice radishes. Mince chervil and chives over this. Then into the salad, cube French bread spread with cheese. Dress with olive oil, salt and pepper, and vinegar. Remove the *chapon*.

## Lettuce Salad with Mint

1 head lettuce
tiny onion tops or chives
at least 6 sprigs spearmint
olive oil

salt
black pepper
vinegar
hard-boiled eggs (optional)

Pull apart, wash, and dry head of lettuce. Heap in salad bowl, mince in tiny onion tops or chives and spearmint. Dress with olive oil, salt and pepper, and vinegar. Hard-boiled eggs may be added, or sliced tomatoes.

## Tomato and Thyme Salad

*romaine*
1  *garlicked* chapon (*page 155*)
2  *peeled tomatoes*
*paper-thin onion slices*

10  *thyme tips*
*olive oil*
*salt*
*black pepper*
*vinegar*

Fresh thyme and fresh tomatoes have a strong affinity for each other, making a delicious salad combination. Heap romaine that has been pulled apart in the salad bowl. Throw in garlicked *chapon*. Slice in tomatoes and add slices of onion separated into rings. Bruise about 10 thyme tips, cut them up, and add. Dress with olive oil, salt and pepper, and vinegar. Remove the *chapon*.

## Bitter Salad (Insalata amara)

How often has this beloved bitter salad of the Italians revived a loitering appetite and made a reluctant diner ready to eat the full meal that was to follow. Its acrid sharpness is a spur to food awareness.

*chicory or* radicetta *leaves*
1  *garlicked* chapon (*page 155*)
2  *hard-boiled eggs*
*tomatoes* (*optional*)

*bulb of a new onion*
*olive oil*
*salt*
*black pepper*
*vinegar*

F    ROSEMARY

Cup up the fresh, new leaves of the small-rooted chicory or *radicetta*. Add *chapon*, and slice in hard-boiled eggs. Tomatoes may be added if desired. Mince over all the onion bulb. Dress with olive oil, salt, pepper, and vinegar. Remove the *chapon*.

## *New Leek Salad*

Unless you know the robust yet gentle flavor of leeks you are not fully flavor-wise. These savory roots must be given careful washing, for sand often hides among the leaves tightly nested just above the bulb.

3 *young and tender leeks*          *olive oil*
1 *large tomato*                          *salt*
*romaine*                                     *black pepper*
1 *teaspoon each sweet basil*      *vinegar*
   *and chervil*
1 *garlicked* chapon *(page*
   *155)*

Cut up coarsely the white parts of leeks. Cut a tomato into sections and add these and the leeks to a bowl of romaine. Sprinkle with sweet basil and chervil. Add *chapon,* and dress with olive oil, salt, pepper, and vinegar. Remove the *chapon.*

## Cauliflower Salad

Cauliflower, if properly cooked, is one of the best salad ingredients. It should be steamed just until it is tender, but still white and firm. If boiled until limp, pink, and wretched, it is neither tempting nor palatable.

*1 small head cauliflower*
*salt*
*½ cup boiling water*
*curly endive*
*4 slices Bermuda onion divided into rings*
*1 garlicked chapon (page 155)*
*2 small stalks celery thinly sliced*

*1 tablespoon chervil*
*1 tablespoon minced sweet basil or tarragon*
*olive oil*
*salt*
*black pepper*
*vinegar*

Separate head of cauliflower into medium pieces, heap them in a saucepan, sprinkle with salt, and add boiling water. Put over a slow flame, cover, and steam until barely tender. Drain and chill.

Fill the salad bowl two-thirds full of curly endive. Add onion rings, *chapon,* and celery. Lay on the cauliflower, topping with chervil and mixed herbs. Dress with olive oil, salt, pepper, and vinegar. Remove the *chapon.*

## String Bean Salad

cold steamed string beans
escarole
2 green onions with tops
   and bulbs shredded
2 sprigs summer savory
   minced
6 or 8 nasturtium flowers
   washed and dried

olive oil
salt
black pepper
garlicked chapon (page
   154)
vinegar

Mix beans and an equal bulk of escarole, plus onions, and summer savory. Cut nasturtium flowers into salad. The finely chopped tender seed pods may be added in season. Dress with olive oil, salt, pepper, vinegar, and *chapon* of bread, removing the *chapon* after mixing.

## Hodgepodge Salad

This salad makes a delightful lunch, served with French bread lightly toasted under the broiler, then rubbed with garlic and buttered.

any three salad greens
tomato sections
sliced onions
sliced cucumbers
cold vegetables
1 can tuna shredded
chervil or parsley

sweet basil
garlicked chapon (page
   154)
olive oil
salt
black pepper
vinegar

Fill your bowl with salad greens. Lay over the top tomato, onions, cucumbers, and any cold vegetables, such as string beans, beets, peas, or potatoes, that you have. Top it with tuna, chervil or parsley, and sweet basil. Throw in a *chapon* of bread rubbed with garlic, and dress with olive oil, salt, pepper, and vinegar. Remove the *chapon*.

## MORE ELABORATE SALADS

You no doubt have muttered by now — "To the Devil with her *chapon* of bread, olive oil, and vinegar! Doesn't the woman know any other salad dressing but that?"

Everything in good time. For, while the plain salad with French dressing is the one dearest to the heart of the true gourmet, he or she also plays around with more fancy salads in his or her lighter hours, and obtains no mean results.

Elaborate salads, or those with rich dressings, are good for luncheons, where they do not have to rival other richness in food. But dinners are not such good times for them. They fill up the guests at the wrong time, leaving no room for further food subtleties.

But they do have a place in life, so by all means let us have them. Here are a few favorites, just to start on.

### *Avocado Salad*

The avocado is, to the majority of diners, a favored salad ingredient. The classically simple version is the serving of halved, unpeeled avocados sprinkled with salt and lemon juice. Eaten with crisp crackers they are truly ambrosial. The confirmed avocado eater likes them with no seasoning but their own richness. I confess I use only a shake of Tabasco sauce. Or try this:

romaine
escarole
1  cucumber minced

1  tomato in sections
1  tablespoon minced chives

DRESSING:
2  tablespoons lemon juice
5  tablespoons olive oil
salt

black pepper
1  fully ripe avocado peeled
   and minced

Fill a bowl with the romaine and escarole in equal parts. Add cucumbers, tomato, and chives. Add the dressing. Toss gently but thoroughly, so that as much of the avocado as possible will coat the greens.

## Avocado with Fresh Dill

Halve lengthwise a large avocado, sprinkle with ½ teaspoon fresh minced dill over each half, and season with lemon juice, salt, and paprika.

## Red Onion and Tomato Salad with Sweet Basil

This is a pretty red and green salad, and if served very cold is refreshing and appetizing.

| | |
|---|---|
| *curly endive pulled apart and cut into bits* | DRESSING: |
| *tomatoes peeled and sliced* | ¼ *cup chopped sweet basil* |
| *sweet red onions thinly sliced* | ¼ *cup chopped parsley* |
| | 4 *tablespoons olive oil* |
| | *red-wine vinegar* |
| | *salt* |
| | *black pepper* |

On each salad plate prepare a thin nest of endive. Over this arrange tomato slices, then onion slices separated into rings. Then make the dressing. Crush and mix basil, parsley, and oil together in a mortar and pestle, then add vinegar and salt and pepper to taste. Your own palate will dictate the amount of vinegar. Mix well. Pour the dressing over the salads, and set in refrigerator 10 minutes before serving.

## Garden Salad

Salad greens topped with marinated vegetables and dressed with a tasty dressing make a distinguished first course to a dinner.

2  *sliced cooked beets*
12  *ripe pitted olives*
*romaine*
*endive*
*escarole*
*thin onion rings*
*thin bell pepper rings*

MARINADE:
½  *cup red-wine vinegar*
4  *tablespoons olive oil*
1  *clove garlic halved*
1  *teaspoon tarragon*
½  *bay leaf broken up*
1  *Japanese chile halved*

6  *sprigs fresh thyme*
*salt*

DRESSING:
6  *tablespoons olive oil*
3  *tablespoons red-wine vinegar*
4  *tablespoons tomato catsup*
6  *sprigs thyme minced*
1  *teaspoon sugar*
*salt*
*black pepper*

Let beets and olives marinate 2 hours, then remove. Fill a large salad bowl with equal parts romaine, endive, and escarole. Mix them well, and dress with half of the dressing.

When greens are dressed, strew beets and olives over them, then add onion and pepper rings. Scatter the remaining dressing over the top and serve at once.

## Tomatoes Royal

How good these are on a hot day, as they come cool and colorful, fresh from the refrigerator. They are welcome accompaniment to a supper of Spanish beans and tortillas, or to any other one-dish meal.

| | |
|---|---|
| *large, firm peeled tomatoes* | *salt* |
| *chopped spearmint, chives,* | *black pepper* |
| *or green onion tops* | *thyme* |
| *olive oil* | *vinegar* |

First prepare the tomatoes by cutting them into ¾-inch slices and sprinkling them with the spearmint, chives, or onion tops. Do not use more than one of these at the same time. Salt and pepper each slice and dot freely with olive oil. No vinegar is needed at this time.

Fill the salad bowl with a mixture of greens. Strew chives and thyme over the mixture, and dress with olive oil, salt, pepper, and vinegar. Portion out on salad plates, and on the top of each lay the dressed tomato slices.

## Our Bean Plate

This salad, hearty and vegetably, is one that we serve at a buffet supper, for it is a salad, but also a vegetable dish. We serve it confidently, and our guests enjoy it.

1 *9-ounce package frozen green lima beans*

1 *9-ounce package frozen cut green beans or same amount fresh green beans*

1 *16-ounce can garbanzo beans drained*

2 *anchovy fillets chopped*

½ *teaspoon wild marjoram (oregano)*

*curly endive, escarole, or leaf spinach cut or pulled into bite-sized pieces, enough to cover the platter on which the salad is to be assembled*

DRESSING:

6 *tablespoons olive oil*

2 *tablespoons red-wine vinegar*

1 *green onion with tops minced*

2 *tablespoons parsley minced*

*salt*

*black pepper*

Cook the two packages of frozen vegetables or the fresh ones separately until just tender and drain well. Put the lima beans, green beans, and garbanzo beans into separate bowls. Mix the dressing ingredients and dress each dish of beans, saving some of the dressing for the greens. Add the anchovy fillets and the wild majoram (oregano) to the garbanzo beans. Let the 3 lots of vegetables marinate in the dressing for 2 hours.

Then prepare a large enough platter to accommodate them, laying on it first a layer of curly endive or escarole or leaf spinach, dressed with the same simple dressing. Arrange the three types of beans in three separate belts across the platter. Serve, passing a bowl of Sour Cream Dressing on the side.

## Sour Cream Dressing

| | |
|---|---|
| *1 cup sour cream* | *1 teaspoon chopped sweet* |
| *1 tablespoon red-wine vine-* | *pickle relish* |
| *gar* | *thin sweet cream as required* |

Mix the first three ingredients, then slowly whip in enough sweet cream to make a spreadable, even runny consistency.

## MEAT SALADS

Now for a few salads of cold meat. They may not be orthodox but they are good American fare.

## French Salad of Cold Roast Meat

A cherished little old brown cookbook, dog-eared and worn with a hundred years' use (but not mine!), gave me this salad. The recipe lies between one for "Stewing Sorrel" and another for "Frying Herbs the Staffordshire Way." It is undoubtedly the most inspired way of serving cold roast that one can imagine.

The way it was done in 1840, with very slight changes, is as good now as then:

Chop three anchovies, a shallot, and some Parsley, small; put them into a bowl with 1 tablespoon of vinegar, 2 of oil, a little mustard, and salt. When well mixed, add by degrees some cold roast or boiled meat in *very thin slices;* put in a few at a time, not exceeding two or three inches long. Shake them in the seasoning, and then put in more; but cover the bowl close, and let the salad be prepared three hours before it is eaten. Garnish with Parsley.

This rule I use by making the marinade as directed, but adding enough chopped rosemary, sage, and spearmint to make a good tablespoon in all.

Serve this on Sunday night for supper, with French bread and such green things as celery, Florence fennel (finocchio), radishes, and new onions.

## Lamb Salad

This is a variation of the above salad, using sliced cold roast lamb, and no other herbs than minced fresh spearmint and chives.

## Bollito Salad

If you have acquired the European habit of making a pot of broth each week, you find yourself now and then with some extra boiled beef on your hands. Some like it cold with mustard, or hot with horseradish, but a third good way of enjoying this meat is to make an Italian meat salad of it.

| | |
|---|---|
| *about 3 cups cold, lean* | *salt* |
| *boiled beef cut into small* | *black pepper* |
| *cubes* | *olive oil* |
| *1  large red onion cubed* | *red-wine vinegar* |

Combine beef and onion. Salt to taste and use lots of black pepper on it. Dress first with enough olive oil to slightly moisten it, then use plenty of red-wine vinegar in it, taking care that the vinegar taste predominates over the oil. Serve this in company with a bowl of plain green salad (page 157).

We ate this dish for years before we discovered justification for our taste. Not that we needed it — but we were delighted to find the food-minded Mr. Thackeray putting into the mouth of Fitzboodle an ecstatic endorsement of this very dish of ours. "*Bouilli* with onions — delicious," was Fitzboodle's opinion of it.


## SOME SALAD DRESSINGS


It is fun to know lots of salad dressings. They are top-notch in the way of culinary surprises. These more complicated dressings are not mixed on the salad, but prepared in advance, usually in quantity so that one may keep some on hand. They are used by adding to the salad and tossing just before serving, or by spooning over an arrangement of salad fruits (page 149,) salad vegetables or roots (pages 147–148), or salad trimmings (pages 151–152) on a bed of greens previously seasoned with olive oil and vinegar. This latter salad arrangement is served without tossing.

The principal thing to remember in serving a salad with special dressing spooned over its top is not to put your fruits, vegetables, etc., on a nest of greens that have had no seasoning. If you do, no matter how much dressing you put over the top, your salad will have spots that taste flat.

## Epicurean Salad Dressing

12 tablespoons olive oil
3 tablespoons red-wine vinegar
6 tablespoons tomato catsup
2 dozen capers
1 tablespoon Worcestershire sauce
2 dashes Tabasco sauce

2 tablespoons lemon juice
2 cloves garlic halved
1 heaping teaspoon sugar
2 sprigs fresh sweet basil minced
6 cloves
salt
black pepper

Mix all ingredients together, beat well, and allow to stand overnight. The next morning remove garlic; otherwise it will be too strong. ½ *pint*.

Use this dressing on:

    Mixtures of salad greens with chives
    Salad greens, cucumbers, and onion
    Salad greens and steamed cauliflower
    Salad greens, radishes, sliced eggs, shredded celery
    Salad greens, onion rings, steamed baby artichokes

August Vollmer often drops his role of criminologist to don a chef's cap in his own kitchen. His New Orleans background bred in him a feeling for the best in food flavor. For his friends he makes a salad dressing that is finer than any I have ever known; and as he serves it he tells of his Negro mammy, Black Mary, who gave its secret to that little Vollmer boy of other days.

## Black Mary's Creole Salad Dressing

**FIRST STEP:**

1 *level tablespoon granulated sugar*

1 *level teaspoon French mustard*

2 *tablespoons olive oil*

1½ *tablespoons vinegar*

*salt*

Mix and stir sugar and mustard thoroughly until sugar is dissolved and mixture creamy.

Pour oil into this mixture a few drops at a time, as in making mayonnaise, stirring all the while, until mixture is smooth and has caramel-like consistency.

Add vinegar slowly, stirring.

Add salt to taste.

**SECOND STEP:**

2 *cloves garlic*

1 *bell pepper, seeds removed*

4 *green onion tops*

2 *heaped tablespoons minced parsley*

*black pepper*

Put garlic, pepper, onion tops, and parsley into a chopping bowl and chop until the mass is reduced to a fine pulp and is smooth. The extreme fineness of this is very important, and is a matter of long chopping. Don't quit too soon. Or you may choose to mix in a blender, if yours chops without added liquid. Add a liberal sprinkling of black pepper.

**THIRD STEP:**

Place green pulp in with the first mixture and beat with an egg beater for 15 minutes or longer.

FOURTH STEP:
Add salt to suit your taste.

TO SERVE:
Pour 4 tablespoons of the dressing on the salad and serve with very thin slices of buttered toast. The best salads for this dressing are those of sliced tomatoes or prawns, served on a nest of seasoned greens such as romaine or butter head lettuce dressed to taste with oil and vinegar. 2 *servings*.

The best way of managing to eat enough of this really superlative dressing is to make lots of the first mixture at one making, for it will keep. Then prepare the green mixture and add it as it is needed.

## Herb Salad Dressing

This is an ideal dressing for that good old American standby, hearts of lettuce.

| | |
|---|---|
| 2 *heaping tablespoons mayonnaise* | 2 *cloves garlic halved* |
| 1 *tablespoon tomato catsup* | ¼ *teaspoon prepared mustard* |
| ½ *teaspoon Worcestershire sauce* | 1 *tablespoon minced herbs: thyme, marjoram, spearmint, sweet basil, and any other you fancy* |
| 2 *dashes Tabasco sauce* | |
| 3 *dashes angostura bitters* | |

Mix all ingredients well, let stand 1 hour, then discard garlic. This dressing will keep as long as mayonnaise will keep, so it is advisable to double or triple amounts, for more salads later on. 2 *servings*.

## Anchovy Dressing

6 *tablespoons olive oil*
2 *tablespoons wine vinegar*
*salt*
*black pepper*
1 *teaspoon minced chives*

1 *teaspoon minced chervil and parsley mixed*
½ *teaspoon minced thyme*
6 *anchovy fillets*

Mix all ingredients except anchovies. Chop anchovies in a bowl until they are fine, then add to dressing. Mix again. This dressing is good on tomatoes or on green mixtures. *3 or 4 servings.*

## Green Salad Dressing

This dressing, made in the indicated quantity and kept in a refrigerator, will keep well for several weeks.

⅔ *teaspoon dry mustard*
⅔ *teaspoon salt*
¼ *teaspoon black pepper*
1 *teaspoon paprika*
2 *cups olive oil*
⅔ *cup red-wine vinegar*

3 *dashes Tabasco sauce*
2 *cloves garlic halved*
2 *sprigs spearmint*
2 *sprigs sweet basil*
½ *cup very finely chopped parsley*

Put dry ingredients into a jar, wet with a little oil, and blend. Add gradually vinegar, Tabasco, and garlic. Bruise sprigs of herbs and add, together with parsley. Let stand 2 hours, then remove garlic and discard. After 24 hours remove the herb sprigs. Shake well before using. *10 to 12 servings.*

## Potpourri Dressing

Use recipe for Green Salad Dressing (above), omitting

the herb sprigs and parsley. Instead use 1 cup minced green herb leaves, all well bruised. Such combinations as thyme, sweet marjoram, rosemary, and parsley; chervil, savory, burnet, and basil; or any other you may like, may be used. Let stand 24 hours, then strain. If the dressing is left too long on the herbs it will be too strong. *10 to 12 servings.*

For you, then, are these green, appetite-teasing, health-bringing salads, the sort we Americans serve so often. Try them. If you want to change a bit the balance of the ingredients, that is personal taste. Remember, however, to under- rather than overseason. For in too much seasoning lies the road back to that palate-deadening habit of "dusting with salt and pepper" that too many of us need to forget.

How fortunate that we today are learning the healthful properties of greens and salads. Otherwise we might be saying with the poet of early Britain:

> Beware of saladis  .  .  .  and fruits rawe,
> For they make many a man haue a feble mawe.

Instead, we can exult with Sydney Smith,

> O green and glorious! O herbaceous treat!
> 'Twould tempt the dying anchorite to eat;
> Back to the world he'd turn his fleeting soul
> And plunge his fingers in the salad bowl.

## ❧ EIGHT ❧

## Brain Food

THE flavor of fish is so different from that of meats, yet its food properties are so similar, that one suspects the Creator of inventing fish to keep man from tiring of meat, or vice versa.

Since time began men have pulled from the water the creatures that lived therein, and eaten them with gusto. No doubt they first ate them raw, for which we cannot feel envy. But the first discovery of the fine flavor that cooking gives this food — that thrill we may begrudge them.

Fish was fair food in biblical times, as the Sermon on the Mount testifies. The Greeks, in their sea-girt land, valued fish, and wrote verse to their praise:

> A little polypus, or a small cuttle-fish,
> A crab, a crawfish, oysters, cockles,
> Limpets, solens, mussels and pinnas,
> Periwinkles, too, from Mytilene take;
> Let us have two sprats, and mullet, ling,
> And congor-eel, and perch and blackfish.

In every land, in every time, men have known the varied wealth of the waters, and have found it good.

The taste of fish, though delicious, is so delicate that it might almost be called, in some instances, weak. In fact, fish is one of the foods that usually does not stand well alone. It needs the addition of seasonings to make it fully enjoyable.

The loophole in that statement was left purposely, to allow me to speak about trout. Otherwise that grand fish would make a liar out of me, for it is one fish that may be cooked with pepper and salt, in such lowly fat even as drippings, and be a gastronomic triumph, needing nothing for perfection. Some of you may know other types that share this distinction. If so, let us include them under the exception. But generally speaking, fish needs zipping up just a little, to be quite interesting.

There are in our vast sea-girt and stream-latticed continent so many kinds of edible fish, and so many possible ways of preparing them, that anything less than a tome could only flick the subject, barely touching it. But whatever the type of fish to be cooked, it will be the best of its kind if herbs are used in its preparation.

For simple cookery that abounds in flavor the brown-paper cookery method is a masterpiece. Seeing it first in an article by George Rector, that maestro of maestros, I adapted it to my herbish habits, and liked it mightily:

## Fish in Brown Paper à la Rector

| | |
|---|---|
| *fish ( see below )* | *black pepper* |
| *olive oil* | *½  teaspoon chervil* |
| *salt* | *¼  teaspoon thyme minced* |

Use any small, sweet fish up to 6 inches in length, so that several may be served to each person. Clean, scale, behead, and wash them, and dry thoroughly. For each fish over 6 inches, and for 3 or 4 together if under that, cut a large oval of heavy brown paper, making its diameter about 2 inches longer than the fish. Oil the paper thoroughly on both sides until limp. Or use cooking foil or parchment. Fold down the middle, and lay the fish between the two halves. Add salt and pepper, chervil, and thyme. Bring the edges of the oval together, crimp, and roll up toward the fish firmly until the package looks like a peach turnover. Preheat the oven to 350°, lay the package on the rack, and let it bake 30 minutes. If the paper begins to scorch brush it with oil. After the first 15 minutes turn over. When done cut off edges of paper with scissors and roll the fish out on the serving plate. *1 serving.*

## Broiled Fish with Herbs

Salmon or halibut, or any large sweet fish, may be broiled in slices. A medium-sized fish may be broiled whole.

First rub the fish with olive oil or melted butter, and season with salt and pepper. Then make a paste of butter and minced herbs such as thyme, fennel, and parsley, and set it aside. Place fish under a 400° broiler, first close to the flame so it will brown. Turn, brown other side. Then lower oven to 300° and move fish a little lower, away from the flame. Cook until tender. When tender remove to a hot platter, spread with herb butter, and serve with lemon.

You will discover other combinations of herbs you like for this, for nearly all have an affinity for fish. Remember not to drown the fish in flavor, for its own taste is so delicate that it must not be obliterated.

## Pan-Fried Fish

Roll salted and peppered fish in corn meal or cracker dust, and lay in frying pan whose bottom is barely covered with bubbling olive oil. Cook slowly until brown on both sides and tender. Serve with Lemon-Herb Butter or with Tartar Sauce (page 184).

## Whole Fish with Herbs

| | |
|---|---|
| 1 *whole fish, such as white-*<br>*fish or rock cod, about 2*<br>*pounds* | 1 *green onion* |
| | ½ *clove garlic* |
| | 1 *tablespoon minced pars-*<br>*ley* |
| *olive oil or melted butter* | |
| *salt* | *small sprig thyme* |
| *black pepper* | *small sprig marjoram* |
| *broth (pages 83–84)* | ½ *leaf sage* |
| SAUCE: | 1 *tablespoon catsup* |
| 2 *tablespoons butter* | |

Wash and dry fish, then rub it with oil or butter, salt and pepper it, and lay it in a roasting pan. Pour in a little broth, and cook in a 350° oven until tender.

Meanwhile make the sauce. Melt butter, mince in onion and garlic, and cook gently 5 minutes. Add parsley, and other herbs minced together. Stir, cook 5 minutes more, add catsup, mix well.

When fish is done take up on hot platter and pour the sauce over it. 2 *servings*.

## Small Fish Stuffed and Baked

| | |
|---|---|
| 4 *fish such as fresh sar-*<br>*dines, pilchards, smelt* | 1 *cup toast crumbs* |
| | ½ *small onion* |

½  clove garlic
 1  tablespoon olive oil
 1  tablespoon grated Ro-
    mano cheese
 1  teaspoon parsley

⅓  teaspoon thyme
 2  tablespoons pine nuts
salt
black pepper

For this recipe one may use fresh sardines or pilchards, or small smelt or surf fish.

Open up the fish along their bellies and clean them. Wash and dry thoroughly. Make stuffing as follows. Mix crumbs with chopped onion and garlic which have been cooked 5 minutes in olive oil. Add other ingredients, salting and peppering to taste.

Stuff the fish, then rub them with a little olive oil and salt and stand them on their backs side by side in an oiled pan. Bake until tender (about 20 minutes to half an hour) in a 400° oven. 2 *servings*. Double or triple for more servings.

## Baked Halibut with Butter Paste

 1  2-pound slice halibut
several thin slices fat salt
    pork
onion slices
½  bay leaf, broken up
black pepper

 4  tablespoons butter
 3  tablespoons flour
½  teaspoon salt
cayenne pepper
cracker meal
 3  strips bacon

Wipe halibut. In a baking dish arrange salt pork slices and over them a layer of sliced onions. Sprinkle over that the bay leaf, then pepper the mixture and over it lay the halibut. Make a paste by creaming butter with flour, salt, and a little cayenne. Spread paste evenly over fish. Scatter cracker meal over this, then lay on bacon. Cover whole with buttered paper or foil and bake 1 hour at 300°. Remove paper or foil last 15 minutes to brown. 2 *servings*.

## Baked Stuffed Bass

1 2-pound bass

STUFFING:
2 tablespoons butter
½ onion
1 clove garlic
2 stalks celery
2 leaves sage
¼ teaspoon basil minced
¼ teaspoon summer savory minced
¼ cup chervil minced
⅓ cup white wine

4 slices whole-wheat toast made into crumbs
¼ cup grated Romano cheese
salt
black pepper
olive oil

BASTING LIQUOR:
¼ cup white wine
¼ cup hot water
1 tablespoon olive oil
salt

Wash the cleaned fish thoroughly, wipe dry, salt and pepper the inside surface.

Preheat the oven to 325° and make stuffing. Melt butter, and in it fry the minced onion, garlic, and celery, cooking slowly so as not to burn. When yellow, add herbs, and stir well. Cook 2 or 3 minutes more. Then pour in wine, and allow mixture to cook 5 minutes, then add to toast made into crumbs. Put in cheese, season to taste with salt and pepper.

Oil the stuffed fish with olive oil, salt and pepper its entire outer surface, and bake in an oiled pan in the oven. Baste every 10 minutes, until it has cooked 30 minutes with the basting liquor.

Then turn heat a little higher, stop basting and let brown for 10 minutes. Serve hot. 2 *servings*.

## Baked Fish with Tomato Sauce

2 pounds fish
½ onion sliced

1 clove garlic sliced
3 tablespoons olive oil

1  can tomato sauce or 3      *black pepper*
    *large peeled tomatoes*     ⅓  teaspoon rosemary
    *minced*              1  teaspoon parsley
*salt*

For this recipe use either a slice from a large fish, a 2-pound whole fish, or several smaller ones. Lay it or them in a baking dish, then make the sauce. Cook onion and garlic in oil for 5 minutes. Add tomato sauce or minced tomatoes, salt and pepper, and rosemary. Cook 20 minutes stirring every 2 or 3 minutes.

Pour the sauce over the fish. Cook in 325° oven, covered, until tender, then remove cover, let dry off a little, sprinkle with chopped parsley and serve, surrounded by sauce. 2 *servings*.

## Fish Steak with Dressing

1  *small fish steak*            *and parsley*
*olive oil*                 *salt*
2  *teaspoons bread crumbs*    *black pepper*
1  *tablespoon butter*        1  *egg*
1  *shallot chopped*        1  *slice bacon*
1  *teaspoon mixed herbs,*    1  *lemon*
    *such as thyme, chervil,*

Wash and dry the fish, oil its surface, and rub with salt and pepper. Then make the dressing. Mix together bread crumbs, butter, shallot, minced herbs, and salt and pepper, then bind with egg — always 1 egg, regardless of the number you are serving. Spread dressing on steak, place bacon on top, and bake in a preheated 325° oven for 30 minutes. Dot with minced parsley and serve with lemon slices. *1 serving.* Increase as needed for any number of diners.

## Boiled Fish with Lemon-Herb Butter

"Boiled fish," if properly cooked, isn't boiled at all, since for such delicate-textured flesh boiling would be ruinous. No matter whether the cooking be done in wine, fish stock, court bouillon, or just plain water, a gentle poaching is the treatment needed. Suppose, then, we "boil" a piece of salmon in court bouillon.

Make the court bouillon on pages 186–187, gauging the amount of cold water to be used by the size of your piece of fish, which should barely be covered by the liquid in a suitably shaped pan or kettle. If the fish is not a thick piece, better wrap it in cheesecloth to preserve its shape.

Sponge off your fish with a cloth wrung from cold water, lay it in a kettle, and carefully pour in the hot court bouillon. Let it come to a boil; then reduce heat and let it merely simmer. Cook until the flesh shrinks away from the center bone, or until tender but not crumbly — about 30 minutes will be sufficient for a 4-pound piece of fish. Gently lift the fish from the liquid, drain thoroughly, and arrange on a hot platter. Melt some Lemon-Herb Butter (page 185), and pour over it. Garnish with lemon wedges and serve hot with steamed, buttered potatoes.

## HERB SAUCES FOR FISH

Dean Swift said that fish should swim thrice — in the sea, in butter, and "at last, sirrah, it should swim in good claret." To my mind a fourth immersion is desirable, in a cunningly created sauce. Fish and sauce — what a pair. They go hand in hand, an admirable duo. The slight richness of the sauce, if starred with the greenness of sweet herbs, is welcome addition to broiled, grilled, or fried fish. Serve in a small side dish, or pass in a boat at the table.

## Tartar Sauce

1  cup mayonnaise
1  teaspoon chopped chives
1  teaspoon tarragon
1  teaspoon chervil
1  chopped gherkin
1  teaspoon capers

dash cayenne pepper
prepared mustard to taste
  (optional)
1  chopped olive
wine vinegar to taste

Mix all ingredients except vinegar, then put that in slowly until the proper tartness is obtained. Approximately 1 tablespoon will be necessary.

## Thousand Island Dressing

½  cup mayonnaise
¼  cup tomato catsup
½  minced green pepper
1  minced peeled cucumber
1  teaspoon Worcestershire
  sauce

¼  teaspoon dry mustard
2  sliced cooked beets
  minced
1  teaspoon chives
½  teaspoon tarragon
½  teaspoon chervil

Mix all ingredients and whip thoroughly. Serve in a boat at the table.

## Lemon-Herb Butter

½  cup butter
1  tablespoon grated lemon
  peel
½  teaspoon basil

½  teaspoon chervil
1  teaspoon parsley
bit of chives

Cream butter and lemon peel until well mixed. Add finely chopped herbs. Spread on fish while very hot.

## SHELLFISH

Fresh shellfish were once the peculiar privilege of those who live near the sea. They learned by experience how to manage the "monsters of the deep"; how to de-shell a tiny pink shrimp, or to prepare a crab for the table.

But inland dwellers can also enjoy these foods now through the art of our expert American canners and freezers. Thus all of our country can know them for the excellent fare they are, and can serve them in the infinite variations which they afford us.

## Crabs

Clarence E. Edwards in *Bohemian San Francisco* said, "One has to come to San Francisco to partake of the king of shell fish — the mammoth Pacific crab . . . while the crab is found all along the coast it is prepared nowhere as deliciously as in San Francisco." Cracked and with no dressing, it is ambrosia. If this crab has been cooked in court bouillon, is flavor is truly superb.

## *Court Bouillon*

Court bouillon is a mixture or broth in which French cooks boil fish and shellfish, in order to give them more distinct flavor. After the bouillon is mixed, put it on the fire and boil for 20 minutes until the seasonings have imparted their goodness to the water and wine. Then cook the fish in this seasoned water, and let it cool in it. You will have truly delicious fish.

½ bottle dry white wine
handful chopped parsley
 2 cloves garlic halved
 1 onion minced
 2 cloves
 1 stalk celery with leaves
 1 teaspoon minced thyme

 1 bay leaf
 1 Japanese chile
 5 peppercorns
 1 slice lemon
 1 tablespoon salt
cold water

Add all ingredients to the cold water, using enough of it to make a liquid to cover the amount of fish to be cooked. Boil 20 minutes, then put in the live shellfish. For a small crab or for shrimps, cook 20 minutes. For a large crab or a lobster, 30 minutes. Take from heat; let fish cool in bouillon.

This bouillon may be boiled down over a brisk fire until reduced to one-third its original quantity. This makes a superior essence of fish, and may be used for fish sauces or to make fish aspic.

Now, what to do with the crab when he is cooked and cooled. If you like, crack him and eat him plain. Or with mayonnaise. Or perhaps you would prefer a Crab Louis, a glorified crab salad that is a meal in itself.

## Crab Louis

 1 cooked crab
lettuce
olive oil
salt
black pepper
vinegar or lemon juice
 1 large firm tomato
 2 hard-boiled eggs
chives

parsley
LOUIS DRESSING:
½ cup mayonnaise
 4 tablespoons tomato
   catsup
 4 tablespoons chili sauce
 1 teaspoon finely minced
   celery leaves
 1 teaspoon chervil minced

Clean the cooked crab, remove the body meat, and crack the legs. Make a nest of lettuce that has been seasoned with olive oil, salt, pepper, and vinegar or lemon juice (page 159), and on it spread the shredded body meat.

Make the Louis Dressing and cover the salad with it. Over the dressing slice the tomato, edge the platter with the cracked crab legs, and crown with a ring of egg slices. Sprinkle chives and parsley over all. Serve chilled. 2 *servings*.


## Spaghetti with Crab

Recipe on page 233.


## Abalone

The abalone, clinging to seaward rocks under his iridescent house, is one of the most delicate seafoods known. Its meat, beaten to tenderness, cooks to buttery perfection. To George Sterling fell the privilege of putting into song the excellence of this shellfish. Verse after verse he made in its praise, always with this refrain:

> Ah! some folks boast of quail on toast
> Because they think it's tony;
> But I'm content to owe my rent
> And live on abalone.

If you know this dish you can understand such enthusiasm. If you are uninitiated, try it and be convinced.


## Sautéed Abalone

| | |
|---|---|
| 2 *eggs beaten* | ⅓ *cup Parmesan cheese* |
| 1 *clove garlic chopped* | ¼ *teaspoon thyme* |

1 tablespoon chopped
   parsley
salt
black pepper

6 slices beaten abalone
cracker crumbs
olive oil
lemon

Mix beaten eggs, garlic, cheese, herbs, and salt and pepper. Dry abalone slices, dip in this mixture, then in cracker crumbs, and fry in oil in a moderately hot pan until a very light brown on one side. Cook no more than 3 minutes on each side. Turn carefully, lightly brown on other side. By this time the meat should be creamy and tender when stuck with a fork. Serve very hot with lemon quarters on the side. *2 servings.*

## Shrimps

Use fresh shrimps if you can, and thank Fortune for the privilege. Otherwise canned or frozen ones can make for you dishes that are full of goodness.

In using fresh shrimps which are uncooked, boil them in heavily salted water, for they absorb little of what is put in. Or they may be cooked in court bouillon (page 186–187).

## *Shrimp Cocktail*

⅓ cup whole Pacific coast
   or broken Eastern or
   Southern shrimps
2 tablespoons tomato
   catsup

1 tablespoon sherry wine
1 tablespoon lemon juice
dash Tabasco sauce
¼ teaspoon chives minced
salt

Mix catsup, sherry, lemon juice, Tabasco, chives, and salt to taste. Add shrimp, serve chilled in cocktail glasses. *1 serving.*

This same sauce may be used for shredded crab, lobster, or tiny raw oysters.

## Stewed Shrimps

Make a Neapolitan sauce (page 234) and to it add 3 cups shelled shrimps. Cook slowly 10 minutes. Serve with hot boiled rice and grated Parmesan cheese.

## Cioppino

Italian fishermen on their sea trips revel in a divine dish called *cioppino*. Easy to make, it takes few ingredients, and with bread is a whole meal. This *cioppino* is a fish medley, whose variable contents may include firm white fish such as rock cod, sea bass, or barracuda (never halibut or salmon), and shellfish such as lobsters, crabs, clams, and prawns.

The most delicate *cioppino* is entirely a shellfish conclave, of crabs, cockles, and prawns. This is how it is made:

1 *large live crab*
2 *dozen unshelled prawns*
2 *dozen live cockles or but-ter clams in their shells*
SAUCE:
1 *large onion*
1 *clove garlic*
½ *cup olive oil*
½ *cup dry white wine*
1 *large can solid-pack to-*
*matoes*
¼ *can tomato paste*
2 *cans tomato sauce*
½ *cup water*
½ *bay leaf*
½ *teaspoon thyme*
½ *teaspoon marjoram*
1 *teaspoon parsley*
1½ *teaspoons salt*
⅛ *teaspoon pepper*

Boil crab, allowing 8 minutes to the pound (with shell), and cool it in the water in which it was cooked. When cold clean it, remove and shred the body meat, and crack the legs. Cook prawns in salted water 15 minutes, then drain. Wash thoroughly the outsides of cockles or clams.

In a tall pot lay first the cockles or clams in their shells, then the prawns in their shells, then the cracked crab legs.

Over all this spread the shredded crabmeat taken from the body.

In another pan make the sauce. Mince onion and garlic and fry slowly in olive oil for 20 minutes. Add wine and cook 10 minutes more. Add tomatoes, tomato paste, and tomato sauce, and ½ cup water. Stir well, add herbs and seasonings. Cook slowly 1 hour, stirring frequently.

When sauce is done pour it over the fish previously arranged in the tall pot. With a long-handled fork move fish around gently so the sauce may run to the bottom of the pot. Cover and cook slowly no more than ½ hour from the time it begins to bubble.

Serve this stew in soup bowls, with a green salad and thick slices of French or Italian bread. No utensils except fish forks are used. The sauce is eaten by dunking the bread in it. Shells are picked up in the fingers, opened, and the fish extracted with the forks.

Just a few tips about serving this dish. To each guest give a large 36-inch-square tea towel to be tied bib-fashion about the neck to protect clothes when the tomato sauce begins to fly. Beside each plate place a generous pile of paper napkins, so that each diner may renew his or hers when the old one has gone to ruin, as it soon will. In the center of the table, in lieu of a centerpiece, place a large empty bowl to receive the worn-out napkins and the fish shells — in other words, a bone yard.

Then invite your most dignified friends, tie them up in bibs, and watch the ice melt into good fun. *4 servings*.

## Bouillabaisse

This fish dish, like *cioppino*, is not exactly a soup, nor yet a stew. It is nothing less than a meal, all by itself, with French bread for its handling, and nothing else, unless one wishes to range alongside its steaming delicacy a bowl of green salad. But forget hostessing worries then, for the dinner is complete. Later on plump and rosy fruit may deck the table, with small coffees and a liqueur.

| | |
|---|---|
| 2 *dozen mussels or clams* | *salt* |
| 1 *quart boiling water* | *cayenne pepper* |
| 1 *large onion* | 1 *cup dry white wine* |
| 2 *cloves garlic* | *pinch saffron dissolved in* |
| ½ *cup olive oil* | *the wine* |
| 1 *teaspoon thyme* | 1 *can whole clams* |
| ½ *bay leaf* | 1½ *pounds solid white* |
| ½ *cup chopped parsley* | *boneless fish such as* |
| 2 *cups tomato juice* | *halibut* |
| *juice of 1 lemon* | 2 *crabs* |
| ¼ *of a lemon rind grated* | |

First, in making bouillabaisse a broth of clams or mussels must be made. Scrub mussels or clams and drop them into the boiling water. Cook slowly 1 hour, then strain off the broth for use in the food, and discard the fish. If you are hurried, 3 cups canned clam broth may be used.

C   SAFFRON

Now for bouillabaisse: Fry minced onion and garlic in oil for 20 minutes. Add thyme and continue cooking. Add broth enough to cover the amount of fish and crabs you have, bay leaf, parsley, tomato juice, lemon and rind, salt and cayenne. Bring to a slow boil and simmer 10 minutes. Then add wine and a pinch of saffron, clams and raw white fish. Put in enough hot water to bring the liquid over the fish in the kettle. Cook 10 minutes slowly. Meanwhile, clean the crabs, take out and shred the body meat, and crack the legs. Then add the meat and legs to the bouillabaisse. Heat to just below the boiling point. Serve in soup plates with hot French bread on a separate dish. *4 servings.*

Of fish as food, we might speak as Dr. Boteler, according to Izaak Walton, spoke of strawberries: "Doubtless God could have made a better berry, but doubtless God never did."

## ❧ NINE ❧

## *One-Dish Meals*

THAT little old brown cookbook which was quoted before is here beside me again. Its dog-eared pages so faithfully echo the tastes and habits of other times. Representative menus of the year 1840 take up a number of pages — and such menus!

For example, under the heading "Family Dinners" are found such refections as these:

Knuckle of Veal Stewed with Rice

Apple Sauce    Bread and Butter    Potatoes

Loin of Pork Roasted

Pudding

or

Peas [*sic*] Soup

Potatoes    Boiled Fowl    Broccoli

Roasted Beef

Benton Sauce

Apple Pie

If one wanted in those days to drop family simplicity and put on just a little style, such a meal as the following was suggested:

Minced Veal
garnished with fried crumbs

| Small Meat | Hot Apple Pie | Potatoes |
|---|---|---|
| Pie | in change for soup | in a Form |
| Stewed Onions | | Beans and Bacon |

Saddle of Mutton

Mind you, these were examples of simple family meals a hundred years ago. Perhaps such eating was all right for the good old days when quantity was paramount, and housemaids as numerous as cranberries in a bog. But today, we Americans do our own cooking, and the trend is more and more toward real simplicity, so such "simple dinners" are inconceivable.

Instead, we dine with the least possible fuss. If we are truly informal, we feast in bucolic homeliness on one-dish meals, and know true comfort and simplicity. After such meals we think fondly of Pliny the Elder, who once unburdened his mind so aptly on this matter:

> Their best and most wholesome feeding is upon one dish and no more and the same plaine and simple; for surely this huddling of many meats one upon another of divers tastes is pestiferous.

Blessed be the one-dish dinner. It is the free, genuine meeting of healthy appetites with sturdy goodness and unpretentious plenty. A meat pie with golden, dimpled crust, or a steaming pot of vegetable soup, accompanied by garlicked bread, a salad — these with robust wine are something to content a crying appetite.

There are many dishes suited to the serving of "one-dish" meals, dishes that have in them the principal requirements for a balanced meal, so that, accompanied by a green salad, bread, and cheese in the absence of meat or eggs, they are complete diet. Such meals are especially good for informal entertaining of friends, where the thing to be desired is hearty hospitality unencumbered by the ceremony and stuffiness of a formal dinner.

There is a relaxing spell in simple hospitality that takes no note of "salads before meats," "serve from the left, take off from the right," and all of the rest of the precious mumbo-jumbo of conventional dining. Just the casual warmth of welcome implied in the family-style service sets guests at ease, and loosens tongues otherwise wary with too much formality. Try a few such dinners. This is the way they go.

First, set the table with your brightest and most informal set of dishes. Let the table covering be colorful. Use a great centerpiece of pure-hued flowers or bright fruits. Peasant wine jugs and vivid tumblers — all your most spirited table beauty is in order now. A gay basket of thick slices of French or Italian bread, and in a pottery or wooden bowl the green salad, crisp and inviting, as the first course, or, as we Mazzas do, after the main dish, to refresh the palate.

Then the main dish, served in brave-toned casserole or ruddy terra-cotta. Perhaps it is a tamale pie studded with olives, and its inevitable companion piece, red beans; a fine meat stew topped with flaky biscuits; or a tureen of fragrant French onion soup, Melba-ed toast crusts riding its waves.

Whatever your choice for the main course, whatever type the green salad, let the dessert correspond in simplicity. Cheese with wafers and a dish of fruit, or the most unassuming of ices; and with them after-dinner coffee, followed by a liqueur or not, as your custom may be. But never, O never follow such a nobly modest meal with a too-sweet, creamy, or sugary dessert, or with cake. That is like a plumed bonnet atop a Grecian-robed maiden.

The recipes for these main dishes are varied, covering many types of food, and they will provide rounds of homely goodness with which none should quarrel.

## *Meat Pie with Biscuits*

| | |
|---|---|
| 2 pounds boneless beef in cubes | small piece bay leaf |
| 2 tablespoons flour | 12 coriander seeds crushed |
| 2 tablespoons lard | salt |
| 1 large onion | black pepper |
| 1 clove garlic | 1 cup diced celery |
| 4 cups boiling water | 2 potatoes |
| 1 teaspoon marjoram | 1 carrot |
| ½ teaspoon thyme | 1 tablespoon sherry wine |

Roll meat in salted and peppered flour and fry until brown in lard. Remove meat and in the fat cook minced onion and garlic slowly 10 minutes without browning. Return meat, add hot water, herbs, and seeds, and salt to taste. Cook slowly 3 hours. Then add vegetables cubed, and enough more hot water to show through meat and vegetables, but not cover them. Cook 1 hour more, or until vegetables are entirely tender. Add more salt then if tasting shows that it is needed. Add sherry, then take from fire and let stand at least 3 hours or overnight in the refrigerator to let the dish blend. When ready for dinner heat the stew, lay uncooked baking-powder biscuits closely over the top, and bake in a hot oven until biscuits are done. *6 servings*.

## *Tamale Pie with Red Beans*

The red beans must be soaked overnight in plenty of cold water.

| | |
|---|---|
| 1 large red onion | ½ green pepper chopped |
| 1 tablespoon lard | salt |
| ½ can corn | ½ cup yellow cornmeal |
| ½ can tomatoes | 6 ripe olives |

½ cup cooked chopped
   meat or same amount
   ground beef browned in
   oil
1 egg

cayenne pepper
chili powder
1 teaspoon wild marjoram
   (oregano)

The best herb to use to secure the typical Mexican flavor in this dish is wild marjoram (oregano), 1 teaspoon being enough for this recipe.

Cook onion, minced, in lard until tender, then add corn, tomatoes, green pepper, and salt to taste. Set to boil, and gradually stir in cornmeal. Cook 20 minutes, stirring often. Add meat, mix well, and allow mixture to cool. Add beaten egg, olives, seasonings, and herb. Pour into buttered casserole and bake 45 minutes at 350°. Serve with Mexican Sauce and Red Beans. *4 servings.*

## Mexican Sauce

2 tablespoons butter
1 small onion chopped
1 green pepper chopped
1 clove garlic chopped
½ cup bouillon

1 can tomatoes
2 teaspoons chili powder
salt
black pepper

Cook onion, green pepper, and garlic in butter 10 minutes. Add bouillon, or 1 bouillon cube dissolved in ½ cup water. Add tomatoes, chili powder, salt and pepper to taste. Cook together 1 hour, stirring frequently. This sauce makes a good topping for an omelette, too.

## Red Beans

1½ cups red beans soaked
    overnight in cold water
 1 heaping teaspoon salt
 3 green onions chopped
    with tops

1 clove garlic chopped
½ teaspoon cumin seed
3 tablespoons olive oil
¼ cup chopped parsley

Soak beans overnight. In the morning drain, renew water, enough to cover to twice their depth. Add salt, 1 onion, garlic, cumin. Boil slowly until very tender — about 2 hours. By this time water should be almost cooked away. Add oil, the remaining 2 green onions finely chopped, tops and all, and parsley. Taste for salt, and add more if needed. Mix well, let stand 10 minutes on back of stove, and serve with tamale pie.

## Cassoulet

This dish hailed originally from the honorable city of Toulouse, where they say the natives approach its preparation with due solemnity. As made there, its cooking requires about 10 hours, which is enough to make anyone solemn; but as we make it in this country, its time of preparation is comfortably shortened.

small piece fat bacon
 1 onion chopped
 1 clove garlic chopped
 1 cup dry white wine
 4 tablespoons tomato
    sauce
 2 cups lima-bean liquor
½ Japanese chile without
    seeds
½ teaspoon thyme

black pepper
2 cups cooked lima beans
2 large pork chops cut in
    two
2 large loin lamb chops cut
    in two
flour
olive oil
1 slice mettwurst (sausage)
    2 inches thick

Put bacon in a saucepan and fry it until the fat is cooked out. Add onion and garlic and cook slowly 10 minutes. Add wine, tomato sauce, lima-bean liquor (from cooking the lima beans). Stir, add Japanese chile, thyme, and a generous amount of black pepper. Cook slowly 5 minutes. Add lima beans, and mix well.

Pour this mixture into a large casserole. In a frying pan brown floured chops in olive oil. Then lay them on top of the bean mixture in the casserole. Over them scatter sausage cut in small pieces. Press meat into the liquid, cover casserole, and bake in 300° oven 1 hour. No salt is added until the dish is half done, for the mettwurst is salty and may supply all that is needed. So at the end of half hour taste for salt, and add more if necessary.

At end of cooking time cover top of cassoulet with a layer of buttered crumbs, and brown under the broiler flame. Serve in casserole. *4 servings*.

## Pepper Stew

| | |
|---|---|
| 3 *large dry onions* | 3 *large tomatoes* |
| 1 *small clove garlic* | 2 *large potatoes* |
| 4 *tablespoons olive oil* | 1 *teaspoon marjoram* |
| 5 *large green bell peppers* | *salt* |
| 2 *fresh green long chili peppers* | *black pepper* |

Cook sliced onions and minced garlic in oil for 20 minutes, but do not allow to brown. Remove stems and seeds from peppers and cut into 2-inch pieces. Peel tomatoes and cut up. Peel potatoes and cut into 2-inch squares. Keep each vegetable separate.

Add peppers to oil and onions and stir well. Add tomatoes, salt and pepper to taste, and marjoram. Stir again, then cook slowly 20 minutes. Add potatoes last, stir, cover, and cook slowly 2 hours. Stir at least six times during cooking. When half done, taste for salt seasoning, adding more if needed.

This makes a thick, fragrant stew somewhat akin to that Provençal favorite called ratatouille, but having the lagniappe of tender pieces of richly seasoned potato rising out of it. Eat it with hot buttered bread. With a green salad, followed by fruit and savory cheese for dessert, it makes a perfectly balanced dinner. If possible cook it in the morning, or, better, the day before it is to be used. Its flavor improves with age — up to a certain point, of course. By the way, we often scatter a judicious amount of grated Romano cheese over each portion before serving. It is unbelievably good. *4 servings*.

## Chicken with Rice

This is one version of the ubiquitous arroz con pollo of the Spanish-speaking nations. It may be slightly American in spots, due to its sponsor's nationality, but it still has plenty of Latin taste.

| | |
|---|---|
| 1   2½-pound chicken | ⅓   teaspoon cumin seed |
| salt | 8   coriander seeds crushed |
| black pepper | 1   teaspoon wild marjoram |
| flour |     (oregano) |
| 4   tablespoons olive oil | ½   cup chopped parsley |
| 1   large onion | ¼   teaspoon saffron dissolved in 2 tablespoons hot water |
| ½   bell pepper | |
| 1   carrot | |
| 1   clove garlic | ½   cup red wine |
| 2   tomatoes | ½   cup rice |
| ⅓   teaspoon nutmeg | |

Cut up chicken, roll in seasoned flour, and brown in oil. Remove to a dish and keep warm. Grate or shred onion, bell pepper, carrot, and garlic, and fry in the oil in which chicken was browned. Add peeled and cut-up tomatoes, then add all herbs, seeds, spices, and wine. Cook 10 minutes, then stir well, and return chicken to this sauce. Add enough hot water to cover, and stir to mix. Cover pot and cook slowly 2 hours, stirring several times to keep from sticking. Then add rice, and cook slowly until rice is tender, *without stirring*. Serve on a platter with chicken in middle surrounded by rice.

## Curry Dinner

Perhaps you will say that curry powder is not an herb. But glance with me through a list of the materials that go into the making of a good curry powder. There are green ginger, coriander seeds, cumin seeds, garlic, turmeric, chile, and peppercorns. Surely that is enough herbal justification for squeezing in a curry recipe, since it is a good one.

You who have never liked curry, do not turn away. Perhaps you have encountered only that jaundiced agglutinant that too often, under the mask of "curry sauce," ruins otherwise good foods. You'll find this curry different — rich with native goodness, fragrant as incense, and hunger-teasing to the last morsel.

*4 pounds lean lamb diced, or*
*1 4-pound hen cut up*
*flour*
*4 tablespoons butter*
*liquor from 1 can mushrooms*
*2 cups water*
*salt*
*1 clove garlic minced*

*1 large onion sliced thin*
*3 stalks celery cut thin*
*1 heaping tablespoon curry powder*
*2 rounded tablespoons flour*
*canned mushrooms*
*broth*
*½ cup evaporated milk*

Dust lamb or chicken well with flour and brown lightly in butter. Remove from pan and add to mushroom liquor, water, and 1 teaspoon salt in another kettle. Cook, simmering until meat is tender. If chicken is used remove from bones and dice. In pan where meat was browned put garlic, onion, and celery, stir well, and cook slowly 10 minutes. Add curry powder and flour mixed, stir well, cook 10 minutes. Add mushrooms well drained, stir well; then add broth, made by dissolving either chicken or beef bouillon cubes in boiling water (1 cup to 1 cube) and milk, stirring in slowly. Cook, stirring, until sauce begins to thicken. Add lamb or chicken, salt to taste, cover, and cook half an hour. If sauce becomes too thick add a little boiling water. Remove from fire and let stand at least 2 hours, though preferably overnight, to blend flavors.

When preparing the dinner, make ready these various accompaniments to the curry:

Boil, separate, and chop whites and yolks of 8 eggs
Steam 2 cups raisins or currants
Steam 2 cups chopped apple
Fry crisp 1 pound bacon cut in small pieces
Toast 2 cups shredded coconut
Chop 2 cups roasted unsalted peanuts
Split lengthwise and fry 6 bananas
Fry chopped onions sufficient to make 2 cups when done

Keep all these ingredients warm while steaming 3 cups rice, measured dry (use 4 cups if there are to be 12 persons).

Heat meat and curry mixture.

Place meat and curry in a large bowl, the rice in another, the relishes in others of suitable size. When serving, the host places a fried banana on the plate, then rice, and the curried meat over the top. The relishes are passed so that the guests may help themselves to some of each one, which they put on their plates and eat with the rice and curry. *8 to 12 servings*.

A tin of Bombay duck, which is a dried-fish preparation from India, is a delicious accompaniment to this meal. It may be secured from quality grocers. However, it is not necessary.

Curry such as this is a splendid buffet supper, for it is truly a one-dish meal. Serve with it only celery, olives, chutney, sour pickles, and a drink — no bread, no salad, no vegetables. For dessert there is just one dish that is right — pineapple ice, and black coffee.

If you want your company to come again, serve this curry. Greater praise hath no man.

For a family curry one can use leftover lamb or chicken in smaller amounts, prepare them in the same broth in the same way, and reduce the quantity and number of relishes as wished. As a way to use up leftovers it is ideal.

# *POLENTA*

Italian folk dust off their appetites and go to work when they smell polenta in the kitchen. This is a sort of grand-opera version of cornmeal mush, arrayed in the most richly colorful and tasty mushroom sauce it is possible to imagine. The result is so rhapsodic that to describe it merely as corn-meal mush is an insult.

To make this dish it is necessary to have a cornmeal that is especially cut for this use, rather than the fine variety we Americans are used to. This other, coarser meal is called "polenta meal," or *granturco,* and is obtainable in all Italian groceries, and in large cities in many markets.

## Polenta

2 *cups cold water*           2 *cups boiling water*
1½ *cups polenta meal*        1 *teaspoon salt*

Moisten polenta meal with cold water and stir until well mixed. Gradually, by spoonfuls, add this moistened meal to the boiling, salted water in the top of a double boiler. Stir after each spoonful is added to prevent lumping. Place over boiling water and let cook 3 hours without stirring.

## Chicken and Polenta

1 *fryer*                     1 *stalk celery*
*salt*                        ½ *cup chopped parsley*
*black pepper*                1 *teaspoon rosemary*
*flour*                       ½ *cup dried mushrooms*
2 *tablespoons olive oil*        *soaked in 1 cup hot*
2 *tablespoons butter*           *water*
1 *large onion*               2 *cans tomato sauce*
1 *clove garlic*

Cut up chicken, roll in seasoned flour, and brown in oil and butter. Mix and chop onion, garlic, celery, parsley, and rosemary. Remove chicken from pan, and in the fat slowly cook above chopped mixture for 10 minutes without browning. Wash mushrooms and soak in hot water 10 minutes, then drain, saving water, and chop them. Add mushrooms to onion, garlic, etc., in pan, stir well, add tomato sauce, mushroom water, and salt and pepper to taste. Sir well, return chicken to this sauce, seeing that all pieces are submerged. If necessary to do this add a little hot water. Cover and cook slowly about 1½ hours, or until chicken is thoroughly tender.

Serve meat in the center of a platter, surround it with *polenta,* and cover all with the sauce. Sprinkle with grated Romano cheese. *4 servings.*

## Hare with Polenta

Follow above recipe, substituting a 2½-pound hare for the chicken.

## Pork and Veal with Polenta

Use Chicken and Polenta recipe above, substituting for chicken 1½ pounds veal stew meat without bones, and ½ pound pork without fat, cut into cubes.

# EGGS AND THINGS

Are you one of that great group of people that thinks an omelette something to be served only at breakfast? Then you are missing a lot of fun. For omelettes, properly made and rightly considered, are one-dish meals of high degree. Let come a warm day when rich meats and filling vegetables fail to arouse enthusiasm, and a tender, aromatic omelette can capture the favor of any diner.

There are various sorts of omelettes. The French kind, in a thousand guises; the Italian *frittata,* changefully packed with tender vegetables; and our own housewives' pride, the "puffy" or soufflé omelette. All are dinner or supper dishes of the first order.

The French omelette is made of whole eggs beaten very slightly. It is cooked quickly in a heavy-bottomed, smooth pan, then (in theory) rolled into a bolster to be served with great dispatch. Actually, it is neater and more possible to fold it over once, and let that suffice.

As to the popular idea that omelette-making is a strange and elusive art that only one of Gallic blood can master, that is pure drivel. Disregard your national background and go to work on omelettes, and you'll see.


## *Omelette with Fine Herbs*

Hunt out an 8-inch frying pan with a smooth interior, for that is the proper vessel for the making of a 4-egg omelette. There is also on the market a folding omelette pan that allows one to pour half the egg mixture into each side, cook it, adding any filling desired to one side only just before folding the pan over. *Voilà* — an omelette that comes out easily and well.

| | |
|---|---|
| 4 *eggs* | 1 *teaspoon chopped parsley* |
| *salt* | ½ *teaspoon chopped chives* |
| *black pepper* | 2 *tablespoons butter* |

Beat eggs lightly, for excessive beating ruins this type of omelette. Add salt and pepper in good proportion. Add herbs and mix slightly. Melt butter in pan so it covers the bottom, then roll pan so the butter coats the sides. When butter is bubbling briskly, but is still uncolored, pour in the eggs. They will begin to cook at once.

Now don't go away. You have to stay by an omelette. As soon as its edges are set, run a spatula under its center so that all the uncooked portion of the egg will run underneath the cooked part. Do this from time to time, watching that it does not scorch, for you know what burned eggs taste like! When the omelette is a sort of pretty *café au lait* underneath and creamy on top, fold it over in the middle, coax it diplomatically off on a hot platter, and serve as fast as you can get to the table. Omelettes wait for no one. 2 *servings*.

OTHER FINE-HERB COMBINATIONS
    Besides parsley, chervil, and chives, other combinations

may be used to vary the herbal-omelette program:

> parsley, sweet basil, and chives
> parsley, burnet, and chives
> parsley, chervil, and shallots

Or you may mix parsley, chopped shallots, and a few slices of fresh mushrooms that have been sautéed in butter and drained. Then, too, you may go original on your family and devise your own combinations, developing a repertoire of omelettes that will make you an omelette *virtuoso*, or *virtuosa*, as the case may be. Fillings may be added just before folding the omelette: shredded sharp cheese, sautéed onions, or ditto mushrooms, are good for a starter.

## Spanish Soufflé Omelette

A soufflé or puffy omelette is just what the name suggests. In this type the egg whites and yolks are separated. The whites are whipped to a froth, the yolks to a cream. Combined, they cook into a fluffy affair that melts in the mouth. Make it so it will stand up full and proud when served, instead of collapsing like a tired horse, and you will have a dish the family will hail with delight.

The secret of preserving the shape of a soufflé omelette is slow cooking, so that the bubbles in the egg mixture do not have a chance to collapse. This is one time when the standard advice on cooking eggs quickly does not hold.

A savory Spanish Sauce tops this, to its vast enhancement.

| | |
|---|---|
| 2 *tablespoons butter* | *black pepper* |
| 4 *eggs, separated* | 1 *tablespoon grated Romano cheese* |
| 3 *tablespoons hot water* | |
| 1 *teaspoon salt* | |

Place an 8-inch skillet on the fire, put the butter into it, and keeping it at a low flame, heat skillet and melt butter, running it well up on the sides.

Beat the egg whites very stiff. The yolks beat until creamy, then add the hot but not boiling water and the salt and pepper. Mix well, fold in beaten whites, and pour mixture into skillet. Leave over low fire until it is brown on the bottom, then place under the broiler in a preheated 400° oven to lightly brown the top. Test with cake tester and if it does not come out clean, set on oven shelf until done. Remove from stove and with a sharp knife carefully cut the omelette once across. Lift one half out and put on a warm platter. Cover with one half the Spanish Sauce. Lay over it the other half of omelette, add rest of sauce. Sprinkle with cheese and serve at once. *4 servings.*

## Spanish Sauce

| | |
|---|---|
| 1  *clove garlic* | *black pepper* |
| 2  *tablespoons olive oil* | ½  *bay leaf* |
| 1  *onion* | ½  *teaspoon wild marjoram* |
| 1  *can tomato sauce* |     (*oregano*) |
| ½  *teaspoon cumin seed* | ½  *Japanese chile without* |
| ⅓  *teaspoon salt* |     *seeds* |

Peel garlic, split lengthwise, and run toothpick through each piece. Brown slowly in oil, then mince in onion and cook slowly 10 minutes. Add sauce and seasonings and cook at medium heat 15 minutes. Remove garlic and toothpicks. Add more salt if taste demands it, before serving.

This by no means covers the question of eggs as a dinner dish. *Frittata*, too, will furnish you with variety now and then. These luscious vegetable-egg dishes, which Southern Europe does so well, deserve special attention. Latins fear not to combine eggs with almost any sort of fresh vegetable, making delectable one-dish meals. String beans, zucchini, baby artichokes, asparagus, spinach, green peas — any of these join with eggs to make the dinner hour an event.

The basic secret of all such dishes is the same. Previously cooked and herb-seasoned vegetables are cooled, then mixed with gently beaten eggs. The whole is cooked as a soufflé omelette, on the stove top until the bottom is cooked, then finished under a slow broiler flame. This is not folded like a French omelette, but is cut into a number of wedges like a pie.

## *Frittata of Zucchini or Asparagus*

| | |
|---|---|
| 3 *tablespoons olive oil* | *same amount solid-pack* |
| 1 *onion* | *salt* |
| 1 *clove garlic* | *black pepper* |
| 5 *small zucchini or tips* | 1 *teaspoon sweet marjoram* |
| *from* 1 *pound asparagus* | *or thyme* |
| 1 *large fresh tomato or* | 9 *eggs* |

Into an iron skillet with olive oil slice thinly the onion and mince the garlic. Cook slowly 10 minutes, then into it cut either zucchini or asparagus. Add peeled and cup-up tomato, salt and pepper, and herb. Stir well, cover, and cook until vegetables are tender. Take from stove and cool. Beat eggs lightly in a bowl, salt and pepper them, and into them stir the cooled vegetable mixture. Mix well, then pour back into skillet. Cover and cook over slow fire until the sides of the *frittata* shrink away from the pan. If the middle puffs up puncture it several times with a knife point. Place in a pre-heated 300° oven under the broiler flame to finish cooking. Cut into pieces like a pie, and serve at once. 6 *servings*.

## Frittata with Cheese

| | |
|---|---|
| vegetable | salt |
| 2 cloves garlic | black pepper |
| 5 tablespoons olive oil | ⅓ cup minced parsley |
| 1 onion | 1 teaspoon herb* |
| 9 eggs | ½ cup grated Romano or |
| 1 cup grated toast crumbs | Parmesan cheese |

First, prepare any one of the following vegetables:

      1 pound French string beans   .
      1 dozen tiny artichokes halved lengthwise
      1 pound chopped fresh spinach (not frozen)
      1 pound green peas
      1 pound zucchini sliced

The preparation consists of steaming them, or cooking in a very small amount of water, until they are fork-tender. Drain and cool them.

Brown garlic, which has been halved and speared with toothpicks, in 2 tablespoons of the oil in an iron skillet. Add onion thinly sliced, and cook slowly until yellow. Remove garlic and discard. Beat eggs lightly in a bowl and to them add crumbs, salt, pepper, parsley, minced herb, cooled onion and oil mixture, the remaining 3 tablespoons olive oil, and the cheese. Add whatever cooked vegetable is to be used, mix well, return to skillet. Cook as in Frittata of Zucchini or Asparagus (page 210). *6 servings*.

Still we are not quite finished with the egg question. There is also, for a light and tasty meal, the profane but sacred Italian dish known in the parlance as "Eggs in Hell" (*uova*

---

\* Herb — for string bean omelette, 1 teaspoon summer savory
           for artichokes, ½ teaspoon rosemary
           for spinach, 1 teaspoon thyme and dash nutmeg
           for peas, 1 teaspoon sweet basil
           for zucchini, 1 teaspoon marjoram or thyme

*in purgatorio*). Those who take their Dante seriously may disagree with this translation, but it's near enough for the layman.

## Eggs in Hell

| | |
|---|---|
| 4 tablespoons olive oil | 1 teaspoon minced parsley |
| 1 clove garlic | salt |
| 1 onion | black pepper |
| 2 cans tomato sauce | 8 eggs |
| ½ teaspoon minced thyme | thin slices of French bread |
| ½ teaspoon minced sweet | dry-toasted in the oven |
| basil | grated Romano cheese |

Heat oil in a saucepan that has a tight cover. Split garlic lengthwise and run a toothpick through each piece. Brown slowly in oil. Add minced onion, cook slowly 10 minutes until yellow. Add tomato sauce and all herbs and seasonings. Cook 15 minutes, stirring often. When done, remove garlic and toothpicks and discard. Into the sauce break the eggs, spacing them in it. Spoon sauce over them, cover closely, and cook slowly for 20 minutes, or until eggs are cooked through. Serve eggs and sauce over toast slices and sprinkle with cheese. *4 servings.*

## CODFISH

Codfish is a fellow that inspires no tepid tolerance. He is either loved or hated. Some people swear by him as a delicacy, and eat him frequently with great gusto. Others shudder at the mention of his name, and leave the house when he comes in.

If you belong to the Codfishist Party, try this some night:

## Codfish Stew

| | |
|---|---|
| 1 *pound dried codfish* | 2 *cups tomato juice* |
| ⅓ *cup olive oil* | 2 *cups boiling water* |
| 2 *large onions* | ¾ *teaspoon salt* |
| 1 *large clove garlic* | 1 *cup chopped parsley* |
| 1 *long dry chile* | 12 *peppercorns crushed* |
| ⅛ *teaspoon nutmeg* | 1 *teaspoon sesame seeds* |
| ½ *teaspoon marjoram* | about 10 *cumin seeds* |
| 1 *teaspoon thyme* | 4 *potatoes* |
| ¼ *cup white wine* | |

Soak codfish in cold water to cover for 6 hours or overnight. Drain, renew water, and bring to a boil. Drain, wash, and shred.

In oil place minced onions and garlic, long chile with seeds removed, nutmeg, marjoram, and thyme. Cook slowly 15 minutes. Add shredded fish, wine, tomato juice, boiling water, salt, and parsley. Crush peppercorns and seeds in a mortar and add them. Mix well, cook slowly 1 hour, stirring frequently. Add potatoes, which have been peeled and cut into 2-inch squares. Cook 3 hours more. *4 servings*.

This dish is better cooked one day and eaten the next.

## EGGPLANT

The colorful aubergine is another of those individuals which is either adored or anathematized. This recipe for eggplant is one way of serving it so that almost everyone enjoys it.

### Eggplant Casserole

|   |   |
|---|---|
| 1   *eggplant* | *flour* |
| 1   *egg* | 1   *can tomato sauce* |
| 1½  *teaspoons salt* | ½   *teaspoon marjoram* |
| 2   *tablespoons olive oil* | 1   *tablespoon sherry wine* |
| ½   *pound soft Monterey*<br>     *jack cheese* | *salt*<br>*black pepper* |

Wash and slice eggplant without peeling, making it into ¾-inch slices. Beat egg thoroughly and add ¾ teaspoon salt. Heat oil in a skillet. Slice cheese in thin slices. Dip each eggplant slice in beaten egg, then in flour, and sauté until delicately brown on both sides. Oil a casserole of ovenware, lay in a layer of eggplant, then one of cheese, until all of both are used. Have the top layer of cheese.

Pour tomato sauce into pan where eggplant was sautéed, add remainder of salt ( ¾ teaspoon), herb, pepper, and sherry. Stir until it boils, then pour over the eggplant. Bake in slow oven, covered, for 1 hour, basting with the sauce in the casserole every 10 minutes. The last 15 minutes remove cover and allow dish to brown. *4 servings*.

### Artichokes and Peas

For a real vegetarian dish, chuck full of all sorts of vitamins, try this mixture of fresh green peas and artichokes.

Serve it with a dish of sliced cheese to supply the protein, a salad and French bread, and know that you have dined.

| | |
|---|---|
| 2 *dozen baby artichokes* | 1 *cup dried mushrooms* |
| 2 *pounds green peas shelled* | *hot water* |
| 2 *tablespoons olive oil* | ½ *teaspoon rosemary* |
| 2 *cloves garlic* | 2 *cups chopped parsley* |
| 2 *large onions* | *salt* |
| 2 *cans tomato sauce* | *black pepper* |

Wash artichokes, peel off tough outer leaves, and cut off the tops about 1 inch down. Cut each artichoke in 2 pieces. Cover with boiling water, add shelled peas, and cook together for 15 minutes. Drain.

Make this sauce:

Heat olive oil and in it brown halved garlic cloves that have been speared with toothpicks. Add onions minced, and cook in oil 15 minutes. Add tomato sauce. Wash mushrooms, cut up, and soak in 2 cups hot water 10 minutes. Then add, with their water, to sauce. Put in herbs and seasonings and cook slowly ½ hour. At end of this time taste for salt seasoning, adding more if necessary. Remove garlic and discard. Add this sauce to the drained vegetables, stir well, pour into an oiled casserole, and bake in a slow oven 1 hour. *6 servings*.

This is one dish that should not be made one day and eaten the next. It is much better made and eaten at once.

## Chick Peas (Ceci)

Perhaps you call these knobby legumes *garbanzos*. Or you may only say "Spanish peas" and hope the grocer or restaurateur will know what you mean. By any name, this favored diet of the Basque, the Spaniard, and the Italian is worth knowing. Delicate in taste, it is delicious boiled with no other seasoning than salt, or made into a sort of stew.

2  *cups chick peas*
*salt pork 2 inches square*
3  *onions*
1  *clove garlic*
2  *quarts boiling water*
1  *teaspoon thyme*

1  *Japanese chile without*
   *seeds*
*salt*
*black pepper*
2  *tablespoons olive oil*

Soak the chick peas overnight, then drain. Cube the pork, fry until all its fat is cooked out. Discard the bits of pork which are now dried out, but save the fat. In it cook minced onion and garlic until soft and yellow. Add onions and garlic to chick peas, together with boiling water, thyme, chile, salt and pepper to taste. Stir well, simmer slowly 5 hours, stirring frequently. Add olive oil, mix well, and serve. *6 servings.*

Do not try substituting butter for oil in this dish, for butter and chick peas do not go well together. To avoid soaking and cooking the raw *ceci*, which is quite tedious, one may use plain canned *ceci*, usually sold under the Spanish name of *garbanzos*. They are already simmered to a fine tenderness.

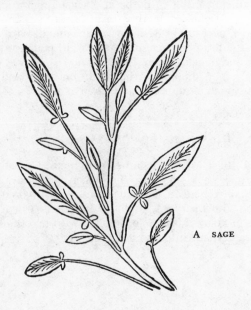

A  SAGE

## Spanish Corn Pie

The Spanish Dons of early California feasted on such dishes as this. My recipe for this delicacy is called "Aunt Dell's Spanish Corn Pie." She is not my Aunt Dell, nor the Aunt Dell of anyone I know personally. But when you taste her corn pie you will bless her, as she must have been blessed often in a long, useful past.

4   medium-sized onions
1   green pepper
1   clove garlic
3   tablespoons olive oil
2   pounds boiled beef or leftover roast, or steak that has been ground
1   cup raisins, seeded or seedless
½   cup liquid from olives

seasonings to taste (for example, salt, black pepper, cayenne pepper, sage, cumin seed, nutmeg, or wild marjoram [oregano])
3   large cans corn
olives
hard-boiled eggs
pieces of cooked chicken
butter
paprika

"First grind onions, pepper, garlic. Fry in oil until soft. Then add beef, roast, or steak. Add raisins, olive liquid, and seasonings to taste. Simmer and strain canned corn, or cut a like amount of fresh corn from cobs and simmer, then strain. This must not be mushy. Line a baking dish with half the corn, then into the center pour the onion and meat mixture. Into it insert olives and egg slices, and scatter over with chicken. Cover with remainder of corn, dot with butter and paprika, and bake ½ hour at 350°." Then — *come con gusto, amigos mios! 6 servings.*

If you like simplicity, and believe that the world needs it, you will appreciate these gastronomical approaches to it. They will help rid your life of the double curse of labored hospitality.

## ❧ TEN ❧

# Spaghetti and the Rest of the Family

YEARS AGO "Italian spaghetti" was a dish that America knew only in its more intitiated circles. The general run of citizens had never tasted its subtle flavor, never known its satisfying deliciousness. It was left to foreigners.

Today things are different. Americans whose pedigrees are rich with Mayflower stock yearn after spaghetti. Sedate dowagers and stately elders and seasoned travelers are as likely to visit Latin quarters in search of *pastasciutta* as are the emancipated youngsters.

Perhaps that word *pastasciutta* needs explaining. Literally "dry pasta," it means just that — any of the spaghetti- or macaroni-like food forms. Since we have adopted the word "pasta" and made it a familiar part of our language, "pasta" we shall call them throughout this book.

In many households such a dish as spaghetti or other Italian pasta is preferred to almost any other food. Fragrant with seasoning, rich with goodness, it is often employed as a Sunday dinner, looked forward to as roasts, chicken, or steaks are longed for elsewhere. Spaghetti and her sister pasta are, in this country, the most misunderstood class of foodstuffs on the roster of victuals. They can be so delicious, and they often are so horrid. What are the reasons for this Jekyll-and-Hyde character of the Pasta Family members? For one thing, they are too often made of the wrong material. Also, there is sad lack of knowledge in their cookery.

The pasta, of which there are many more than the familiar spaghetti, macaroni, and *tagliarini,* should be made of semolina, a flour from a hard type of wheat rich in gluten content. In this country the best semolina comes from Kansas, and is made of "durum wheat." Pasta *properly* made of durum-wheat semolina is likely to be good pasta.

Much of this domestic durum-wheat-semolina pasta is made after Italian methods, and sold largely in stores catering to those who have learned its superiority. It is sold in bulk, by the pound.

Many of our American manufacturers make and sell pasta of ordinary wheat flour — make it in the same forms as the semolina pasta, but without its merits. Or worse still, they use semolina flour, but somehow manage to go wrong in the making, so that the pasta is not good. Either of these two products is sold in American stores, and is largely consumed by Americans. Between them and really good semolina pasta there is a universe of difference.

The distinguishing feature of semolina pasta is its horny toughness before it is cooked. A true child of Italy can tell at a glance whether pasta is good or poor. This horny, hard type takes long to cook, in comparison with the American product. But when it is done the difference is fully apparent. Semolina emerges from the kettle firm, clean, smooth. No starchy residue clings to it. Most American pasta, on the other hand, are what the name implies — soft and gummy.

So if you want to know how really appetizing spaghetti or other pasta can be, find a good Italian store and buy real horny, tough semolina pasta.

## Cooking Pasta

Next in order of importance comes cookery. We here in America are apt to cook our pasta to death, and eat them when they are in a limp, collapsed state. To so use this delectable food is to abuse it. The true pasta-eater prefers his or her spaghetti, macaroni, and so on cooked to a point which we should call "almost done." They call it *al dente* — that is, so its texture is still firm enough to be felt under the teeth. It holds its shape, instead of collapsing, as our American pasta are liable to do when cooked.

Pasta is always cooked in a large kettle of generously salted, rapidly boiling water. It is closely watched, and stirred occasionally with a long-handled fork to keep it from sticking. Most good pasta, with the exception of the finely cut types, takes from 15 to 25 minutes to cook, depending on the size. When it is almost done it should be tested often so that it may be taken from the fire at just the right moment.

When the pasta is just tender but still retains its shape — *al dente* — lift the kettle from the fire and run cold water from the tap into it. About 3 cupfuls should be enough. This is to cool the boiling water sufficiently to stop the cooking, which otherwise would continue, ruining the pasta's consistency.

Pour the pasta into a colander and drain it thoroughly, tossing it to be sure that all the water is out. If any should remain it would dilute the sauce or dressing used and make it runny — and what food heresy is equal to runny sauce?

Please, if you cook the long, spaghetti type of pasta, don't break it up into small pieces to make it easier to eat! It loses its true identity when broken up, and you lose half the fun of eating it. Perhaps you are thinking that if you leave it in long strands you have to eat it by "inhaling" it, after the manner of comic-strip Italians. Such antics are really not necessary. It is only a matter of a little practice to learn to roll it around your fork and slip it into your mouth. This is surely a thousand times better than herding short bits of spaghetti around a plate with a fork, trying to persuade them to stay together long enough for you to get them inside yourself. So we must have a little lesson on:

## Eating Pasta

The larger pasta usually come already cut up, so they can be eaten piece by piece. But those long strands of spaghetti or *tagliarini* are many an American's Waterloo. May I tell you how to tame their wriggling lengths?

Seat yourself at the table, before you a plate of long pasta, ready to be eaten. Take your fork in your right hand, a soup spoon in the left. If you are left-handed, reverse these directions. Hold the spoon in the usual position, except that the tip of its bowl you rest lightly on top of your heap of pasta. With the tines of the fork pick up about three strands of pasta, no more. Bring them, on the fork, to the spoon, and rest the tines of the fork on the inside of the spoon bowl, thus pinning the pasta down. Now, with your fingers, turn the fork slowly away from you, winding the pasta around it. When the fork has been completely turned several times, entirely winding the pasta up on it, secure the ends on the tines by a quick jab. There you are, with a neat, compact mouthful of pasta, and no need of inhaling.

But beware — don't take four, five, or six strands on your fork instead of the prescribed three. You will roll and roll, seeing your mouthful growing and growing, and presently you will find yourself with an immense blob of food that will never go into your mouth without ruining your face.

The first few times you try it the pasta will slip and wriggle away from your grasp, and you will swear it can't be done. But try again. Soon you will be rolling, and flipping, and eating, with an insouciance that will make you the envy of the dining room. You will have one more accomplishment to your credit. Anyone who has tried knows that eating spaghetti gracefully is no mean accomplishment.

## The Pasta Family

We are apt to run the names spaghetti, *tagliarini, vermicelli,* macaroni, off our tongues, and consider the pasta family adequately discussed. But there are others, many others. In fact, there are about fifty different Italian pasta forms. The only way to truly understand the great variety of them is to visit an Italian macaroni factory or a large Italian market. There you may see box after box spread out before you, waiting for customers, and offering to them *vermicelli, fettucine, farfalle, gnocchi, orzi, rigati, rigatoni, maccheroncelli, lasagne, mostaccioli, pennini, occhi di perce,* and so on and on. Fascinating shapes and sizes, all good food.

Truly, you can do far worse than to spend some time getting acquainted with spaghetti and family. They are absorbing, versatile, appetizing, and inviting.

## Dressing Pasta

You have read this far. Now perhaps you pause to fume, "All very interesting — but I can't serve nude, unadorned pasta. How about a few instructions on draping it to send out in company?"

That is a subject all by itself. Since pasta is preeminently the food of Italians, and since they have learned more about its preparation than any other people, it is natural to deal with such food as it is prepared by the Italians. Especially is this true in view of the odd and dreadful manipulations which some other nations go through in cooking and dressing pasta. "Macaroni pudding," "spaghetti with cream sauce," "macaroni custard," "spaghetti timbales" and such heresies send long, shuddering shivers down the spine of any real pasta enthusiast. So let us stick to the Italian way of preparation.

O cuisine of Italy, what atrocities are committed in thy name. "Italian spaghetti" has become a synonym for any mass of limp, sticky pasta hiding unhappily in a swamp of indifferently flavored tomato sauce.

Another misapprehension under which many cooks labor is that "Italian style" is one single, set way of cooking and dressing pasta. Haven't you heard utterances such as "Look at that recipe. That's not Italian-style sauce. It should be cooked in such and such a way." What the speaker does not realize is that while the recipe he or she describes may be true Italian style the other also may be equally faithful.

Italy is a region of diversities. The Genoese differ from the Venetians, who in turn are unlike the Neapolitans or the Sicilians. These differences manifest themselves in many ways, but in none more clearly than in their ways of cookery. While a basic principle runs through the entire business of Italian cookery, giving it a fundamental kinship, each region has its own distinct variations of the treatment of food. So when we say "Italian spaghetti" we may mean any of a thousand dishes, depending on the part of the country in which it originated.

## Tomatoes and Pasta

Tomatoes play a considerable part in the preparation of pasta sauces. They appear in a number of forms for use in cookery. To the average cook these various guises are mystifying indeed. Many a bewildered person has puckered his or her brow and worried: "Tomato sauce, tomato paste, tomato puree, tomato soup, solid-pack tomatoes, fresh tomatoes —

how can I ever know which one to use?" It does take a little
knowing. But once understood, the secret will be a valuable
one in cookery.

## TOMATO SOUP

First, let us settle one question once and for all. Too many
are the recipes for so-called Italian sauces that cheerfully
direct the cook to "add one can of So-and-So's tomato soup."
Please throw such recipes in the wastebasket. Not that Mr.
So-and-So's soup is not good — it undoubtedly is all right as
soup. But *never use tomato soup to make Italian sauce*. Nine
times out of ten it is highly seasoned according to the taste of
Mr. So-and-So's chef. When you add it to your sauce, you at
once rob yourself of the privilege of doing any subtle flavoring according to your own ideas. You may stand forever and
season with this, that, and the other thing, but when you
finish the sauce will be Mr. So-and-So's sauce, not yours. So
don't use tomato soup to make sauce.

## "MUSHROOM GRAVY"

There are many ready-cooked "Italian mushroom gravies"
on the market, advised by manufacturers as ideal for dressing pasta. Mushroom gravies of a sort they may be, but no
one can ever make me believe they are Italian. They are
usually overseasoned, and not satisfactory to the experienced
palate. Better make your own — you will have better flavor,
and *more mushrooms*.

## TOMATO PASTE

Grocery shelves the country over hold slender, tall cans of
"tomato paste," *conserva di pomidoro*. It may be procured *con
basilico* or plain. *Con basilico* means that the tomato paste
is seasoned with sweet basil. The uninitiated are prone to
consider *conserva di pomidoro* the proper form of tomatoes
to use in real Italian sauces. They cook with it alone, and

find themselves with an unpleasantly strong sauce, not really subtle enough to be enjoyable. The reason for this unwelcome strength is that tomato paste is pureed tomatoes that are reduced by heat, either sun or artificial, to about half their bulk. Thus it is twice as strong as other tomato preparations, and must be used accordingly. Its sharp strength must be tempered with some milder form of tomatoes, such as fresh tomatoes peeled and chopped, solid-pack tomatoes with juice, tomato sauce, or tomatoes with puree of trimmings. All of these, except, of course, the fresh tomatoes, can be bought in cans. Use them in the proportion of about 2 tablespoons of tomato paste to 2 cups of any of the others. Tomato paste is used to lend a tomato flavor without bulk, as in soup, or to provide taste emphasis, as in sauces. It should not be used alone.

## TOMATO SAUCE

Eight-ounce or picnic size cans of "tomato sauce" are familiar stock in American grocery stores. This sauce, if of good quality, is suitable for use either alone or with fresh tomatoes, solid-pack tomatoes, tomatoes with puree of trimmings, or tomato paste.

## SOLID-PACK TOMATOES

Solid-pack tomatoes, in large or medium cans, are always available at the grocer's. They are very usable, being peeled, whole unseasoned tomatoes in their own juices. It is this lack of seasoning that makes them the best substitute for fresh tomatoes.

## TOMATOES WITH PUREE OF TRIMMINGS

Tomatoes with puree of trimmings are closely related to solid-pack tomatoes, and can be used in their stead. They are less expensive, and have also the virtue of making lighter sauces than solid packs.

FRESH TOMATOES

Fresh tomatoes in season are the best material for Italian sauces. There is a lightness and savor about a sauce of them which can never be matched when canned fruit is used. Hot-house tomatoes, on the other hand, are too flavorless for this use. In using fresh tomatoes peel them and cut them small, then cook them longer than canned tomatoes in any form. Like solid-pack tomatoes, they are better with a little sauce or tomato paste added for binding.

CAUTION!

Many recipes purporting to be Italian instruct the cook to "thicken the sauce with a little flour." Please, never, never! The rich goodness of tomato pulp is the only thickening needed or wanted by one who has ever tasted a truly orthodox sauce.

## Pasta Pointers

Since all pasta are actually cooked in the same way it would be useless to repeat the cooking instructions in the recipe for each dish. But it will be best to give a few pointers so that novices will not have the pasta cold and clammy by the time the sauce is done.

First: your pasta will take from 15 to 25 minutes to cook, but don't plan on just that amount of time, for it takes time to heat the water, in a large pot or kettle, about ¼ full. There should be enough water for the pasta to swim freely and not be crowded. With this fact in mind, put your kettle of water on long enough ahead so it will be boiling about a half hour before dinner is to be served. Then, *when the sauce and every-thing is ready*, throw the pasta into the actively boiling water and let it cook.

Second: don't cook the pasta, dress it, and then let it stand. Don't even think you can put it in the oven to stay hot while you eat the salad. In a true Italian meal the pasta is the first course served at the table, the salad coming second, or even after the meat. This is expressly so that the pasta can be served immediately after it is cooked. So train the family to be ready for dinner before you cook and dress your spaghetti.

Third: a secret given to me by a restaurateur, who in his restaurant was able to serve pasta to his guests at a moment's notice, yet have it always firm and clean — never sticky or overcooked. This is how he did it. He cooked his pasta hours before he needed it, and before the rush of business began. But he took it from the water while it still was slightly under-done. He drained it, and — this is extremely important — washed it thoroughly under the cold-water tap, in a colander. Thus any starchy residue, which might have caused it to stick together as it cooled, was washed out, leaving it smooth and clean. Then he set it aside. But as the business hours drew near, he heated another kettle of water, well salted (about 2 heaping tablespoons to a gallon or more of water). When a customer ordered pasta, Joe put the amount needed for the order into a colander, sank it into the boiling water, and left it there about 20 seconds. Then he lifted it out, drained it well, dressed it, and sent it out to a well-pleased customer.

This method is invaluable when serving pasta to guests. The fuss of last-minute cooking is eliminated, and what a boon that is. One can cook pasta the morning of the day of one's dinner, then at the last minute heat it up, and go cool and calm to serve the guests.

Before we go on to the actual recipes, a few pointers on applying the sauce to the cooked pasta may not be amiss. There is a bit of a trick to it.

First, there is the matter of something to serve in. Instead of picking a dish at random from the shelf and hoping it will fit the food, why not once and for all outlaw all such hybrid receptacles? Why not provide your household with a large platter to be officially known as The Spaghetti Platter? Pick one that is long, but not too deep. As to materials, French terra-cotta is the finest, for it may be heated on the stove before using, with no danger of ruining its glaze. Then too, the rich natural color of the clay heightens the appetizing appearance of the dressed pasta surprisingly. Mexican pottery, such special ware as Corning, or the casseroles one finds in such gratifying variety in these imaginative days, all are "not only beautiful but neat," as someone conveniently said.

The first step in dressing pasta is to have the platter and all dressing materials, butter, sauce, cheese, or whatever you are using, at hand where the mixing is to be done, before the pasta is taken from the stove.

Now, for the sake of illustration, suppose you are dressing your pasta with some type of sauce. After making certain that the pasta is drained thoroughly, spoon into the bottom of the warmed platter a little lake of sauce. On it put about half the pasta. Over that spoon (don't pour) a third of the sauce. With tablespoon and fork turn the pasta over and over as if you were mixing a salad. Add the rest of the pasta and another third of the sauce. Over the top spoon the remaining third of the sauce, and send to the table at once.

Please note that nothing has been said about adding grated cheese while mixing the dish. It is a ticklish business, that of cheese, for there are cheeses and cheeses. Some go stringy and sticky when encountering heat, while others retain their tender consistency and are fully manageable. So, unless you are sure of your cheese, better pass it at the table, letting each diner top his pasta with it.

Which brings us to the subject of:

## Grating Cheeses

Two types of grating cheeses are all I have found that do not string or stick. Both are imported from Italy — Romano and Parmesan. If you can obtain good qualities of these cheeses, you may add them to the sauce layer by layer in the above dressing operation, and they will stand up as they should.

But too many other types of grating cheeses, such as domestic Parmesan or Romano, dry Monterey, or the familiar kinds sold ready grated in cellophane envelopes, are very apt to misbehave. Under the heat of the sauce they agglutinate into long, tough strings that adhere to the bridgework in distressing fashion. Beware of such cheese.

Ways of dressing pasta range all the way from the engagingly simple to the entrancingly elaborate. There are sauces of wondrous construction whose cooking takes an entire day. Others, equally delicious in their simplicity, can be made in little more than a trice.

In many opinions the best dressing for pasta is nothing more than grated Romano or Parmesan cheese and *plenty* of good butter. If it is tossed until thoroughly mixed, it almost defies surpassing. The long pasta, such as spaghetti or *tagliarini,* are best suited to this treatment.

## Spaghetti with Butter and Cheese

¾ pound pasta cooked, drained, and piping hot (page 220)
6 tablespoons butter cut into small pieces
6 tablespoons grated Romano cheese

Put butter with hot, well-drained pasta in a saucepan with a tight cover, adding cheese. Put on the cover, then shake the pan briskly up and down, as if shaking a cocktail, for 5 minutes. Turn the pasta out onto a hot platter, and eat it while it still smokes.

To an appetite tired with rich living this homely dish presents a restful savor second to none. *3 to 5 servings.*

A slightly more elaborate version of this dish, but one having a bit more dash to its taste, is:

## *Spaghetti with Chives or Green Onions*

Just before shaking the above Spaghetti with Butter and Cheese, add ½ cup minced chives or ¼ cup minced green onions, using tops and bulbs. Stir well, cover the dish, and shake as directed. Serve before the heat has wilted the greens. This is a delightful dish, and the chives or new onions, being mild, do not stay long on the breath.

Nor is butter the only unguent used in preparing plain pasta. The cooks of Italy, they tell me, are wont to dash into the kitchen at the last minute and stir up a dish that rivals more elaborate concoctions. It is called simply:

## *Spaghetti with Garlic and Oil*
### *(Spaghetti aglio e olio)*

¾ pound spaghetti cooked,    6 tablespoons olive oil
   drained, and still hot    3 to 5 cloves garlic, accord-
   (page 220)       ing to taste

Put oil into a pan and add garlic, split lengthwise. Don't shy from this amount of garlic, for it is left in only to flavor the dish, and is not eaten. Fry garlic slowly in the oil until brown on both sides. Then pour the garlic and oil on the hot, drained pasta and toss until well mixed. Eat the pasta at once, leaving the garlic on the plates. *3 to 5 servings*.

Up and down the long and wiggly length of Italy's coastline dwells a race of enthusiastic fish eaters. They pull the big monsters and the little demons of the deep from their cool homes, and do a fine lot of cooking with them. Probably no fish of all their multitudinous kinds is more loved by them than the salted anchovy. This delectable fishlet is added to Spaghetti with Garlic and Oil to make of it:

## Spaghetti with Garlic, Oil, and Anchovies (*Spaghetti aglio e olio con acciughe*)

This dish is made as in the preceding recipe, except that just before the oil and garlic are added to the pasta 20 anchovy fillets, cut into ½-inch pieces, are added to the oil. But they are not cooked in it, for that melts them and ruins their flavor. Add them after the oil and garlic are taken from the stove.

If salted anchovies are used they are washed, boned, and drained. If anchovy fillets in oil are your choice, they should simply be cut up. Remember that 1 salted anchovy is equal to 2 fillets, and judge amounts accordingly.

Sometimes anchovies are wanted, but at the same time the cook has a yearning for tomato sauce. In that event a more elaborate anchovy sauce is in order, one where the flavors of the fish, tomatoes, and herbs, blended, make a tempting dressing for the pasta.

## Spaghetti with Tomatoes and Anchovies (*Spaghetti al pomidoro con acciughe*)

| | |
|---|---|
| 1 clove garlic | salt |
| 1 medium-sized onion | black pepper |
| 4 tablespoons olive oil | 10 anchovies (20 fillets) |
| 2 cans tomato sauce | ¾ pound spaghetti cooked |
| 1 teaspoon sweet basil | (page 220) |
| ½ bay leaf | Romano cheese |

Fry minced garlic and onion in oil, then add the tomato sauce and seasonings. Cook slowly 20 minutes, stirring often. Add anchovies, stir, let stand 5 minutes. Dress hot spaghetti or *tagliarini* with this, adding grated Romano cheese. *3 to 5 servings.*

Since it is in character to group together all dishes which have a tang of the sea, we must not miss *pasta alla marinara.* Though it is innocent of fish, yet it tastes strongly of them, leaving uninitiated eaters guessing as to the source of the savor. No involved list of ingredients enters it, and no lengthy rite attends its concocting. Yet it repays the small effort of its making with rich and satisfying flavor.

## Pasta alla Marinara

| | |
|---|---|
| 6 *cloves garlic* | ½ *bay leaf* |
| ½ *cup olive oil* | 1 *teaspoon thyme* |
| 1 *large onion minced* | *salt* |
| 2 *cans tomato sauce* | ⅛ *teaspoon black pepper* |
| ½ *cup water* | ¾ *pound macaroni or spa-* |
| 1 *heaping teaspoon wild* | *ghetti cooked (page* |
| *marjoram (oregano)* | *220)* |

Peel garlic cloves, halve each lengthwise, and through each piece run a toothpick. Cook them slowly in olive oil in a sauce-pan until they are lightly browned. Add onion, stir, and cook 10 minutes slowly. Then add tomato sauce, water, and all herbs and seasonings. Stir well, cook slowly ½ hour, stirring often. When cooked, remove garlic and toothpicks and discard. The sauce is ready to use. Dress the cooked, drained, and still hot pasta with it. Put a small nutmeg grater on the table with a whole nutmeg in it, so that each diner may grate a dash of fresh nutmeg over his dish of pasta. Serve without cheese. *3 to 5 servings.*

This sauce lends itself well to spaghetti, macaroni, *rigatoni, mostaccioli,* or lasagne. Frankly, it is a slightly odoriferous sauce, tasting strongly of garlic, and is better for the Saturday night preceding a dateless Sunday than any other time. So much garlic as this, even in essence, may scent your breath. So don't say you weren't warned; but it is grand eating.

## Spaghetti with Crab

Spaghetti with crab is a dish to remember, to pray one may encounter often, to value in eating as a privilege. As a meal it needs no accompaniment other than a large salad, preferably with a few vegetables incorporated in it.

First, procure a large-sized crab. Take off the legs and crack them. Clean the body, and cut in four pieces. Wash all pieces well.

| | |
|---|---|
| ½ cup olive oil | ½ cup chopped parsley |
| 2 onions | ½ cup dry white wine |
| 1 clove garlic | salt |
| 1 can solid-pack tomatoes, or 4 large fresh ones | black pepper |
| | 1 pound spaghetti |
| 1 can tomato sauce | |

Into oil mince the onions and garlic and let cook slowly 10 minutes. Add pieces of crab still in the shell, and cook for 10 minutes covered. Add solid-pack tomatoes (if fresh tomatoes are used peel them and cut them up) and tomato sauce. Add parsley, wine, salt and pepper to taste. Stir well and cook slowly 20 minutes. Remove crab and continue cooking the sauce for 1 hour or more. When done return crab to sauce and reheat. Cook spaghetti (page 220), drain, and dress with the sauce, laying the crab aside in a warming oven to be served as a separate course. *4 to 6 servings.*

Dear to the hearts of Neapolitans is pasta with a simple sauce, tomato-red and with no meat to complicate its flavor. So easy to make, so inexpensive, and so enchantingly good. Even those who cry after meat sauces will find this a welcome variation.

## Neapolitan Pasta (Pastasciutta alla Napolitana)

4  tablespoons olive oil
2  cloves garlic
1  onion
5  tablespoons minced green pepper
1  carrot
2  cans tomato sauce
salt

black pepper
1  teaspoon minced thyme
1  teaspoon minced marjoram
¾  pound spaghetti or macaroni cooked (page 220)
grated cheese

Into olive oil mince garlic and onion, and grate or shred pepper and carrot. Cook slowly 10 minutes. Add tomato sauce and all seasonings, stirring well. Cook for 20 minutes, stirring often. Dress hot, drained pasta with this, and serve with cheese. *3 to 5 servings.*

A Genoese conceit is that of dressing pasta with a sauce so thick with green herbs that it smells sweetly of the garden patch. It is an unusual sauce in that quantities of fresh herbs are used. Almost any type of pasta is suitable for use with this dressing.

## Pasta with Herb Sauce (*Pasta all'erbe*)

½  onion minced
 1  clove garlic minced
 6  tablespoons olive oil
 1  cup chopped parsley
 1  cup mixed minced green
     herbs: basil, thyme, and
     marjoram
½  cup dry white wine
½  cup dried mushrooms
 2  cans tomato sauce

 2  cups broth (pages 83–
     84) or hot water
pinch each allspice, cloves,
     and nutmeg
salt
black pepper
¾  pound pasta cooked
     (page 220)
Romano or Parmesan cheese

Cook onion and garlic in oil for 10 minutes, then add minced herbs, stir well, and add wine. Cook 10 minutes more. Soak mushrooms in enough broth or hot water to cover, and after 10 minutes drain and chop, saving liquid in which they were soaked. Add tomato sauce, broth or hot water, mushrooms and their liquid, and all seasonings to the herbs and wine. Stir well and cook slowly 1 hour, stirring frequently. When half done add more salt if needed.

Dress hot cooked and drained spaghetti or other pasta with this sauce and either Romano or Parmesan cheese. *3 to 5 servings.*

A very little ground round steak, no more than the amount needed for flavor, makes the simplest of the meat sauces for *pastasciutta*.

## Pasta with Sauce of Ground Meat
### (*Pastasciutta con salsa di carne macchinata*)

2 ounces lean salt pork
½ pound ground round steak
2 cloves garlic
½ cup dry white or red wine
½ cup dried mushrooms
hot water
¼ teaspoon rosemary
1 teaspoon sweet basil
1 tablespoon minced parsley

pinch cinnamon and allspice
1 large can solid-pack tomatoes, or 4 peeled fresh tomatoes
½ can tomato sauce
salt
black pepper
¾ pound dry pasta cooked (page 220)
grated cheese

Cut salt pork into small pieces and fry in saucepan until fat is cooked out of them. Remove pork and discard, saving fat. Add ground meat in little pieces and brown quickly. Then add minced garlic and cook slowly until yellow. Soak dried mushrooms in hot water to cover for ten minutes. Add wine to saucepan, cook 10 minutes, then add the rest of the ingredients, cutting up the mushrooms and adding also the water in which they were soaked. Cook slowly 1 hour, stirring often. Add more salt if needed, at end of first half hour of cooking.

Dress hot, well-drained pasta with this, and serve with grated cheese. *3 to 5 servings*.

## Pasta with Veal Sauce

Use the above recipe, substituting ½ pound leg of veal cut into inch pieces for the ground beef, omitting the basil, and increasing the rosemary to 1 teaspoon.

## Pasta with Sauce of Veal and Pork

Use the recipe for Pasta with Sauce of Ground Meat (page 235), substituting for the ground beef ½ pound each of lean pork and veal cut into inch pieces, and for herbs using 1 teaspoon minced rosemary and ½ bay leaf.

## Pasta with Steak Rolls (*Pasta colle braciuole*)

8  4-inch squares of round steak
1  medium onion
1  clove garlic
6  tablespoons olive oil
1  tablespoon grated Romano cheese
½  well-beaten raw egg
¼  cup pine nuts (optional)

½  pound puffed raisins
¾  teaspoon salt
dash black pepper
pinch nutmeg
flour
¾  pound dry pasta cooked (page 220)
Romano cheese

SAUCE:
½  onion
2  cloves garlic
1  can solid-pack tomatoes or tomatoes with puree
1  can tomato sauce
½  Japanese chile without seeds

⅛  teaspoon black pepper
½  teaspoon rosemary
salt
½  bay leaf
½  teaspoon sweet basil

Have the butcher cut the squares of round steak, and if bottom round is used pound them. They should be between ½ and ¾ inch thick.

To make the filling, fry onion and garlic, minced, in 2 tablespoons of the oil for 10 minutes, then cool. When cold add other ingredients, chopping the raisins well. Mix thoroughly.

Divide filling into 8 portions, place 1 on each of the pieces of meat, roll the meat up well, and tie with string loosely, but well enough so the filling will not escape in the cooking. Dust each roll with seasoned flour and brown in the remaining 4 tablespoons olive oil. Remove them from pan, and in it make the sauce: Cook minced onion and garlic for 10 minutes in the oil remaining in pan after browning meat. Add tomatoes, sauce, and seasonings, mix well, then put in the meat rolls. Cook slowly 2 hours, stirring often.

When meat is tender, cook the pasta. Remove meat from sauce, take strings off the rolls, and slice each of them through once. Arrange them on a serving platter and spoon over them enough sauce to moisten a bit. Put them into a warming oven.

Dress pasta with remaining sauce and grated Romano cheese. Serve pasta first, then meat as a separate course with vegetables. Or if wished, the meat may be laid around the edge of the pasta platter. *3 to 5 servings*.

There is a little island in the Adriatic Sea which is called Curzola. Its Italian cookery is tinged with a slight touch of the neighboring East. There they turn out a noble dish of macaroni with a heavy, utterly delicious spicy sauce fruited with plump prunes. Perhaps it is hard to imagine prunes in a macaroni sauce. Yet when once you taste it you will never cease to praise this excellent dish. Its Italian name reflects the dark color of the sauce.

# Macaroni from Curzola (*Maccheroni sporchi*)

1 pound boneless beef cubed
⅓ cup olive oil
1 onion
2 cloves garlic
2 cans tomato sauce
⅓ teaspoon cinnamon
⅓ teaspoon nutmeg
⅓ teaspoon allspice
½ cup dry red wine
salt
black pepper
18 dried prunes without pits
½ pound macaroni
Parmesan cheese

Brown meat in oil, then remove. Mince onion and garlic, cook in oil slowly 10 minutes. Add tomato sauce, spices, and wine, and salt and pepper to taste. Return meat, stir well, and cook slowly ½ hour. Add prunes and cook for another half hour, stirring often to prevent sticking.

Cook macaroni, drain, and dress with the sauce and grated Parmesan cheese. 2 *to 4 servings.*

A well-made and cunningly seasoned casserole of lasagna is a masterpiece that will make a party or exalt a family dinner to party status. Yet happily, if this recipe is cut to a quarter of its quantity, it can be served *à deux* with equal success.

## Minerva's Lasagna

MEATBALLS AND SAUCE:
⅔ pound ground beef
⅓ cup bread crumbs
3 tablespoons chopped parsley
⅛ teaspoon black pepper
1 beaten egg
¼ cup sweet milk
3 tablespoons grated Romano cheese
4 tablespoons olive oil
2 cloves garlic chopped
½ large dry onion chopped
1 #2½ can solid pack tomatoes, picked to pieces
2 cans tomato sauce

½ *Japanese chile without*
  *its seeds*
⅛ *teaspoon black pepper*
 1 *teaspoon sweet basil*
*salt*

LASAGNA:
 1 *teaspoon olive oil*
*boiling water*

12 *ounces lasagna (very*
   *wide noodles)*
 1 *pound mozzarella cheese*
   *thinly sliced*
 1 *pound ricotta cheese*
   *blended with ⅓ cup*
   *sauce from the meatballs*
 4 *ounces grated Romano*
   *cheese*

Combine beef, bread crumbs, parsley, half the pepper, egg, milk, and cheese, mix well with hands, and shape into small balls about 1 inch in diameter. Brown in the 4 tablespoons olive oil in a large, deep pan. The pan must be large enough to hold a lot of sauce, to be made and cooked with the meatballs. When the balls are lightly browned add garlic and onion, and cook slowly until onion is yellow. Then add tomatoes, tomato sauce, chile, the remaining pepper, basil, and salt to taste. Mix well and cook slowly, uncovered, for 1 hour, stirring often. Set aside until you are ready to assemble and bake the lasagna.

Now have the remaining ingredients prepared all in one area, ready to use. Take the meatballs out of the sauce, and set the sauce over slow fire. Fill a large kettle ⅔ full of water, add the olive oil to prevent boiling over, and place over high flame. When water reaches a rolling boil add lasagna, push down into the water, and return to a rolling boil. Cook until pasta is about three-quarters done then drain and rinse in a colander under the cold water tap until pasta is no longer covered with starch. It should be clean and not stick together.

Oil a large oven casserole or an oblong baking dish sold as a "lasagna pan." In the bottom spread several tablespoons sauce, then add a layer of lasagna laid in orderly overlapping fashion. Next spread ⅓ of the sauce, which has been mixed well with the ricotta, a layer of mozzarella slices, another layer of sauce — this one without ricotta. If more lasagna and mozzarella remain, repeat in layers as above, ending with mozzarella, over which arrange all the meatballs, the remaining sauce, and the Romano cheese.

About an hour before serving time bake in a 350° oven, uncovered, for 45 minutes, then serve. Behold, *un miracolo!* Food for the upper-echelon gods, as well as for you and me and those we want to honor. *8 servings.*


If one dish can spell Italy, that dish, to us Americans, is ravioli. Plump little squares of fulsome flavor, housed in tender pasta, moistened with a sauce of mushrooms, tomatoes, and sheer goodness — no wonder we are often willing to content ourselves with ravioli of inferior quality, cloaked in a pseudo-mushroom-gravy that would cause good Marco Polo to rise in his grave.

Why Marco Polo? It is whispered that Italy borrowed the secret of the delectable ravioli from China. Some go even further and say that it was Marco Polo, returning from the court of the Great Khan, who brought the recipe from Cathay. True or not, it is undeniable that to this day the Chinese serve a food significantly reminiscent of ravioli, with Oriental trimmings, of course.

Anyhow, it is a pretty story. One likes to picture swaggering Marco, that prince of boasters, hanging around the hearth of an ancient Italian kitchen, telling the cook how to prepare this strange foreign food. Judging from the results visible today, he succeeded pretty well.

We are apt to think that ravioli can be eaten only in a restaurant, suspecting their making a fearsome lot of work. Actually, they can be made at home, and without too much trouble. The homemade variety is well worth the effort, having a delicacy and balance of flavor that far surpasses most of the commercial kinds; and the sauce — none of that sharp, overseasoned liquid that too often mantles the restaurant ravioli. Instead, a sauce that tastes as if it had been born for that particular crop of pasta.

## Ravioli

There are three distinct steps in the preparation of this dish, but none of the three is really arduous. So don't be dismayed at the length of these directions.

First, the sauce must be made and heated before the ravioli are cooked. I usually make the sauce the day before I need it.

## Sauce for Ravioli

Use either the sauce from the recipe for Pasta with Sauce of Ground Meat (page 236) or that from Pasta with Herb Sauce (page 235) for these ravioli.

## Pasta

| | |
|---|---|
| 2 *cups flour* | 1 *tablespoon olive oil* |
| ½ *teaspoon salt* | *water* |
| 1 *egg* | |

Sift flour and salt together. Beat egg with oil and stir thoroughly into flour. Add carefully enough cold water to make a stiff dough. Knead for 15 minutes, or until quite smooth. Then let stand 30 minutes. Roll on a board into a very thin sheet. Cut in 3-inch strips the length of the dough, using a very sharp knife.

FILLING:

⅓  pound lean pork
⅓  pound very tender beef
10  leaves Swiss chard with-
     out stems
 1  cup chopped parsley
½  teaspoon marjoram
½  teaspoon thyme
¼  onion
 2  small cloves garlic

3  tablespoons olive oil
1  tablespoon butter
salt
2  slices stale French bread
2  eggs
3  tablespoons grated
    cheese, Romano or Par-
    mesan
pinch nutmeg and allspice

This filling should be made the day before the ravioli are to be made, and allowed to gather flavor overnight.

Grind the meat fine, and chop the chard, parsley, and herbs. Mince onion and garlic and in a pan, fry them slowly 5 minutes in oil. Melt butter in another pan, add salted meat, and let cook 5 minutes.

After the meat has cooked 5 minutes, add the chard to the oil, onion, and garlic mixture, and cook it 5 minutes. Then add the chard mixture to the meat and cook them together for 5 minutes. Add stale bread finely cut up, mix well, and cook the entire mixture 5 minutes. Pour into a bowl, let cool and add eggs, cheese, and spices. Taste for salt seasoning, and add more if needed. This is now ready for the ravioli.

One scant teaspoon of the filling is enough for each of the ravioli. Down the length of the 3-inch strips of dough deposit teaspoonfuls of filling, keeping all in a row on one side of the strips. When all are on, fold the strips lengthwise, so that the empty side of each strip covers the filled side. Press together between the heaps of filling and all the way along the edge. Then cut apart so that each filled covered square is separate. A sharp knife may be used if care is taken to have all sides of the squares closed after cutting. But a ravioli wheel is better for this, as it is more efficient.

Cook the ravioli in a kettle half full of well-salted boiling water, using a good handful of salt to insure enough seasoning. *Take care that they are not overcooked.* Usually 10 minutes will do them nicely. Remove carefully with a strainer, so they will not be broken. Drain well, place on a hot platter, and spoon over them the sauce which is named above, and either Romano or Parmesan cheese. 6 *servings*.

A long and noble file of names, these pasta dishes, and material for fine eating. Well-balanced, appetizing, economical they are, and they may well do their part in coaxing Americans from a steak-and-chop diet.

Hunt up a good pasta store and stock your pantry shelves. Such wares keep quite well, so what you do not cook one week will do for the next, and for many others after that. Try the various shapes. Perhaps you will find yourself with an unsuspected passion for "little ribbons" (*fettucine*), or "butterflies" (*farfalle*), or some other of the numerous fantastic forms that pasta takes in an Italian factory.

## ❧ ELEVEN ❧

# The Thousand Faces of Rice

RICE is a versatile grain, capable of assuming inviting food forms. In the Eastern countries she is garbed in gay raiment, and loved by all people. Europe dresses her well and entertains her often. But in America she wears a drab uniform, a never-changing habit that bears no adornment, exerts no allure. It is scant wonder that we fail to see any vast attraction in rice.

With revolutions the talk of the day, why not a rice revolution? Why not a massed movement to liberate rice from her gray existence in our land, to bring her out into the world reborn, newly clad, ever desirable?

Somehow, the thought of grown men and women eating rice with sugar and cream as a dinner dish is revolting. It is tantamount to seeing solid citizens regaling themselves with sugar sops! For a breakfast cereal such a combination may be all right — but not at dinner.

As far as rice is concerned, there is no need for stark, flavorless eating as long as risotto, chow fan, jambalaya, gumbo, or any other of the myriad interesting dishes into which it enters are open secrets. The best of all these is the fact that they are simple dishes. For there is no necessity of disguising rice's identity to make it good. Just a little trimming here, a bit of fixing there, and the result is a dish inferior to none.

Of course there is rice, and then there is rice. Some are good, others are better, and a few are perfect. To buy and use any type without knowing the ins and outs of the matter is to risk mediocrity in rice cookery.

Too many types of rice have the tragic tendency to cook to a gummy, adhesive consistency that is truly a "paper-hanger's delight." A food chemist might be able to explain why this is. Being just a woman who cooks and eats rice with appreciation, I can only say that it is so, and go on to rejoice that some types of this food are not so cursed.

There is "China rice," which has excellent cooking qualities. Its grains are short and chubby, about half the length of long-grain rice. In its best quality it cooks to a dry, fluffy lightness.

"Brown Rice," which is unpolished rice, is another good cooker. It is rice in the original package, so to speak, with the full amount of mineral salts, calcium, phosphorus, and iron that the good Lord gave it. So if you value food properties along with good taste, use brown rice. But remember to allow extra cooking time, for it breaks down slowly.

In the larger cities of America it is possible to get rice that is imported from Italy. Slightly brown, it has not been so ruthlessly polished as our own white rices and those from the Orient. The grains are large, yet they cook quickly, and *if they are not stirred while cooking* will never be soggy.

There is also wild rice, a delicious luxury food, the seed of a wild grass, the bounty of the fields. Mixtures of wild and domestic rice are procurable, already mixed and ready to cook. If you have not used it, try this blend, following the instructions on the package.

Any of those rice types, as well as some discriminatingly chosen American rices, will give you dry, fluffy food when prepared according to the best tenets of their cookery. As to those tenets, they are easy to follow, and hold true for almost any method of rice cookery.

1. Rice, with a very few exceptions, should never be stirred while cooking. Perhaps a few whirls at the first, just to mix it with the other ingredients — but don't stir it at intervals during its cooking. Stirring makes soggy rice.
2. In order to avoid stirring use plenty of whatever it is being cooked in: oil, butter, broth, water, etc. Turn the fire low and let it simmer until tender. Cover the pot closely, and let the grains steam into plump fluffiness — unless you are boiling rice, in which case:
3. Keep boiling rice briskly bubbling in plenty of well-salted water. Have the fire turned up so that the water moves actively at all times, for that keeps the rice from sticking to the bottom of the kettle.

## Boiled Rice

For those of you who cling stubbornly to boiled rice, who adore it, crave it, and want no other, it is allowable that you are partly right. For boiled rice, imaginatively handled and properly prepared, can be pretty fine eating.

For 1 cupful of rice, enough for 4 to 6 servings, use 2 teaspoonfuls of salt and 3 quarts of water. Wash the rice thoroughly in a sieve, rubbing it between the hands until the water from it runs clean. This washes off all the starchy residue that might cloud the cooked rice.

Have the water boiling violently in a large saucepan, and add the rice by small handfuls so that the boiling does not stop. Use a medium high heat to keep the water briskly agitated during the entire cooking process. Do not stir, for the boiling keeps the grains from sticking. When the rice is soft enough to be crushed between thumb and fingertips, drain it in a colander. Run cold water through it many times, then drain again and reheat in the colander over boiling water. If the rice used is of a good type, every grain will stand alone, plump and tender.

There is another way to cook rice, the Oriental way, easier and as good, especially for amounts of raw rice up to and including 1 cup. I learned this once from our Chinese laundryman, for in my learning days everything was grist to my mill.

## Steamed Rice

| | |
|---|---|
| ¼ cup raw rice for each serving | ¼ teaspoon salt for each serving |
| 2 cups water for each cup of rice | small lump butter |

Wash rice thoroughly in several waters, until the water runs clear. Drain. For your cooking choose a heavy saucepan with a lid. Measure in the water, twice as much as the rice you are cooking, and bring it rapidly to the boil. Add salt and butter, the latter to keep the kettle from boiling over. Scatter the rice slowly and evenly over the pan bottom, shake to level. Return water to boil, then lower the heat to a low setting, and put an asbestos mat over the burner for the pot to set on. First lay a paper towel over the pot, then put on the lid over it. This helps keep the steam in. Now go away for 20 minutes, and don't open the pot. After that time the rice should be cooked, but slightly al dente. If you prefer it entirely soft, return the towel and cover, and cook 5 minutes more. And never stir until you take the rice off the stove to serve it.

Boiled or steamed rice may be served as an accompaniment to stews, curries, gravies, Chinese dishes, and such foods as will provide flavor to augment its own rather weak-kneed taste. Or it may be used as the basis for various dishes of distinct character.

# DISHES MADE FROM BOILED RICE

A dish refreshing in its simplicity, but tasty to the nth degree, is:

## Rice with Herbs

| | |
|---|---|
| 4 tablespoons butter | 3 tablespoons chives |
| 1 clove garlic (optional) | 1 teaspoon each basil, |
| 2 cups hot boiled rice | thyme, and savory |
| (page 247) | 1 teaspoon parsley |
| salt | ⅛ teaspoon paprika |
| black pepper | |

Melt butter in top of a double boiler. Add hot rice, salt and pepper to taste, and herbs chopped fine and mixed. Stir in paprika, mix well, cover, and heat to serving temperature over hot water. Serve hot.

If you like garlic, brown a split clove of it in the butter before turning in the rice. Let garlic steam with rice, but discard it before serving. *4 servings.*

## Rice with Eggs

This is a pleasant reminder of chow fan, that Oriental classic. Let no one accuse me of trying to give Chinese recipes. This is an entirely different dish, made of different ingredients, but it does have a Chinese flavor.

| | |
|---|---|
| 2 tablespoons olive oil or butter | salt |
| | black pepper |
| 1 onion | 1 teaspoon paprika |
| 2 cups boiled rice | ½ cup cream |
| 6 thin slices cervelat sausage | 4 eggs |

Heat oil or butter in a skillet, add to it minced onion, and cook slowly until onion is yellow and soft. Add rice, sausage finely minced, and seasonings. Cover closely and steam on a slow fire 2 or 3 minutes, then add cream and stir well. Heat, add beaten eggs, and scramble over slow fire until eggs are fluffy, but not too solid. Serve at once, for the heat in them will finish their cooking. *4 servings*.

Rice masquerading in a yellow frock is this next dish. Easily prepared, it is a supper dish that has an appealing delicacy.

## Rice with White Wine and Tuna

| | |
|---|---|
| 1 clove garlic split | few drops lemon juice |
| 2 tablespoons olive oil or butter | salt |
| | black pepper |
| ½ small onion minced | ½ teaspoon marjoram |
| ½ stalk celery minced | 2 cups cooked rice (pages 247–248) |
| 1 large can tuna with its oil | |
| ½ cup dry white wine | ¼ cup cream |
| ½ teaspoon curry powder | 1 green onion with tops |
| ½ teaspoon paprika | |

Cook garlic halves in oil or butter until brown, then add onion and celery and sauté 10 minutes. Remove garlic and discard. Add flaked tuna and its oil, then the wine. Stir, cook 5 minutes. Add curry powder, paprika, lemon juice, salt, pepper, and marjoram. Stir well, add rice, mix thoroughly, and taste for salt. Add more if necessary. Cover and cook 20 minutes. Add cream 5 minutes before serving. Serve with finely minced green onion sprinkled over it. *4 servings.*

## RISOTTO

Another way of treating rice to make it utterly delicious is first to fry it in its raw state to a lovely golden transparence in oil or butter, then add liquids, which may be of various kinds, to finish the cooking. To many minds this is regal treatment for rice. It becomes more than a cereal, little less than a culinary miracle.

Here the exception to that rule of not stirring cooking rice enters, for the frying rice must be stirred frequently to save it from scorching. But after the liquid is added, *there should be no more stirring.*

Dishes of rice cooked in this way are many and diverse, but the grandpapa of them all is:

D     SUMMER SAVORY

## Milanese Rice (Risotto alla Milanese)

2 tablespoons butter
2 tablespoons olive oil
1 cup raw rice
1 onion
½ clove garlic
3 to 4 cups chicken stock
  (page 84) or bouillon
pinch powdered saffron

2 tablespoons white wine
salt
black pepper
½ cup dried mushrooms
lump butter
½ cup grated Parmesan
  cheese

Melt butter in skillet and add oil. When hot add rice which is unwashed but has been rubbed well in a towel. Stir well to coat it with oil and butter, then spread evenly over the pan bottom and let brown, stirring frequently to keep from burning. The last few minutes of frying add minced onion and garlic and allow them to brown also. Have stock or bouillon hot. (If desired, bouillon cubes dissolved in hot water may be used, or canned bouillon or chicken broth.) Add a cupful to the rice, and also add the saffron, which has been soaked in the wine, the wine itself, and salt and pepper to taste.

Cover and cook slowly without stirring from 20 to 30 minutes, adding more stock when that cooks away. Meanwhile soak the well-washed mushrooms in a little hot bouillon for 10 minutes. Cut them up and add to the rice, with the bouillon in which they were soaked, the last 10 minutes of its cooking. When all the bouillon has been used and the rice is tender and dry, put a lump of butter the size of a walnut on the top of the rice. Sprinkle with the cheese, stir lightly to mix it in. Serve at once. *4 servings*.

## Rice Savory with Herbs (*Risotto all'erbe*)

| | |
|---|---|
| 1   cup raw rice | pinch allspice |
| 2   tablespoons olive oil | 2   tablespoons chopped green |
| 2   tablespoons butter |    herbs in equal amounts: |
| 1   small onion |    parsley, marjoram, thyme, |
| 1   clove garlic |    basil, and rosemary |
| 2   tablespoons white wine | 4   bouillon cubes |
| ½   teaspoon salt | 4   cups hot water |
| 1   teaspoon paprika | |

Rub rice clean with a dry towel, but do not wash. Mix and heat together oil and butter in a skillet or earthenware casserole. Add minced onion and garlic, and the rice. Let fry over a slow fire until rice is translucent, stirring frequently to prevent burning. When translucent add wine, seasonings, and green herbs. Stir well. Dissolve bouillon cubes in hot water and keep hot in a pan on stove. Pour a cup of it over rice, stir once, then cover tightly. Cook slowly until this bouillon is dissolved, then add another cup. Continue this process until rice is tender and bouillon used up. Do not stir after first bouillon is added. Serve this risotto with raisins cooked in half white wine and half water, with a little allspice added. *4 servings.*

## Rice with Tomato Sauce (*Risotto al pomidoro*)

| | |
|---|---|
| 2   tablespoons olive oil | salt |
| 2   tablespoons butter | black pepper |
| 1   cup raw rice | ½   cup dried mushrooms |
| 1   small onion | ½   cup hot water |
| ½   teaspoon wild marjoram | ½   cup tomato sauce |
|    (oregano) | 1   cup broth (pages 83–84) |
| ½   teaspoon sweet basil | |

Heat oil and butter in skillet or flat earthenware casserole, add rice rubbed clean with a cloth, and finely minced onion. Cook slowly, stirring frequently. When onion and rice are translucent, add minced green herbs and salt and pepper. Meanwhile soak mushrooms, which have been carefully washed, in hot water. Drain, saving water. To that water in a small saucepan add tomato sauce and broth. Keep this mixture hot, and add 1 cup of it to the rice. Cover and cook slowly until liquid is taken up. Add another cup and cook again. *Do not stir.* Continue this process until rice is tender. If there is not enough liquid to finish the cooking add hot water with a little butter in it. The last 10 minutes of cooking add the chopped mushrooms, gently stirring them in. When completed this dish should be dry and fluffy, with no visible liquid. *4 servings.*

## Rice with Pepper Sausage
### (*Risotto con salsiccie peperone*)

The salamilike sausage used in this dish is a typical Italian cooking sausage about 1¼ inches in diameter. The inside of the skin, next to the meat, is coated with red pepper, making it a piquant but not violent seasoning agent. Dried before it is used for cookery, this sausage keeps very well. When buying it in the Italian markets, ask for it as "peperone sausage," and be sure it is the dried kind, not fresh.

| | |
|---|---|
| 1 *cup raw rice* | 4½ *cups hot water* |
| 2 *tablespoons olive oil* | ½ *cup dried mushrooms* |
| 2 *tablespoons butter* | ½ *teaspoon salt* |
| 1 *small onion* | *black pepper* |
| ¼ *teaspoon rosemary* | 1 *tablespoon grated Romano cheese* |
| 1 *3-inch piece sausage* | |
| 4 *bouillon cubes* | |

Pick over rice and rub clean in dry cloth. Heat and mix oil and butter in a skillet or flat earthenware casserole. Add rice, minced onion, rosemary, and the sausage peeled and cut up. Brown all slowly, stirring frequently, until rice is golden brown. Have bouillon cubes dissolved in 4 cups of the hot water. Soak mushrooms in the remaining ½ cup of hot water, then drain and add that water to the bouillon. Keep this liquid hot. Ladle 1 cup of it into the rice, salt rice to taste, and add pepper. Cook slowly until liquid is cooked away, then add another cupful. Do not stir. Continue this process until rice is tender. A few minutes before it is done add chopped mushrooms and stir them in very gently. Finish cooking, add cheese, and stir in softly. Serve at once. The rice should be dry and fluffy and there should be no liquid visible. *4 servings.*

All of these are typical risottos. They take about 1 hour to cook, and each makes an excellent main dish for a meal, or a meat accompaniment.

Our Mexican neighbors to the south of us also welcome rice to their tables. A dish that is as Mexican as tamales and fully as intriguing is *sopa de arroz.* Literally "rice soup," it is actually of the same consistency as risotto.

## Sopa de Arroz

4   *tablespoons olive oil*
1   *cup raw rice*
½   *cup minced onions*
2   *cloves garlic*
1   *cup tomato sauce*
4   *cups broth (pages 83–84) or 4 bouillon cubes in 4 cups hot water*

½   *teaspoon each chopped spearmint and wild marjoram (oregano)*
1   *tablespoon chopped parsley*
*small pinch cumin seed*
*salt*
*black pepper*

Heat oil in skillet or terra-cotta casserole with flat bottom. Add rice, and stir over slow fire until it is translucent. Add onions, which have been finely minced, chopped garlic, tomato sauce, and 1 cup hot broth or bouillon. Add herbs, stir well, season with salt and pepper. Stir again, cover, and cook over slow fire. When more broth is needed add a cupful and continue cooking without stirring. Cook until rice is fluffy. Serve at once. *4 servings.*

# PILAF

Eastern countries bestow upon rice the care in preparation that befits an important part of their diet. Whether the dish be labeled *pilaf,* or *pilau,* or *pilaw* depends on how your ear renders into English lettering the sounds from Indian, Turkish, or other Oriental tongues. But the dishes represented by these names are cooking secrets to be carefully learned and often practiced. Here is one pilaf, or whatever you may choose to call it, that rarely fails to please.

## Indian Rice without Meat

| | |
|---|---|
| 1  *cup butter* | *scant ⅓ teaspoon saffron* |
| 1  *cup raw rice* | *dissolved in 2 tablespoons* |
| 2  *onions* | *water* |
| 6  *peppercorns* | ½  *cup seeded raisins* |
| 5  *cardamom seeds* | 12  *blanched almonds* |
| *dash cinnamon* | 4  *cups broth (pages 83–* |
| *salt* | *84)* |
| ½  *bay leaf* | |

Melt half the butter in a saucepan and add the rice which has been rubbed in a towel. Cook slowly, stirring often, until translucent. Add the rest of the butter and the minced onions, and cook slowly 5 minutes. Then add peppercorns and cardamoms crushed in a mortar, cinnamon, salt, bay leaf broken up, and saffron. Put in raisins and almonds, and add a cupful of hot broth. Cover, set on slow fire, and cook without stirring. When broth is absorbed add more. When rice is done all the liquid should be evaporated, and the rice be tender and fluffy. Do not stir after adding the liquid. *4 servings*.

## Torta

A Latinized version of our own too-often tasteless "rice ring" combines fascinating seasonings and ingredients, with a result that is tantalizingly savory. This torta is of Italian-French origin, and is cooked in a ring mold. Turned out on a large round platter, its center is filled with heaped green vegetables skillfully seasoned. It is a pretty dish, and one that serves guests at luncheon or buffet supper with temptation and fulfillment.

| | |
|---|---|
| *4 tablespoons olive oil* | *½ cup dried mushrooms* |
| *1 cup raw rice* | *1 bell pepper* |
| *from 2 to 2½ cups hot water, as needed* | *2 eggs* |
| *salt* | *1 tablespoon mixed herbs minced: marjoram, basil, and thyme* |
| *black pepper* | *½ cup chopped parsley* |
| *2 tablespoons butter* | *½ cup Parmesan cheese grated* |
| *1 large onion* | |
| *1 clove garlic* | |

Heat 2 tablespoons of the oil in a skillet, add raw rice, and cook slowly until translucent, stirring often. Add 2 cups hot water and 1 teaspoon of salt. Cover tightly, place over slow fire, and cook without uncovering for 20 minutes (longer for unpolished rice).

Meanwhile put the other 2 tablespoons of oil and the butter into a small frying pan, add minced onion and garlic, and fry 10 minutes slowly. Wash the dried mushrooms in lukewarm water, drain, chop, and soak in the ½ cup hot water.

When rice is cooked turn it out into a bowl, add to it fried onion and garlic, mushrooms, and the bell pepper, which has been chopped. Mix well, and let stand several hours.

When ready to complete the dish add one by one the beaten whole eggs, then the chopped herbs and the cheese. Season to taste with salt, and turn into a buttered ring mold. Bake in moderate oven ½ hour. Turn onto a hot platter. Fill center with broccoli or Swiss chard that has been steamed, chopped, and sautéed in oil with garlic (pages 284 and 266–267), or with carrots seasoned with butter, salt, and pepper. Serve at once. *4 servings*.

There they are, some of the thousand faces of rice. They are attractive, for rice is a royal grain, and deserves royal cookery. Make savory rice dishes your own, and never think that "rice for dinner" means sugar and cream!

# TWELVE

# Some Vegetables

Cling to thy home! If there the meanest shed
Yield thee a hearth, and shelter for thy head,
And some poor plot, with vegetables stored,
Be all that Heaven allots thee for thy board,
Unsavory bread, and herbs that scattered grow
Wild on the river-brink or mountain-brow;
Yet e'en this cheerless mansion shall provide
More heart's repose than all the world beside.

IT WOULD take faith to believe that such a home as that described by Leonidas would furnish heart's repose to restless,
acquisitive moderns. A mean shed, vegetables, herbs, unsavory bread — men and women today want more than that
to cover them with contentment. A ten-room shed, perhaps,
with a patio and a game room, and the last word in electric
stoves; with two baths and a powder room, of course, provided it were near enough to the chain stores and the movies.

A rereading of Henri Charpentier's idyllic picture of his
dream-retreat for his old age brought on that bit of philos-
ophizing. A little house he plans for, and a tiny poultry run,
with a cock to keep his hens company; a goat, a neat pigsty, a

plump porker; a kitchen garden laced with bright flowers; his Philomene in the kitchen, and Henri himself bringing to her a basket of his own dewy-fresh vegetables. And, says he, "When I handed her the basket . . . I would also hand her a bouquet of flowers, and . . . utter such compliments as would make us both sing while the dinner was cooking."

Henri, you would know how to find heart's repose even in a shed on a river bank.

But this is not getting on with my vegetables — and what is a dinner without vegetables? Green, yellow, white, red — multicolored crispness from carefully tended market gardens. Such gardens in themselves are beautiful. Van Gogh saw their beauty in panorama, and painted them true and lovely on lasting canvas. Day after day such neat-rowed plots yield their best for us, that we may gain pleasure and health from vegetables on our tables.

We Americans have a wealth of vegetables, but in the past we rarely have done anything subtle with them. We have boiled them impartially, regardless of their nature, sluiced them with butter, and eaten them. For some vegetables such scant dressing is proper treatment — for green corn, for instance, and the newest, most tender peas; but timid, retiring vegetables such as squash and carrots have shrunk even further into their weak personalities when given such poor consideration by the cook.

Vegetable cookery is important. It is well worth our while to give the matter our consideration until we have learned how to coax out the flavors hidden in the less aggressive vegetables, how to recognize and tolerate the bolder members of the tribe. What to do with squash, how to treat spinach, when to restrain an onion — these and many others are momentous matters within the Kingdom of the Kitchen. They are worthy of our deep study.

The vegetables are a varied group, testimony to man's innate versatility in adapting Nature to his needs. Of the plants of the earth he has taken leaves, roots, tubers, stalks, seeds and their pods, fruits, flowers, even the fungi that live on them, and has nourished himself. Each of these, dressed with care and ingenuity, can be truly good food.

First there are the green vegetables, or "greens" as they are so often called. Today we eat such food the year round, and take it for granted. But there was a time, not so many years ago, when winter was a white season, gastronomically as well as meteorologically speaking. The winter-vegetable fare was too liable to be confined to potatoes, beans, hominy, and now and then a cabbage dug from the vegetable pit in the frozen dooryard. How sluggish appetites must have become, and how folks must have longed for just one bit of fresh green on their tables.

But in the inevitability of Nature, came spring. The earth was clothed in green, and in *greens*. The housewife went forth and gathered new life for her larder from the fields and the fence corners. That night a grateful family feasted on "greens and pot likker" and knew that the winter was over.

To have many dinners lightened with leafy green vegetables is our privilege today, for there is wide variety available in markets throughout the country. Spinach one day, chard another, with others waiting their turn in the kitchen and the dining room. The trick is to know which to choose, and how to cook them to realize their potential.

## GREENS

Could we but rise *en masse* and demand other greens besides spinach and chard, there are actually enough other species of greens to keep us eating happily the rest of our lives. For instance:

## Dandelion

This bitter-leafed plant makes a delicious addition to a dish of greens, and is more acceptable to the American palate that way than cooked alone. Gathered from the fields, pulled from our own fenced gardens, where it springs up in defiance of the gardener, it should never be thrown away but added to the other greens for cooking or for salad.

## Mustard Greens

Mustard greens are grown in several forms, all of them crisp and pleasing. Some are large and curly, others smaller and smoother in texture. Each has that pungent mustard tang that puts such zest into a meal.

## New Zealand Spinach

New Zealand spinach, also called "mountain spinach," "summer spinach," and *tetragone,* is a trailing plant with fleshy stems and dark green leaves. It is more tender than our common form of spinach.

## Patience Dock

Here's an old-fashioned green straight from Great-Grand-mother's kitchen garden. Tender, a shade sour, since it is of the same family as sorrel, it is "right tasty." Grow it in a corner of your kitchen garden, and cook it as a green, either alone or with spinach.

## Rape or Rapini

Rape, usually called "turnip greens," is used principally by Latin cooks. It is often sold under the diminutive of "rapini," and is tender and tasty. One form has embryo turnips attached, while the other has only an undeveloped root. The entire plant is eaten, and when cooked with pork chops and white wine (pages 114–115) it is truly regal food.

## Sorrel

Mix this beautiful green leaf with your other leaf vegetables in the proportion of two to one, or use it in soup or salad. You will seen then why the French always have a sorrel bed in the garden plot. It is perennial, easily grown, and must only be renewed every three or four years.

Doubtless you all can name others not listed here, but these are enough to remove the odium of monotony from "a dish of greens."

## *Preparation of Greens*

These days we have relegated to the heap of worn-out saws

the idea that "each of us must eat a peck of dirt a year to be healthy." We are concentrating on getting the grit out of our spinach, for we know that it can be done, and without too much trouble.

First, roots harbor dirt, so cut them off and discard them. Then put the greens into a large pan full of hot water from the tap. Move them about gently but firmly in this bath, then lift them out. Pour out the water, rinsing the sediment from the pan bottom. Refill with lukewarm water, return greens, and let soak 5 minutes. Then gently wash again, lift out, and again change the water. Give them a third bath. This washes off all the sand, eliminates the laborious washing of leaf by leaf, and does not injure the leaves.

## Cooking Greens

Greens are easy to cook, but they must be understood. So many limp, dejected "messes of greens" served in our country are literally what the name implies. Yet each could be a bowl of green goodness begging to be really enjoyed, instead of grimly swallowed.

Too often greens are overcooked, and so lose their shape, their taste, their color, and their general goodness. For instance, fifteen years ago authorities advised cooking spinach "*25 minutes . . . in an uncovered vessel, in a large quantity of water to which has been added ⅓ teaspoon of soda.*" Shades of Vatel! What could remain to be enjoyed?

Greens should never be boiled. They should instead be cooked in their own juice — that is, in the water that is clinging to their leaves. Salt should be scattered among the greens, not put just on the top, for this dish should be evenly salted.

A low fire is needed, to slowly wilt the greens. As soon as they have gone down to half their bulk in the pan, add any other seasonings that are to be used, such as olive oil, bacon fat, or what you wish. Stir carefully, and continue cooking at the same low heat until the greens are wilted to the bottom of the pan, but still retain their shapes as leaves. They are then cooked as much as any leafy vegetables should be. Remove from the fire and serve.

The little bit of "pot likker" that has cooked from them can be used as your family's likes dictate. Some drink. Others dunk. Suit yourselves.

This entire cooking process takes only from 10 to 12 minutes for spinach, 15 minutes or perhaps a little more for such greens as mustard, chard, or rape.

The majority of leafy vegetables are made more pleasing by the addition of a little seasoning besides the salt. By varying these seasonings it is possible to vary this class of foods to a surprising degree.

For instance, olive oil and garlic lend a touch to spinach or any of her sister greens that adds greatly to their delicacy:

## *Spinach with Olive Oil and Garlic*

*1 pound fresh spinach*      *4 tablespoons olive oil*
*salt*                                      *1 clove garlic*

Wash greens (pages 264), and cook them as follows: Cut up slightly, but do not chop. Put into the kettle, salting it by layers, so the salt will be scattered throughout the greens. Cover, put on slow fire, and cook until wilted.

In the meantime brown the garlic, which has been split once lengthwise, in the oil, and set aside to cool.

When greens are wilted to half their bulk pour over them the cool oil and garlic, and lift gently until they are coated with oil. Return to fire and cook until wilted to bottom of kettle. Remove from fire, discard garlic, and serve. *3 servings.*

Greens so cooked will be bright green, have a definite shape and freshness of appearance, and a taste much more satisfying than those cooked longer.

## Spinach with Rosemary

This is a hundred-year-old recipe which proves that even that long ago spinach was appreciated by some. The dish is as delightful today as it must have been then.

Clean and wash a good quantity of spinach-leaves, two handfuls of parsley, and a handful of green onions. Chop the parsley and onions and sprinkle them among the spinach. Set them all on to stew with some salt and a bit of butter the size of a walnut, shake the pan when it begins to grow warm, and let it be loosely covered over a slow oven until done enough. It is served with slices of broiled calves' liver, small rashers of bacon, and eggs fried.

Follow this recipe, suiting it to your needs by using a pound of spinach for 3 persons. If you wish you may add rosemary (½ teaspoon to 1 pound spinach) to the parsley and onions, and know a new delicacy. Serve the spinach in the center of a hot platter, with liver, bacon, and eggs around the edge. It is a tempting supper dish.

## Swiss Chard

Chard, if not too adult, is almost as good as spinach. It should be cut up, leaves as well as stems, and cooked as spinach is cooked. Or try:

## Chard with Herbs

| | |
|---|---|
| 10 to 15 *leaves chard with stems* | 2 *cloves garlic* |
| | 4 *tablespoons olive oil* |

salt                                chives
chervil                             ⅛   teaspoon nutmeg grated

Prepare a bunch of chard for cooking (pages 264 to 265), cutting it up and draining it. Meanwhile brown garlic in olive oil and set aside to cool. Lay chard in kettle, salting by layers, and on each layer scatter a little chopped chervil and chives. Cover and cook slowly 15 minutes. Then pour cold oil and garlic over it, stir well, grate in nutmeg, stir again, and finish cooking. *4 servings.*


## Greens with Bacon

Prepare the greens for cooking (pages 264 to 265), cutting them up coarsely, and put them into a saucepan, salting them in layers. Cook covered over a slow fire until wilted to half their bulk. Meanwhile cut 3 rashers of bacon into small pieces and fry them slowly until brown. Turn them, with their fat, into the greens, stir well, and finish cooking.

Chard, rape, mustard greens, either alone or mixed with sorrel or a few beet leaves, are especially good with bacon dressing. The garlic dressing following is preferable with all of the spinach type of greens.


## Greens with Lemon Juice and Oil

enough greens to make a          2   cloves garlic
    quart when cut up            4   tablespoons olive oil
salt                             2   tablespoons lemon juice

Choose any greens you wish, either alone or in mixture. Wash and drain them (page 264), and put them into a kettle, salting each layer. Cook slowly until they are reduced to half their bulk.

To make the dressing, brown the garlic in oil, adding lemon juice just after browning. Pour the dressing over the greens and finish cooking. Remove garlic and discard before serving. *4 servings*.


# MORE VEGETABLES TO CONQUER


Excellent as greens may be, they are, after all, of no greater relative importance than many other vegetables. Enchanting are the forms Nature has given her vegetable offerings. Shape, color, texture, taste, all differ completely in each type. A small daily adventure, this eating of vegetables.


## Artichokes

Edible thistles, with rich goodness to prod reluctant appetites, and flowerlike form to delight the eye — such are artichokes, as good vegetables as anything ever put on a plate.

But artichokes, to attain such goodness, must be aided a little. Nothing is more dreary than one that comes to you innocent of any seasoning save too little salt, and attended by a dab of unctuous mayonnaise. Compared to the same artichoke cooked cunningly and seasoned with imagination, it is doubly depressing. To cook them well does not necessarily mean going through elaborate preparations. It means simply giving them a chance to show what they, under favorable circumstances, can be.

In the first place, artichokes are rarely sufficiently salted. A little salt, such as is called for in the cooking of other vegetables, makes no impression on this spiny child of Nature. Almost a teaspoon for each can be used with safety, to have them only well salted.

D   WINTER SAVORY

Second, they are usually undercooked. Taken from the kettle while the meat of their leaves is still tough, they are barely
edible. The diner has to fairly pull his or her teeth loose to get
off any meat whatsoever. To really cook artichokes one
should *steam,* never boil, them for at least ½ hour for those
of medium size, longer for larger ones. When they are done
they will be so tender that the cook will be able to thrust a
fork tine completely through them. Better, test them by tasting a leaf. If the meat is creamy and comes off easily, they
are done, and not before.

## Steamed Artichokes with Olive Oil

4  *large artichokes*          3  *level teaspoons salt*
2  *cloves garlic*             3  *tablespoons olive oil*
1  *cup hot water*

There is something in olive oil that makes the personality
of an artichoke bloom like the rose. Its armored austerity
gives way to tenderness.

Remove outer leaves of artichokes. Clip remaining leaf
ends, and wash the artichokes well under the tap. Cut off

stems, peel them, and lay them on tops of artichokes so they will cook tender. They are delicious eating. Peel garlic and cut each clove in two lengthwise. Put one piece among the leaves of each choke. Stand them all in a saucepan into which they fit closely, and which has a good cover. All must stand on the bottom of the pan.

Mix hot water, salt, and oil, stirring until salt is thoroughly dissolved. Pour this mixture evenly over the artichokes, so that the oil and salt will be evenly distributed among the leaves. Cover closely and cook over slow fire for at least 1 hour, or until leaves are thoroughly soft, like butter. Watch that they do not cook dry, adding more water if necessary. But see that the water is never more than barely covering the bottom of the pan, just enough to provide steam.

Cooked this way artichokes require no dressing, and are eaten hot. *4 servings*.

## Artichokes with Mustard Sauce

Cook steamed artichokes with olive oil, cool, and serve with this sauce:

4 *tablespoons mayonnaise*
2 *tablespoons prepared mustard*
1 *teaspoon minced chervil*

½ *teaspoon minced spearmint*
1 *teaspoon minced chives*

Mix ingredients thoroughly, and let stand 1 hour before serving.

## Artichokes with Rosemary

Follow recipe for Steamed Artichokes with Olive Oil (page 269), and just before the kettle is set to cooking scatter 1 teaspoon minced rosemary over the top. *4 servings*.

The artichoke de luxe, however, is one that is stuffed. It gathers heightened character from the savory stuffing put among the leaves and into the center, and emerges an artichokian triumph.

## Stuffed Artichokes

From 4 medium-sized artichokes clip the ends of all but the outermost leaves, which should be removed and discarded. Cut off stems flush with the bottoms, to provide flat surfaces so the artichokes can stand erect. Save the stems. Wash chokes well. Then, holding each in turn under the tap, let the water run hard on them while you, with the fingers, coax their leaves apart until they are like full-blown flowers. Reach down into their centers and pull out the central tuft of leaves, then, with a spoon, coax out the cushion of fuzz you will find and discard it. This makes a hole in the center of each for the stuffing.

## Stuffing

1 *small onion minced*
1 *clove garlic minced*
*artichoke stems peeled and minced*
2 *tablespoons olive oil*
1 *cup dry toast crumbs*
½ *teaspoon minced rosemary*

½ *teaspoon wild marjoram (oregano)*
*dash cayenne pepper*
½ *teaspoon salt*
⅛ *teaspoon black pepper*
¼ *cup hot water*

Cook onion, garlic, and stems in oil for 10 minutes without browning, then add all other ingredients, remove from fire, and mix well.

Fill center holes in chokes with stuffing, then divide the remainder among them, putting it in among the leaves. Stand them up in a saucepan, pour in around them — but not over them — ½ cup boiling water in which 2 tablespoons olive oil and 2 teaspoons salt have been blended. Wet a clean white cloth, lay it in the kettle over the tops of the chokes, and tuck it in around them. Cover and cook on a slow fire 1 hour or until tender. Serve hot. *4 servings*.

While some cooks advocate baking these in the oven, and make no mention of a cloth, that method results in hard, dried-out artichokes. The cloth keeps in the steam and keeps them moist and tender.

## Artichokes Stuffed with Anchovies

Follow recipe for Stuffed Artichokes (page 271), but eliminate herbs (rosemary and oregano). In their stead add 1 tablespoon parsley and 8 chopped anchovy fillets (or 4 salted anchovies that have been boned and washed). Cook as above.

## Beans

Beans are Everyman's food. They feed us often, feed us well and kindly, deliciously and pleasantly. Both dry and green, they are the poor man's bread, the gourmet's delight.

How richly simple must have been the sensibilities of Martial, prompting him to say in epigram:

If pale beans bubble for you in an earthenware pot, then you can often decline the dinners of sumptuous hosts.

There are so many kinds of beans, so many ways of preparing them, that a book could be written entirely on this subject and be affluent reading. But in a general food book, even a few recipes may lead readers and diners to discover new liking for this old food.

*Green Beans*. First come green beans. Hailed with joy as they appear in season, they continue a delight through their time, going out to the tune of our regrets, but even then they can be bought frozen, and be very good. As to which kinds you prefer, that is a personal matter. If you can find "Italian string beans" and once come to know their tender, slightly sweet, and very delicate flavor, you will doubtless prefer them. Their quick cooking habit is enough to recommend them, for they are done in easily half the time other green beans take.

But if Italian string beans are not to be found in your markets, use these recipes for ordinary string beans, for they too are very good fare.

How green beans can blend their tender lengths with a bit of oil, garlic, and herbs. So seasoned, they are delectable served hot, and fully as good cold.

## String Beans with Rosemary

| | |
|---|---|
| 2 *pounds string beans* | 1 *clove garlic* |
| *salt* | ½ *teaspoon rosemary* |
| 4 *tablespoons olive oil* | *black pepper* |

String the beans and cut them in half. Put a layer into a saucepan, salt them, then another layer and more salt, and so on until all are in. Add ½ cup hot water, cover tightly, and steam ½ hour over a slow fire. Cook down the little water that remains. In a frying pan heat the oil. Add garlic split lengthwise and speared with toothpicks, and let it brown on both sides. Add beans to the oil. Add rosemary, stir well, and add a dash pepper and more salt if needed. Cover closely and cook for 10 minutes. Discard garlic and serve beans either hot or cold. *4 to 6 servings.*

This rather thin, but zestful, sauce for string beans makes them authentically Latin, with that correct taste:

## String Beans with Sauce

| | |
|---|---|
| 1 *pound string beans* | 1 *tablespoon minced celery* |
| 2 *tablespoons olive oil* | 1 *tablespoon minced parsley* |
| 1 *small onion* | 1 *teaspoon marjoram or* |
| 1 *clove garlic* | *summer savory* |
| 1 *large tomato* | *pinch cinnamon and allspice* |
| 1 *tablespoon white wine* | *salt* |
| 1 *tablespoon minced bell* | *black pepper* |
| *pepper* | |

Prepare and steam beans as in previous recipe. Make this sauce in another pan:

Heat oil, in it fry minced onion and garlic slowly 10 minutes. Peel tomato and cut into oil and onion mixture. Add wine, pepper, celery, herbs, and spices. Salt and pepper to taste, simmer 10 minutes, then add beans, stir well, cover, and cook 10 minutes more. Serve hot. *2 or 3 servings.*

*Shell Beans.* Next in favor come "shell beans" — beans sufficiently mature to shell out of their pods before cooking, yet not fully ripe, not dry. The three best known and delicious of these are fresh limas, fresh broad beans, and fresh cranberry beans.

*Fresh Lima Beans.* That creamy goodness which is lima beans stands far up in front when the rating of beans begins.

And the best of all the limas are "baby limas," those precious infants that are only half as large as full-grown limas, and as tender as butter. They are adaptable, as youth always is, and lend themselves to various ways of preparation.

## *Baby Limas with Herbs*

| | |
|---|---|
| 1 small onion minced | 2 cups shelled fresh lima |
| 1 clove garlic | beans |
| 2 tablespoons olive oil or | ½ teaspoon marjoram |
| butter | 1 tablespoon parsley |
| 2 medium-sized tomatoes | salt |
| | black pepper |

Mince onion and garlic into oil in a saucepan or terra-cotta casserole, and cook for 10 minutes after it starts bubbling. Peel tomatoes and cut them up in the casserole. Stir well, then add rest of ingredients. Cover and cook slowly 1 hour, stirring every 15 minutes. After first half hour add more salt if necessary. *4 servings*.

## *Baby Limas with Fine Herbs*

| | |
|---|---|
| 2 tablespoons butter | black pepper |
| 2 cups shelled baby limas | 1 teaspoon minced parsley |
| salt | 1 teaspoon minced chives |

Melt butter, add limas, and stir until they are coated with butter. Add good dash of salt, pepper, and enough hot water to moisten but not cover them. (It is better to use less water and watch the dish more closely than to add a lot at first and have too much, for by the time they are done the beans should have no water left on them.) Cover and cook until tender, adding more salt if necessary 5 minutes before they are done. When ready to take up stir in the herbs, cover, and let stand 10 minutes in a warm place, but do not cook further. *4 servings*.

*Dried Lima Beans*. All the preceding recipes for fresh limas are adaptable also to dried limas that have been soaked overnight, drained, and cooked slowly with salt in just enough water so that by the time they are tender their liquor will be cooked down to nothing. This saves for them much flavor otherwise lost in draining them.

*Broad Beans* (*fave*). Broad beans are the beans of history. Cultivated from prehistoric times in the lands of southwestern Asia and northern Africa, they are the ones meant when *beans* are mentioned in historic records of the world's beginnings.

Europe and Asia still use this type of bean. Italy calls them *fave,* and cooks them in beguiling manner. But to us Americans they are "horse beans," scorned by all but those fortunate few initiate to their charm. A little open-mindedness about an unfamiliar food will endow us with another delicious course to serve in fascinating versatility.

Broad beans, horse beans, or *fave,* whichever you may choose to call them, are larger than the laregst limas, and when dry have a thick, heavy outer skin. Some eat this skin, relishing it as part of the bean. Others prefer to peel it off after cooking and eat only the tender inner part. We have found that it is best to leave on the skin when serving the beans hot, while cold beans, in salad, taste better if the heavy covering is removed.

But *fave* also are eaten fresh. Sold in the pods, which are bright green, very fleshy, and slightly downy, they must be shelled out, as only the bean itself is eaten. So full is the native flavor of the fresh beans that, though often cooked with seasonings of various sorts, they give a splendid account of themselves when seasoned only with butter, salt, pepper, and a little cream.

## Fresh Fave with Cream

Don't shrug aside this recipe as one of those murderous "creamed bean things." It is as simple as honesty, and will give you a dish full of unstudied savor when you would shun labored elaboration.

| | |
|---|---|
| 3  *pounds fresh* fave *weighed in the shells* | ½  *cup heavy cream* |
| 2  *tablespoons butter* | 1  *tablespoon chopped parsley* |
| *salt* | |

Don't gasp at buying 3 pounds for 4 persons, for those heavy pods run up the weight wondrously. Luckily, the price per pound is always low. Shell out the beans and put them into a saucepan in which the butter has been melted. Salt them, stir well, add a very little hot water, just barely enough to cover the kettle bottom. Cover and cook slowly until tender, renewing water as it cooks off. When beans are done the water should be entirely cooked away. Add heavy cream and parsley, and lower the fire. Allow cream to heat, but not to boil. Serve at once. *4 servings*.

## Fresh Fave with Summer Savory

Follow the recipe for Fresh *Fave* with Cream (above), adding 1 teaspoon minced savory to the parsley.

Now for the dried *fave*. Remember, they are not so subtle as the fresh ones, and have a more hearty taste. Perhaps you may think them strong at first. But try them again, preferably on a crisp night when winter is near, for they are not hot-weather fare.

## Fave with Ham

| | |
|---|---|
| 1  *clove garlic* | 3  *cups water in which* fave |
| 2  *tablespoons olive oil* | *were parboiled* |
| 2  *green onions with tops* | ½  *cup dry white wine* |
| 1  *slice cured ham* | *salt* |
| 1  *cup dried* fave, *soaked* | *black pepper* |
| *overnight in* 3 *cups water* | 1  *teaspoon wild marjoram* |
| *and parboiled* | *(oregano)* |
| 2  *bouillon cubes* | 1  *tablespoon parsley* |
| | *minced (optional)* |

Brown garlic slowly in oil, then add onion and tops minced, and cook slowly 10 minutes. Add ham cut in small bits, and cook 10 minutes more. Add drained *fave*, bouillon cubes dissolved in hot bean liquor, and wine. Season to taste with salt and pepper, and add wild marjoram (oregano). Cover, cook slowly 4 hours, stirring often. A tablespoon finely minced parsley may be stirred in 10 minutes before serving, if desired. *4 servings.*

## Fave Stew

This is a very hearty soup, with cabbage and everything in it.

| | |
|---|---|
| ½  *pound dried* fave | 1  *clove garlic* |
| 3  *cups boiling water* | 2  *tablespoons olive oil* |
| 1  *teaspoon salt* | ⅓  *cup tomato juice* |
| 3  *dry onions* | |

2 cups broth (pages 83–
84) or 2 bouillon cubes
dissolved in 2 cups hot
fave *liquor*
1 teaspoon minced summer
savory

1 teaspoon minced mar-
joram
1 Japanese chile without
seeds
black pepper
1 cup chopped cabbage

Soak *fave* overnight. The next morning put them into the
boiling water with the salt and cook until tender (about 2
hours). Then make this sauce in a frying pan:

Mince onions and garlic and fry slowly in oil 10 minutes.
Add tomato juice and stir well. Drain water from *fave* and in
2 cups of it dissolve 2 bouillon cubes. Add to tomato juice
mixture. Put in herbs and all seasonings, stir well, and cook
10 minutes. Add this sauce to the drained beans, cover, and
cook slowly 2 hours more, stirring frequently. At end of first
hour add cabbage and continue cooking. When nearly done
taste, and if necessary add more salt.

Savoy, or curly, cabbage is best for this dish. *4 servings*.

*Cranberry Beans*. These pot-bellied beans, freckled with
color, meaty and mealy, are the choicest of all beans smaller
than limas. They cook into tender globules of savoriness,
prime palate-flatterers. "The Queen's Beans" (*fagiuoli della
regina*) the Italians call them, though whether in honor to
the Queen or the bean they do not say.

These beans can be bought dried and shelled, or fresh in
season in their own beautifully mottled pods.

## Fresh Cranberry Beans with Sage

2 pounds cranberry beans
weighed in pods
3 tablespoons olive oil

salt
black pepper
2 leaves sage

Shell the beans and cook them until tender in as little salted hot water as can be managed without burning them. All the water should be cooked away by the time they are tender. Heat oil in a frying pan and put in the beans. Mince in the sage, add salt and pepper to taste, stir well, and cover. Let cook until all the oil is taken up into the beans, shaking the pan from time to time to keep them from burning. Serve hot. *4 servings.*

## Dried Cranberry Beans with Shallots

| | |
|---|---|
| ½  pound dried cranberry beans | or same amount of green onions |
| ⅓  cup olive oil | black pepper |
| 3  green shallots with tops | salt |

Soak beans overnight. In the morning drain, put into freshly boiling water with salt, and cook until tender. Drain, and into the hot beans stir the oil, the chopped shallots or onions with their tops, and mix well. Grind in a good bit of fresh black pepper, add more salt if needed. Serve with garlic bread (page 314) and Tomatoes Royal (pages 167–168), and have cheese for dessert. *6 servings.*

## Dried Cranberry Beans with Chili Peppers

Truly Mexican in their flavor without being fiery are these beans, with their darkly rich sauce of the famous "long chili peppers."

| | |
|---|---|
| ½  pound dried cranberry beans | 3  tablespoons olive oil |
| salt | 1  clove garlic |
| black pepper | 1  dry onion |

1   *teaspoon wild marjoram*          4   *dried "long chilis"*
   *(oregano)*                  1   *tablespoon minced pars-*
¼   *teaspoon cumin seed*               *ley*

Soak beans overnight in water to cover, and in the morning boil in salted water to cover until half done. Drain, *saving the water*. Into a saucepan put the oil. In it fry garlic and onion minced, then add wild marjoram (oregano) and cumin seed.

Meanwhile wash the chilis, removing and discarding their seeds. Boil chilis in 2 cups of the water drained from the beans. After 5 minutes of active boiling, remove them, saving water. Lay chilis on a board to cool, and when cold open them and scrape the inner pulp from the thin skins. Mix that pulp with the water in which they were boiled. Add this water-and-pepper mixture to onion, garlic, and oil. Cook 5 minutes, then add beans, and continue cooking until they are entirely tender. Renew water from time to time as it cooks away. When nearly done taste, and add salt if necessary. When ready to serve stir in parsley. *6 servings*.

# BEETS

## New Beets with Tarragon

4   *hot boiled and peeled*          ½   *teaspoon fresh minced*
   *medium-sized beets*             *tarragon*
1   *tablespoon oil*                 1   *teaspoon sugar*
1   *tablespoon butter*              *vinegar*

Cube beets and toss with oil and butter. Add tarragon, sugar, and vinegar to taste. Serve hot. *4 servings*.

## Beets Pickled with Mixed Herbs

| | |
|---|---|
| 5 or 6 beets | 1 clove garlic thinly sliced |
| 1 small sweet onion | salt |
| 2 bay leaves | black pepper |
| dash nutmeg | olive oil |
| 1 heaping teaspoon minced marjoram | red-wine vinegar |
| | dry red wine |

Boil or steam beets and let them cool. Peel and slice them into ¼-inch slices. Cut onion into thin slices and separate into rings.

Put a layer of beets into a wide, shallow bowl, then a layer of onion. Top with a few broken pieces of bay, a dash of nutmeg, a sprinkling of marjoram, a few slices garlic, salt, and pepper. Repeat until ingredients are all in the bowl. Then blend ⅓ olive oil, ⅓ vinegar, and ⅓ dry red wine, in sufficient quantity to cover the beets. Pour it over them, let stand 1 hour. Remove garlic, drain off the greater part of the liquid, and serve the beets cold. The liquid can be used for a green salad. *6 servings.*

# ❧ THIRTEEN ❧

# More Vegetables

You like your dinner, man; never be ashamed to say so . . . remember that every man who has been worth a fig in this world, as poet, painter, or musician, has had a good appetite and a good taste.

THACKERAY, speaking through the Nestorian Fitzboodle, sums up the sentiments of every announced gourmand, and raises a standard to inspire timid souls with epicurean courage. For food is physical wealth that contributes not a little to man's spiritual richness, so that all of its branches merit our attention in proportion to their variety and the parts they play in our lives.

Vegetables are such a long and toothsome list, so vitally important in pleasing our senses as well as nourishing us, that none can be passed over as nonessential. So another chapter we devote to vegetables, and know that they are worthy of time and effort spent.

# BROCCOLI

Broccoli is cabbage on the distaff side, and has in delicate proportion that characteristic flavor of its tribe. Its flowering heads, prettily green and succulent, are cooked with the tenderer parts of the stems and the smaller leaves.

Broccoli hot or broccoli cold? Each is enjoyable, for this is a vegetable that does well either as an accompaniment to the meat, or anointed with oil and lemon juice and regnant in the salad course.

## *Hot Broccoli*

| | |
|---|---|
| *1  pound broccoli* | *salt* |
| *2  cloves garlic* | *black pepper* |
| *4  tablespoons olive oil* | |

Wash broccoli after soaking it ½ hour in salted water. Save the flower heads, the tenderest stem pieces, and the smaller leaves. Arrange in saucepan or steamer, salting by layers. Add a very small amount of hot water, just enough to cover the bottom of the pan. This will keep the greens from scorching until the water on the leaves collects in the pan: that will be enough to finish the cooking. Cover, cook slowly for 20 to 30 minutes, depending on the age and size of the vegetable. Do not stir, for that breaks it. Take from fire when it is barely tender, and not too soft to retain its shape.

Meanwhile halve garlic cloves lengthwise and run a toothpick through each piece. Brown slowly in oil. Drain broccoli, put into the oil, stir carefully, and let sauté 10 minutes. Add more salt if necessary, a good dash of black pepper, and stir again. Remove garlic, and serve broccoli hot. *4 servings.*

## Cold Broccoli with Lemon Juice

| | |
|---|---|
| 1 *pound broccoli* | *salt* |
| 4 *tablespoons olive oil* | *black pepper* |
| 2 *cloves garlic* | 1 *tablespoon minced chervil* |
| 2 *tablespoons lemon juice* | |

Cook broccoli as in the preceding recipe. Make this dressing:

Set oil to heat in frying pan, and in it brown garlic which has been halved lengthwise and stuck with toothpicks. Add lemon juice and stir well.

When broccoli is tender pour over it the dressing, add salt and pepper to taste, stir carefully. Then chill. Before serving remove garlic and discard, and stir in chervil. *4 servings.*

# BRUSSELS SPROUTS

This vegetable is a first cousin to broccoli, and may be served in exactly the same ways.

# CABBAGE

The delicious cabbage, one of our vegetable standbys, has merit uncounted. To the Greeks in olden days it was medicine as well as food:

> Wife, quick! some cabbage boil, of virtue healing,
> That I may rid me of this seedy feeling.

We today can still find in it "virtue healing" if we will remember that cabbage briefly cooked is food, while cabbage too long cooked is more near to poison.

The glowing red-hued cabbage combines well with caraway seeds, as in this recipe:

## Red Cabbage and Caraway Seeds

| | |
|---|---|
| 2  *pounds red cabbage* | ¾  *cup vinegar* |
| 3  *tablespoons butter* | 1  *tablespoon caraway seeds* |
| ½  *cup brown sugar* | |

Shred cabbage. Melt butter, add sugar, vinegar, and caraway seeds. Add cabbage and cook 25 minutes, stirring often. Serve with roast pork or goose. 6 *servings*.

Herbs or no herbs, you must share a cooking secret my mother taught me. She cooks cabbage into a refreshing, sweet-smelling, delectable dish, and almost in a twinkle. No long stewing or boiling, no overcooking the cabbage until it turns pink and drives you out of the house. Just a short cooking, a little wise seasoning, and a perfect cabbage dish is ready to be eaten. So cooked, this vegetable has none of the disastrous effects so often laid at its door.

## Cabbage in Heavy Cream

| | |
|---|---|
| 2  *cups shredded cabbage* | *salt* |
| ½  *small onion* | *black pepper* |
| 2  *tablespoons butter or bacon drippings* | ½  *cup heavy cream* |

Shred cabbage. Shred onion, cook in fat slowly 10 minutes, then add cabbage, salt, and pepper. Cover, and cook 15 minutes, or until cabbage is barely wilted and tender. Add cream, stir well, let stand covered for 5 minutes off the fire, then serve hot. Do not boil after cream is added. 2 *servings*.

# CAULIFLOWER

Cauliflower — creamy flowerets that can be so good, but are often so bad. Too frequently they creep out from restaurant kitchens, their sullen sogginess masked with congealing butter, their whiteness sullied by overcooking. Then they are only pitiful.

But when they are carefully steamed and taken from the pot while still white and barely tender; when they are sautéed in butter and olive oil, or served cold with oil and red-wine vinegar, dotted with chives, they are full of fine personality.

## Cauliflower Sauté

| | |
|---|---|
| 1 tablespoon butter | salt |
| 3 tablespoons olive oil | black pepper |
| 1 clove garlic minced | 1 tablespoon parsley minced |
| 1 small cauliflower | |

Melt butter and mix with oil in frying pan. In it cook garlic slowly 5 minutes. Have cauliflower cut up and steamed until tender (page 288). Add it to the oil mixture and stir gently until each piece is coated with oil. Add salt and pepper, stir again, cover and cook slowly 5 minutes. Add parsley just before serving. 4 *servings*.

## Cold Cauliflower with Oil and Vinegar

| | |
|---|---|
| 1 *cauliflower* | 1 *teaspoon minced chives* |
| 4 *tablespoons olive oil* | 1 *teaspoon minced thyme* |
| 3 *tablespoons red-wine* | *salt* |
| *vinegar* | *black pepper* |

Steam the cauliflower (below), which has been cut into pieces, until it is barely tender but still white and firm. Drain and chill. Mix other ingredients, pour over cauliflower, and toss as a salad until well mixed. Serve cold, either as a vegetable course or a salad. *4 servings.*

## Steaming the Cauliflower

One does not need elaborate utensils to steam this, or any other, vegetable. Simply pile it in a deep saucepan that has a tight-fitting cover, salt it, and pour in barely enough hot water to cover the bottom of the saucepan. Let steam slowly for about 15 or 20 minutes. When tender but still firm remove from fire, drain, and dress as desired.

## EGGPLANT

This richly mantled thing we call an eggplant and use as a vegetable is in reality a fruit, perhaps the most beautiful of them all. Its color is so full, its form so gracefully mature. Surely it deserves a place of honor as a table decoration for a day before it is cooked.

American cooks formerly were able to think of little to do with an eggplant besides frying it and serving it in its shriveled nudity. To despoil such beauty thus, then to exhibit the revolting result, is unalleviated ignominy. ·

Other countries accord it more courtesy and considera-tion, prizing its taste, performing culinary wonders with it. All over southern Europe, the Near East, and Asia, the egg-plant is important food. Could we learn to give it a larger place in our menus, the gain would be ours.

These recipes for eggplant might logically have been in-cluded in the chapter on one-dish meals, for they make com-plete dishes that need but the addition of bread and salad to be real meals. Cheese for dessert takes up the protein lag.

## Eggplant with Herbs

| | |
|---|---|
| 1 medium-sized eggplant | ½ teaspoon minced mar-joram |
| salt | |
| 2 tablespoons olive oil | ⅓ bay leaf |
| 3 green onions with tops | ½ teaspoon rosemary |
| 1 clove garlic | 1 cup tomato juice |
| 1 tablespoon chopped pars-ley | black pepper |
| | 2 tablespoons grated Ro-mano cheese |

Wash eggplant, cut it into slices about ¾ inch thick, and lay in a skillet or wide terra-cotta casserole, salting each layer. Pour around it ⅓ cup hot water, cover tightly, and cook slowly 10 minutes. In another pan make this sauce:

Heat oil, and in it cook minced onion, including the onion tops, and garlic. When tender add herbs and tomato juice, salt and pepper to taste, and cook 10 minutes.

Pour this sauce over the eggplant, cover, and finish cook-ing, which will take about 20 minutes more. Remove cover, sprinkle with cheese, and put under broiler flame to brown. *4 servings.*

## Eggplant Cutlets

1  eggplant
1  egg
1  heaping tablespoon flour
salt
black pepper

1  clove garlic
⅓  teaspoon rosemary
1  tablespoon bell pepper
olive oil

Peel eggplant and boil until tender in salted water. Drain and mash. Let cool slightly, then add rest of ingredients. Mix well.

Cover the bottom of your skillet with olive oil and bring to the bubbling point. Dip up spoonfuls of the eggplant batter and drop into the oil. When brown on one side turn with spatula and brown other side. Serve with meat. *4 servings.*

## Stuffed Eggplant

If it is possible to secure baby eggplant about 2 or 3 inches long, use four of them. Otherwise, 1 large one will be enough.

eggplant
½  pound ground round
   steak
2  tablespoons olive oil
1  onion
½  clove garlic
½  cup bread crumbs
1  egg
2  tablespoons grated Romano cheese

6  to 8 black Greek olives
1  teaspoon minced sweet
   marjoram
½  teaspoon minced thyme
1  tablespoon minced parsley
salt
black pepper

Wash eggplant, put into a covered dish with ½ inch water, and bake in a slow oven until tender, or parboil. Cool, then cut a slice from the long side. Scoop out the pulp.

Fry steak in oil, then add minced onion and garlic and cook slowly 5 minutes more. Add eggplant pulp, which has been chopped, and the crumbs, and cook 5 minutes more. Cool, and add beaten egg, cheese, minced olives, herbs, and salt and pepper to taste. Stuff eggplant, return to baking dish, and bake in medium oven uncovered for 25 minutes. Serve with garlicked French bread and a salad. *4 good servings*.

# MUSHROOMS

Nero, it seems, called mushrooms "food for the gods." Cannot that temper for him a trifle the history-deep shadow under which he rests? For to be right in even one thing must lighten somewhat the darkness of his villainy.

We here in America are learning as never before the blessed gift of taste improvement that lies in mushrooms, fresh or dried, finding that they will assure for our food that ever-novel gift of Jove, savory surprise.

Since dried mushrooms are used almost entirely as seasoning, they appear in that role all through the book. Fresh mushrooms, however, are exotic vegetables, and as such need thoughtful preparation.

## Fresh Mushrooms

Ways of cooking the edible fungi of this type range all the way from the simplest to the most elaborate. With due respect to the devotees of complicated mushroom dishes, this food is at its best when simply cooked. Its native flavor is so delicate yet so complete that it needs little in addition.

That does not mean that mushrooms should get no seasoning at all. On the contrary, alliance with certain other foods seems only to enhance their own delicacy. Either oil or butter they must have. A touch of garlic they welcome. Salt, of course, is taken for granted. Italy decrees that marjoram, either wild or sweet, should accompany them, calling it aptly *l'erba di funghi*, "the mushroom herb."

## Mushrooms with Marjoram

|  |  |
|---|---|
| 1  pound mushrooms | black pepper |
| ⅓  cup olive oil or butter | 1  teaspoon minced mar- |
| 2  cloves garlic | joram |
| salt | |

Peel mushrooms, both caps and stems, or wipe clean with a paper towel but *do not wash.* Cut them into large pieces. Heat oil in frying pan, and in it brown garlic which has been halved and stuck with toothpicks to facilitate removal. Add mushrooms, salt, pepper, and marjoram. Stir well, and cook slowly about 15 minutes, or until barely tender. If cooked longer they will be tough. Remove garlic before serving. *4 servings.*

## Mushrooms with Chives and Parsley

Follow preceding recipe, substituting for the garlic and marjoram 1 heaping teaspoon chives and 1 tablespoon parsley, which are to be added at the beginning of the cooking. *4 servings.*

## ONIONS

Whole onions, with a little judiciously selected seasoning, make such a delicious vegetable that they often have a place in our menus as an accompaniment for meat. Cook as many onions as you wish servings, and multiply other ingredients in proportion.

### Baked Whole Onions

| | |
|---|---|
| *1  large onion* | *⅛  teaspoon nutmeg* |
| *1  teaspoon butter* | *⅛  teaspoon salt* |
| *1  level teaspoon grated Romano cheese* | *⅛  teaspoon pepper* |

Select fairly large, firm dry onions, matched in size if you are serving a group, so no one need feel slighted. Peel them, and place each on a suitably sized rectangle of foil. Wrap each, twisting the ends to make for easy release when tender. Bake at 400° until tender when squeezed. Meanwhile, cream together butter, cheese, nutmeg, salt, and pepper.

When onion is tender, unwrap and remove from foil, split in half, and spread with seasoning mix. *1 serving.*

## GREEN PEAS

New peas, like mushrooms, are flavorsome enough to need little help from seasoning agents. On the other hand, if they have hung too long on the vine so that they are a bit on the tough side they are better for some dressing up. So the tender little peas it is best to cook almost plain, while those further along in years — or weeks — are reserved for the elaborate recipes.

Peas should never be boiled, for when they are drained half of their goodness is lost. Instead, cook them in a little butter in a tightly closed pan, or in just enough water to cover the pan bottom, so that when they are done the water has cooked away. Then you will have in those emerald globules all their natural tastiness.

Second, peas, to be green and full of flavor, must not be cooked for long. Various methods of cooking them so they will not lose their color have been advanced from time to time. An uncovered vessel, some say, while others, *horribile dictu,* hold out for a pinch of soda. But none disclose the real secret, that peas lose their color because they are overcooked. If they are watched closely and removed from the fire as soon as they are tender, they will remain as green as when they were first shelled.

## Peas in Butter

| | |
|---|---|
| 2  *pounds green peas* | *salt* |
| 2  *scant tablespoons butter* | *black pepper* |

Shell the peas, and if they are washed, drain them well. Melt butter in saucepan, add peas, salt and pepper them, and stir until they are coated with butter. Cover tightly and cook slowly until tender, usually from 12 to 18 minutes. If they threaten to stick add a very small amount of boiling water, and be sure it is all cooked away before serving them. *4 servings.*

Perhaps you want something a little more elaborate. In such case try:

## Peas with Onion

2 *pounds peas*
1 *tablespoon butter*
1 *tablespoon olive oil*
1 *tablespoon finely minced*
 *onion*

1 *tablespoon finely minced*
 *celery*
*salt*
*black pepper*

Shell peas. Melt butter and mix in oil in a saucepan. Add onion and celery and cook slowly 10 minutes, but do not brown. Add peas, salt them, add pepper, and stir until they are coated with oil and butter. Cook slowly until tender, adding 2 tablespoons hot water if they start to stick. *4 servings*.

## Peas and Herbs

2 *pounds peas*
2 *tablespoons olive oil*
*salt*

1 *teaspoon finely minced*
 *herbs, either sweet basil,*
 *thyme, or spearmint*

Shell peas, put them into a saucepan with the oil, salt them, and stir until they are coated with oil. Cover closely and cook until tender, adding 2 tablespoons hot water if they stick. When tender, add herbs, stir well, and let stand 10 minutes in a warm place before serving. *4 servings*.

## Peas in Minted Cream

Cook peas as in Peas with Onion (above). Have prepared half a cup of warm cream in which 6 or 8 leaves of crushed spearmint have been soaked for 1 hour and removed. When peas are tender pour over them the cream, stir well, heat, but *do not boil*. Serve hot. *4 servings*.

For older peas use the recipe for Artichokes and Peas (pages 214–215) or:

## Peas with Ham

| | |
|---|---|
| 1 tablespoon butter | ½ cup hot water |
| 1 tablespoon minced onion | salt |
| ½ clove garlic minced | black pepper |
| ⅓ cup chopped raw ham | ½ teaspoon sweet basil |
| 2 pounds green peas | minced |
| ½ bouillon cube | |

Melt butter and in it cook onion and garlic slowly 10 minutes without browning. Add ham, cook 5 minutes. Add shelled green peas and water with bouillon cube dissolved in it. Stir, salt and pepper to taste, add basil, and cook until peas are tender, stirring several times and adding more broth if necessary. When done all the liquid should be cooked away. *4 servings*.

## SWEET PEPPERS

The large bell pepper is the best of our edible peppers. Mild and kind, it causes no weeping, no flame breathing. For that reason, as well as because it has a fine flavor, this vegetable is a favorite. Fascinating things can be done with it, allowing it to appear as superior food in various guises.

Though a bell pepper is always a bell pepper, there is nothing monotonous about it, once one learns that it doesn't always have to be stuffed with hamburger and baked! For instance, there is such treatment as:

## Peppers with Tomatoes

*1 small onion*
*1 clove garlic*
*2 tablespoons butter*
*2 tablespoons olive oil*
*4 large bell peppers*
*3 large tomatoes*
 *1 teaspoon minced sweet basil*

*½ teaspoon minced marjoram*
*½ Japanese chile without seeds*
*salt*
*black pepper*

Mince onion and garlic and cook in oil and butter for 10 minutes. Wash peppers, remove seeds and stems, and cut into large pieces. Add to the oil, onion, and garlic, stir well, and cook 10 minutes. Skin tomatoes, cut them up among the peppers, add herbs, chile, salt, and black pepper. Stir again, cover, and cook 30 minutes, or until peppers are tender. Add more salt if necessary when nearly done.

If you like hot food substitute 1 long green chili for ½ of one of the bells. But no more, or you will be suing me for writing with intent to do bodily harm. *4 servings.*


## Roasted Bell Peppers

*3 large bell peppers*
*garlic*

*salt*
*olive oil*

Wash and dry the whole raw peppers. Lay them in a slow oven in an iron skillet. Let them roast, uncovered, turning them occasionally, until the entire skin is blistered. They will look burned in spots, but don't let that worry you. Take them from the oven, slit each pepper up the side to let the steam out, and leave them to cool. When cool enough to handle remove seeds and membranes from the insides, then remove the outer skins, which will come off easily if the peppers are not entirely cold. Lay out on a shallow dish, dot with several garlic cloves cut in half. Salt generously and cover with olive oil. Let stand 1 hour, then remove garlic.

Serve these as a cold relish with meat, or as a salad with French bread. Be bold — dunk your bread in the oil, and glare your defiance at all the Grundy family. Just think what they are missing. 2 *servings*.


# POTATOES


Since Elizabethan days when potatoes first became fashionable food in England they have remained easily the most versatile and delicious of the tubers. Cooked simply, they are unbelievably good; yet, given sophisticated treatment and raised from the ranks as *pommes de terre*, they are unspoiled by their added swank.

New potatoes, browned and dripping with butter, perfumed with a shade of garlic and a stippling of fine herbs, are perfect. Equally good are the big mealy ones we call "baking potatoes." But shun, as you would a hoary, bearded germ, the potato that is soggy when cooked. That is the black sheep of the white-potato family.


## Boiled Potatoes with Dill

When serving boiled potatoes chop very fine enough fresh dill to make a teaspoonful, and sprinkle over the potatoes when ready for the table.

## Mashed Potatoes with Chives and Parsley

No less a personage than William Allen White, the Sage of Main Street, recommends "mashed potatoes beaten feather light and made noble by the addition of finely minced Chives and Parsley." In preparing them, dress the potatoes as usual, with pepper, salt, butter, and cream, then add a heaping teaspoon each of chives and parsley at the final whipping. Then, for Beauty's sake, scatter a bit of the green on top.

## Potatoes Bolognese

In Bologna, Italy, that fountainhead whence come so many inspired recipes, potatoes are cooked in such an intriguing way one must perforce disregard their infernal calories, and eat them with abandon. Such rash behavior now and then is balm for the soul.

| | |
|---|---|
| 3 medium-sized potatoes cut in half lengthwise | 1 teaspoon rosemary minced |
| 4 tablespoons olive oil | salt |
| 1 clove garlic minced | black pepper |

Preheat oven to 400°. Cut each potato half into 3 or 4 wedge-shaped sections. In a roomy baking pan, heat olive oil, then add garlic. When oven is ready, add potato sections, stirring until each is oil-coated, and then stir in rosemary. Cook uncovered, stirring every 10 minutes, until all are fork tender. Then add a dusting of salt and pepper, and serve with roasted or broiled meat. *4 to 5 servings*.

## Potatoes with White Wine and Herbs

3  tablespoons butter or olive
   oil
1  teaspoon flour
4  medium-sized raw pota-
   toes
1  clove garlic minced
1  medium onion sliced
salt

black pepper
⅓  cup white wine
⅓  cup broth (pages 83–
   84)
 1  teaspoon minced thyme
    or marjoram
 1  teaspoon minced parsley

Melt butter or heat oil, mix in flour, and brown it quickly. Add sliced potatoes, garlic, onion, salt, and pepper. Fry, turning very often, until they begin to show brown color. Add wine and broth, herbs, and cover closely. Simmer until potatoes are tender and liquor is cooked up. Add parsley, stir well, and serve. *4 to 5 servings.*

Everyone knows baked potatoes, with butter, salt, and pepper. But there are other things that can be done with them, things that will make them absolutely seductive.

## Baked Potatoes with Herbs

4  large potatoes
3  tablespoons  butter
heavy cream
½  teaspoon minced thyme
½  teaspoon chervil

½  teaspoon chives
sage
salt
black pepper
paprika (optional)

Bake potatoes until they are soft when squeezed. Cut a slice from the long side of each, and scoop out the inside. Mash this and mix with butter and enough heavy cream to make a fluffy consistency. Add thyme, chervil, chives, and a tiny bit of sage, for the entire lot of potatoes. Salt and pepper to taste, mix well, and refill potatoes without packing in. Reheat in a slow oven. A little paprika over the tops is decorative. *4 servings.*

## Baked Potatoes with Romano Cheese

Follow recipe for Baked Potatoes with Herbs (page 000), but for the herbs substitute 2 heaping tablespoons grated Romano cheese, and add 1 teaspoon chopped chives and chervil, or parsley.

## SQUASH

The marrow or squash tribe is a large one, and multiform. Of all its members, those most deserving of culinary notice are the long, green squash known as zucchini, or "Italian squash." They have the family delicacy, but a more definite flavor, and enough body when cooked to lend themselves to interesting modes of preparation. There is also a golden variety, which is truly beautiful, and also delicious.

## Zucchini Sauté with Sweet Basil

| | |
|---|---|
| 4 medium-sized zucchini | salt |
| 1 tablespoon butter | black pepper |
| 2 tablespoons olive oil | ½ bouillon cube dissolved |
| 1 small onion | in ⅓ cup hot water |
| 1 clove garlic | 2 tablespoons tomato |
| ⅓ bay leaf | sauce, or 1 peeled fresh |
| 1 teaspoon sweet basil | tomato cut up |
| minced | Parmesan cheese (optional) |

Wash zucchini and cut into thin rounds without peeling. Melt butter and mix with oil in frying pan. In this cook minced onion and garlic for 10 minutes without browning. Add zucchini and all herbs and seasonings, stir well, and add bouillon. Cover and cook 10 minutes, then add sauce or tomato and finish cooking. When almost done add more salt if necessary. A tablespoon grated Parmesan cheese stirred in when serving adds a fillip. *4 servings.*

## Zucchini Sauté with Marjoram

Follow preceding recipe, omitting tomato sauce and basil and substituting 1 teaspoon sweet marjoram and 1 teaspoon minced parsley.

## Zucchini with Rosemary Sauce

| | |
|---|---|
| 4 medium-sized zucchini | stale end of French loaf |
| 1 onion sliced thin | salt |
| 1 clove garlic minced | black pepper |
| ½ teaspoon minced rose-mary | ⅓ cup broth (pages 83–84), or hot water |
| 2 tablespoons olive oil or butter | 1 tablespoon grated Romano cheese |

Wash and slice zucchini without peeling. Fry onion, garlic, and rosemary in oil or butter for 10 minutes very slowly. Then from the stale French loaf shave enough thin tiny shavings to make ½ cupful. Add this to the oil mixture and fry slowly until bread slivers are browned. Add zucchini, salt and pepper to taste, and broth or water. Stir well, cover, and cook slowly until zucchini are tender, stirring frequently. If necessary to keep from burning, add small amount of water. Just before serving stir in cheese. *4 servings.*

## Zucchini Stuffed with Veal and Chard

| | |
|---|---|
| 4 *medium-sized zucchini* | ⅓ *cup grated Romano* |
| 1 *small veal chop* | *cheese* |
| 2 *tablespoons olive oil* | 1 *teaspoon minced mar-* |
| 1 *onion* | *joram or thyme* |
| 1 *clove garlic* | *salt* |
| ½ *bunch Swiss chard* | *black pepper* |
| 2 *eggs* | 1 *teaspoon minced parsley* |

Parboil zucchini 10 minutes, drain, and cool. Split length-wise, take out pulp, and chop finely. Fry veal brown in oil, then put through food chopper. In pan where meat was browned cook minced onion and garlic 10 minutes, then add chard that has been steamed (page 288), drained, and chopped. Stir well, cook until hot, then add zucchini pulp. Mix, cook 5 minutes more. Cool slightly, add beaten eggs, cheese, seasonings, and veal. Mix well and with this mixture stuff zucchini halves. Lay in oiled pan and bake in moderate oven about 30 minutes, or until squash are tender.

If no meat is available, dried mushrooms that have been soaked in hot water, drained, and chopped may be added instead just for flavor's sake. For this recipe use ½ cup measured before soaking. *4 servings.*

## Fried Stuffed Zucchini

These are excellent to serve with rather simply seasoned meat, for they are full of taste and very satisfying. No matter how many you cook, they will not go begging.

| | |
|---|---|
| 1 *6-inch zucchini for each* | 3 *slices bread soaked in* |
| *serving* | *milk* |
| *pulp of zucchini* | 2 *eggs* |

| | |
|---|---|
| 1  clove garlic minced | salt |
| ½  cup grated Romano cheese | black pepper |
| | olive oil |
| ½  teaspoon thyme | butter |

Parboil zucchini, cool, and split lengthwise. Take out pulp, chop finely, add to it bread from which milk has been squeezed, eggs, garlic, cheese, thyme, salt, and pepper. Mix well and stuff zucchini halves. Fry on both sides in mixture of half butter and half oil, gauging amount by number of zucchini used. Take care to brown completely, then serve very hot. *4 servings*.

Then there are the winter squash, so good for pies, for breads, for puddings, but even a little more special as a carbohydrate vegetable in the body of the meal. That lovely green and gold Danish squash is a winter gem, and when its goodness is mixed with the proper seasoning touch, it is really special food. My friend Maurine shared her secret for easy cooking, for which I bless her.

## Baked Danish Squash, Gingered

| | |
|---|---|
| 1  Danish squash | root, or dried root soaked overnight in a little water, then sliced and minced |
| 2  tablespoons butter for each half squash | |
| 1  teaspoon freshly sliced and minced fresh ginger | salt |
| | black pepper |

Wash and dry squash and wrap in a piece of foil, twisting the ends. Lay in an open pan and bake in a 400° oven until soft when pressed. This takes about an hour. Meanwhile prepare the seasoning mix by creaming together all the other ingredients.

When the squash is tender, and you are ready to serve,

unwrap it, split it lengthwise, and with a fork work part of the seasoning paste into the squash meat. 2 *servings*.

Please don't write and ask where to buy fresh ginger. If you don't have a Chinese or Japanese grocer near who can supply it, then I cannot help you. We on the West Coast have them virtually at every whistle stop. This is richness indeed, but we don't take credit for this fortunate fact. We just thank our stars.

# VEGETABLE COMBINATIONS

Dishes composed of two or more vegetables cooked together add interest to a meal. Not the old "peas-and-carrots" dish we know so well, but more unusual mixtures. Some of them sit right down in the same pan or casserole and establish such fine friendships that they make the whole family happy, just to eat them.

## Carrots and Zucchini

| | |
|---|---|
| 2 *cloves garlic* | *black pepper* |
| 2 *tablespoons olive oil or butter* | 1 *teaspoon thyme* |
| | ⅛ *cup water* |
| 1 *small onion* | 2 *tablespoons grated Romano cheese* |
| 2 *large carrots* | |
| 4 *small zucchini* | 1 *tablespoon parsley* |
| *salt* | |

Halve garlic lengthwise, run a toothpick through each piece, and brown slowly in oil or butter. Mince onion, add to garlic, and cook slowly 10 minutes. Cut up carrots and zucchini coarsely and add. Season with salt and pepper to taste, and add thyme. Stir, then add water. Cover and cook slowly until tender, stirring often. When half done remove garlic and discard. When cooked stir in cheese, let stand 5 minutes without cooking, then top with parsley and serve. *4 servings*.

## Celery and Artichokes

For this dish use baby artichokes no more than 2 inches long. If not obtainable, use only the bottoms of the large ones, leaving on enough of the lower portions of the leaves to make up the 2-inch length. The green outer stalks of celery are usable, and provided they are not stringy will cook to better advantage than the very tender inner stalks.

| | |
|---|---|
| 3 *large stalks celery* | 2 *tablespoons olive oil* |
| 6 *small artichokes or 3* | 1 *small onion* |
| *larger ones cut down* | 1 *small tomato* |
| *salt* | 1 *teaspoon minced thyme,* |
| *black pepper* | *or ½ teaspoon rosemary* |
| ½ *clove garlic* | |

Wash celery and cut into 1-inch pieces. If small chokes are used, halve them. Larger ones should be cut down as directed above and quartered. Cover vegetables with boiling water and salt and cook until tender. Drain. Brown halved and toothpick-speared garlic in oil, then add minced onion and cook slowly 10 minutes. Peel tomato and cut it up in oil and onion. Add vegetables, pepper, herbs and stir well. Discard garlic, and cook slowly, with cover on, for 10 minutes. *4 servings*.

# Three-Vegetable Sauté with White Wine

| | | | |
|---|---|---|---|
| 6 | medium-sized artichokes or 10 little ones | 2 | cloves garlic |
| 6 | medium-sized new pota-toes | 1 | tomato |
| ½ | pound green peas | ¼ | cup dry white wine |
| 2 | tablespoons olive oil | 6 | leaves sweet basil |
| 2 | tablespoons butter | | salt |
| | | | black pepper |

Strip off outer leaves of artichokes, cut off leaf tops halfway down, keeping only the bottom parts of the leaves and the hearts. This makes of each a piece about 2 inches long. Quarter each of these. If baby artichokes are used, cut off their spines and halve them.

Scrape potatoes and slice into ¼-inch slices. Shell peas. Heat oil and butter in a skillet or terra-cotta casserole and to it add the garlic cloves halved lengthwise and speared with toothpicks. Brown garlic slowly, then add artichokes and potatoes, stir well, and cook 5 minutes. Add peas and the tomato, which has been peeled and cut up. Stir again, add rest of ingredients. Mix well, cover, and cook slowly until potatoes and artichokes are tender. If necessary to prevent scorching, add a very little hot water from time to time, but never much. When ready to serve, all free moisture should have been cooked up. Discard garlic before serving, and add more salt if necessary. *6 servings.*

May these vegetables serve to lighten many a meal and load your systems with vitamins and joy.

# ❧ FOURTEEN ❧

# The Lovable, Errant Lily

Garlic: a European liliaceous plant (*allium sativum*).
*Liliaceae:* a large family of monocotyledonous plants, the Lily
    family. . . . .
                    *Webster's New International Dictionary,* 1927 *ed.*

WHEN one member of a proud and honorable family goes
astray, onlookers often debate just where to bestow their
sympathy. The family proper, still on its pedestal, has had
a body blow. But the bawdy one, what about him? If he looks
up regretfully at the safe eminence whence he tumbled, then
pity him. But wait! Maybe he likes it better down there where
he is. Can we blame him? Rarefied air, rumor says, is a little
thin for general breathing purposes.

Presumably the Lily Family was once an unsullied unit
of botanical society. The Lilies, the Tulips, the Hyacinths,
even the Asparagus, held their heads high in conscious respectability. They were one of the really fine families, whose
escutcheon bore no visible blot. But, as the saying goes, no
one steps so high that he can't stub his toe. And so it was

with them. One of those nice little Lily girls got involved in a scandal with someone unsavory. The issue, to speak bluntly, was a far from fragrant character, who was given the name of Garlic. The Family wasn't proud of him. He reeked, they said, of vulgarity. So they drew the curtain on the affair and once more withdrew into dull respectability.

But Garlic! He was really an individual, and he was too brash to stay snubbed. He had more fun — went right out and began getting himself noticed. And since personality will take one a long way even without background, he gradually came to be accepted in even the best places. Look at him now. He gets into practically everything. The world, not being able to ignore him, has come to adore him.

Laying foolery aside, garlic is truly an ancient and honorable thing. Along with its cousins, the leeks and onions, it was among the earliest of the seasonings. Ancient Egypt relished it as food, and the Hebrews yearned nostalgically after it in their wilderness wanderings:

We remember the fish, which we did eat in Egypt freely; the cucumbers, and the melons, and the leeks, and the onions, and the garlick. . . .

Numbers 11:5

These are only a few of the peoples who relished the reaching flavor. But it was class-conscious Rome that first looked at it askance. There, as elsewhere, garlic was a favored food of the soldiers, sailors, slaves, and the hoi polloi generally. As the food of the vulgar, the fastidious nobles and wealthy classes scorned its delights and sniffed at its emanation. Could it have been in grudging envy, wanting yet fearing to lower themselves to the "level" of their servants? Horace inveighed against it in his *Epodes*, and reading them hundreds of years later, a witty Frenchman was prompted to write:

Horace, si tu l'avais goûté . . .
Tu aurais mieux aimé ta tête couronnée
D'une chaîne d'ail que de laurier.*

The odium gathered force. While the common folk went on happily devouring their garlic and innocently relishing it, the gentlefolk's noses were increasingly in the air about the matter. But how lucky that the plebeians kept the use of garlic alive. They didn't know there was anything wrong about it, bless them! Gradually, as the centuries passed, their wholesome attitude carried over, and in some countries garlic became customary and accepted seasoning. France, Italy, and Spain, with most of the rest of southern Europe, have ennobled the use of this flavor, with results of evident excellence. But in England and our own America garlic has only recently become widely used, to the vast diversification and benefit of our cuisine. Only when we forget that prejudice, at least to some extent, can our national cuisine approach the excellence it should have.

Victorian England and America reached a new high in abhorring garlic. Even onions were barely tolerated, and then only on occasions of social negligee. Shelley, in a letter to Leigh Hunt from Italy, shuddered at the *déclassé* vegetable, at the same time giving Lord Byron a nasty poke:

What do you think? Young women of rank actually eat — you will never guess what — *garlick!* Our poor friend Lord Byron is quite corrupted by living among these people, and in fact, is going on in a way not worthy of him.

Of course garlic, like politics and religion, is never discussed indiscriminately. It is apt to engender harsh state-

---

* Horace, if you had tasted it . . .
  You had rather be crowned with garlic
  Than with laurel.

ments and sweeping generalizations on the subject, and sometimes the generalizer is put in an awkward position. For tastes change, and the garlic-hater of today is often the garlic-lover of tomorrow. The remembrance that he has previously classed all garlic-eaters as fetid oafs does not add to a convert's peace of mind when he himself joins the barbaric horde. So careful is the watchword.

But here in this book, where no one can answer me back to his or her later discomfiture, a few words can be spoken in behalf of garlic and its fans. The book has a faint reek of the blessed herb anyway. In a nice way it enters into a large part of the recipes. However, all the way through I've saved people's social positions by showing them how garlic can be used discreetly. Now I must speak up for that throng, gourmets all, who have no desire to be discreet about garlic. They love it, in large and noticeable amounts, and would not be ashamed to say so, if it were necessary, which it hardly ever is. This chapter I dedicate to them.

Now garlic, as I have said elsewhere, is a bold fellow and needs a little understanding. The older countries, culinarily speaking, handle him with finesse. They let him speak up when they want him heard, squelch him when the full force of his presence is not desired. The results are marvelous. Good, well-cooked restaurant fare, as well as *pianissimo* versions of the heartier dishes, exhale a gentle *je ne sais quoi* which means garlic firmly leashed. Good peasant cookery, which after all is the real *haute cuisine* of the world, breathes frankly of it.

Ruth Gottfried, in *The Questing Cook*, says that "no cook who has attained mastery over her craft ever apologizes for the presence of garlic in her productions." She further says that her recipes use garlic proudly. I only wish I had thought of those phrases first. As it is, in lieu of originating them, I can only make bold to borrow them.

The recipes in this chapter are for the type of dishes one

might call "Saturday night dishes." That would mean that, barring some heavy Sunday social obligations on the right side of town, one could feel free to eat these dishes on Saturday night, knowing that by Monday morning the garlic would all have cleared away, with nothing but the memory lingering on. For these dishes are well seasoned with the odoriferous bulb, and if eaten on any other night in the week may cause you to be the recipient of hostile glares, or even frank words. There may be things your best friends won't tell you about, but garlic isn't one of them.

Not only is Saturday night a good time to revel in garlic, but such intermissions as vacations can be similarly enjoyed if they are on the isolated side, such as a camping trip or a motor trip *à deux*. Many people do real garlic eating at such times.

A warning is due here, I feel. If you value your palate and wish to keep your taste buds inviolate, do not make constant practice of too heavy garlic seasoning, or any other kind for that matter. The most artistic seasoning, whether of herbs, condiments, garlic, or what, is the subtle sort — seasoning in which the various notes of flavor make themselves known as a beautiful ensemble. Such seasoning adds to the excellence of the food itself, instead of drowning the true flavor in other, extraneous tastes.

Thus it is with garlic. The person who constantly revels in a great deal of garlic, whether raw or cooked, builds for him or herself a taste-destroying habit. The taste buds on the tongue, which allow us to enjoy even the most delicate of flavors, can become so accustomed to strong tastes that they finally cease to detect and register light, subtle ones. Thus the pleasure of sophisticated eating is lost.

Here, then, are the recipes wherein there is a strong note of garlic. You know your lives better than I do. You have long ago found whether or not you can take it or leave it alone and how much your friends will or will not stand. If you are a conformist, you can purge these recipes by cutting the garlic content to 1 clove. If you are a crusader, stage a local garlic revolution. Rugged individualists will be able to take what comes. That is how they became rugged in the first place.

## Saturday Night Salad, with Garlic

A good green sald, of the sorts described in Chapter 7, is a good place to gratify a sudden, unbridled craving for the taste of garlic. Some people there are, I am told, who slice raw garlic in among the greens. Perhaps the less said of that the better. Myself, I like now and then the taste of a special salad dressing mixed up at least twenty-four hours before using, wherein several beans of garlic have lain, giving their all without stint, then discarded. This recipe provides enough dressing for several salads and keeps well. Do not refrigerate, as the oil congeals.

## The Dressing

1 *heaping teaspoon celery seed*
2 *tablespoons brown sugar*
1 *level teaspoon dry mustard*
¾ *cup red-wine vinegar*
1 *cup olive oil*
3 *cloves garlic slightly crushed*

*tops of 3 green onions minced*
1 *teaspoon wild marjoram (oregano)*
1 *teaspoon thyme*
*salt*
*black pepper*

In a mortar crush the celery seed well. If dried herbs are used pulverize them also in the mortar; green ones can be minced along with the onions. Mix sugar and mustard with vinegar, add oil, garlic and onions, and the herbs. Add salt and pepper to suit taste. Keep in a covered jar at least twenty-four hours before using, and shake or beat well before putting on the salad. The garlic is thrown away before the dressing is used.


## Garlic Bread Deluxe

This garlic bread is a fragrantly varied version of the regular thing and makes an outstanding accompaniment to a green salad. Also it does handsomely as an hors d'oeuvre. The recipe is used by courtesy of *Sunset Magazine* in which I previously printed it. Perhaps I should also say, while giving credit where credit is due, that it is a brainchild of my husband.

| | |
|---|---|
| 2 *small cloves garlic* | ⅛ *teaspoon salt* |
| 1 *tablespoon wild marjoram (oregano)* | ⅛ *teaspoon black pepper* |
| | 6 *thin slices Italian or* |
| 2 *tablespoons olive oil* | *sourdough French bread* |

In a mortar or a small heavy bowl mince the garlic and the marjoram (oregano) leaves if green. If dried marjoram (oregano) is used put in the whole leaves. Grind with the pestle or a small wooden muddler, and after they are well crushed together continue to grind, adding the oil bit by bit till it is all in. Add salt and pepper, mix well, and paint on the bread slices with a pastry brush. Put slices under the broiler until lightly brown but not hard and dry. Serve this bread at once while piping hot.


## Spinach and Rice Soup Saloniki

The vigorous flavor of garlic in thick hearty soups sounds a peasant note usually welcome to diners who know their cuisine. This soup is one that makes a meal if well dusted with good cheese and served with crusty bread and a noble green salad. The Greeks, who invented it, must have had a word for it, but since we do not know that word we just make it, give it a regional label, and enjoy it.

| | |
|---|---|
| 4 tablespoons olive oil | dash nutmeg |
| 3 cloves garlic minced | dash allspice |
| 1 large dry onion minced | 5 cups hot broth (pages |
| ¼ cup raw rice | 83–84), or 5 bouillon |
| 1 teaspoon fresh spear-mint minced | cubes dissolved in 5 cups boiling water |
| 1½ cups spinach leaves minced | ½ cup dry sherry wine |
| 3 green onions minced | croutons |
| ⅛ teaspoon black pepper | grated Italian cheese |

In a soup kettle or terrine heat the oil, add garlic and dry onion minced, and cook slowly for 10 minutes. Do not let brown. Add raw, unwashed rice, stir well, spread over bottom of kettle, and turn fire up a bit. Fry rice lightly, stirring often, by which time onion and garlic will be yellow. Add mint, spinach, and green onions, stir, cover kettle, and let simmer slowly for 10 minutes. Add pepper, spices, and broth. Simmer 15 minutes, or until rice grains are tender. Add wine; taste soup for salt seasoning, adding more if necessary. Take off heat and let stand 5 minutes covered. Turn into hot tureen, float croutons on top, and send to the table with a bowl of grated cheese. *4 servings*.

## Crushed Basil Sauce (*Pesto di basilico*)

While on the subject of garlic and soup, that revered Italian soup *minestrone* (pages 78 to 81) traditionally is crowned with a richly scented garlic and basil sauce called *pesto di basilico,* stirred into it just as it is readied for the table. No nobler experiment ever lived to become an unwritten law of regional cuisine. Besides being so good with soup, it is superb dressing for spaghetti or *tagliarini,* topping for broiled fish or steaks, sauce for string beans, or used in lieu of butter on baked potatoes. You may also discover, after you have eaten it and gone about your pursuits after pleasure, that it is very efficacious in getting seats on a crowded bus, or in the movies. However, it tastes fine.

| | |
|---|---|
| 3 *large peeled cloves garlic* | grated Parmesan or Romano cheese |
| 1 *cup chopped fresh sweet basil* | 3 *tablespoons olive oil (approximate)* |
| 3 *heaping tablespoons* | |

A mortar and pestle, or the alternative deep bowl and wooden muddler (not the same one used for your old-fashioneds, I beg of you!) are necessary for the making of this sauce. Into the mortar or bowl mince garlic. Pick the leaves from the stems of the basil, wash them, blot dry with a towel, and mince into the mortar enough to make ⅔ of a cup. With pestle or muddler grind basil and garlic well together, until it becomes a well-mixed green paste. Sprinkle in cheese, grinding with the pestle as you sprinkle. The result will be a somewhat hard ball. To this start adding oil bit by bit, mixing with pestle until you have a smooth paste somewhat the consistency of whipped cream. Three tablespoons of oil should do it, but if not add a bit more. The *pesto* is now ready to use, in any of these ways:

1. Cook ½ pound *tagliarini* or spaghetti as directed on pages 226 to 227. When drained, dress while hot with this *pesto* and serve at once.
2. Make the Italian vegetable soup from recipe on pages 78 to 81. Ten minutes before serving put into a tureen, float *pesto* on the top. Cover, let stand 10 minutes, then stir in well and serve.

3. Steam (page 288) green string beans until tender, then dress with enough *pesto* to make them a thin sauce. Serve hot.
4. Broil steaks, chops, or fish steaks, put a teaspoon of *pesto* on each, spread over the surface, and serve.
5. Bake potatoes in jackets, and when ready to serve slit, squeeze to open, and put a level teaspoon of *pesto* in each potato.
6. This is also good stirred into flaky, hot rice just before serving.

Now — to the meat, to the meat! For we Americans, even in the very act of honoring G.B.S. and his vegetarian cohorts, wonder at them, not understanding such apparently pointless denial. Meat, when priced reasonably, is the stuff of hungry Americans' dreams and the pivot of their meals. Meatless meals we do eat, omelettes, fish, and such, and are often surprised to find that when we must, we can thus be well nourished.

We've cooked meat with herbs and with nice little *sotto voce* touches of garlic elsewhere in this book. But there are those who want now and then a full *fortissimo* of flavor. This dish of lamb chops and rice, which is really a whole meal, vegetable and all, should fill the bill.

C   THYME

## Lamb Chops with Rice and Onions

| | |
|---|---|
| 4 shoulder or loin lamb chops | 4 large dry onions peeled and halved |
| *flour* | 2 cups hot broth (pages 83–84), or 2 cups boiling water and 2 bouillon cubes |
| *salt* | |
| *black pepper* | |
| 3 tablespoons olive oil | |
| ½ cup raw rice | ½ cup dry sherry wine |
| 3 cloves garlic minced | ⅓ teaspoon curry powder |
| 1½ teaspoons sweet marjoram | ½ cup chopped parsley |

First, select a cooking utensil not too deep and with plenty of "floor space" to spread the food out in. A large iron skillet or chicken fryer with cover would be perfect. Dip chops in salted and peppered flour. Heat oil in the iron utensil on the floor of a 500° oven, then in it brown the chops on one side. When they are done on one side turn them over; into the spaces among the chops scatter the raw rice and the minced garlic, stirring well in the oil and then spreading it about evenly. Finish browning the chops, stirring the rice occasionally so it will brown evenly at the same time. When the second side of the chops and the rice are golden, lay the onion halves among the chops on top of the rice. Mix hot broth (or bouillon cubes dissolved in hot water), marjoram, sherry, and curry powder, and pour this mixture carefully over the chops, rice, and onions.

From now on nothing is to be stirred. Reduce oven heat to 325°, leaving the utensil on the floor of the oven. Cover it closely and cook for three-quarters of an hour. Look occasionally, and if the moisture is all cooked away add from time to time about 2 or 3 tablespoons boiling water. Taste for salt when half done, adding more if necessary. Ten minutes before the rice and meat are done add chopped parsley, stirring it *lightly* with a fork into the rice. When done the liquid should have all cooked away, leaving the dry fluffy rice, delectably tender onions, and chops of miraculous flavor. Take up on hot plates, a chop in the center flanked by rice on one side and a piece of onion on the other. Behold, your "plate special." *4 servings.*

## Braised Flank Steak, Sandwich Style

There is braising and braising — braising with the meat on top, vegetables underneath; meat underneath, blanketed with the vegetables; and so on. But this flank steak is different from them all. It has vegetables in the middle, surrounded by the meat.

*1 large flank steak pounded*
*salt*
*black pepper*
*2 cloves garlic minced*
*2 onions sliced thin*
*1 large potato peeled and sliced*
*2 tablespoons sweet basil minced*
*flour*

*2 tablespoons lard or drippings*
*1 tablespoon olive oil*
*½ Japanese chile without seeds minced*
*1 cup celery leaves chopped*
*1 large tomato sliced*
*1 cup boiling water*

Wipe the meat with a damp cloth, then salt and pepper one side. Draw a mental line of demarcation across its width and treat one half of it thus: Scatter on it one of the minced garlic cloves; then arrange on it one of the sliced onions. Over the onion lay the potato slices; then top with a generous sprinkling of salt, some black pepper, and 1 tablespoon of the basil. Fold over this the other end of the steak and pin the edges together with metal skewers. You now have an affair that resembles a fat turnover, with meat in lieu of crust. Roll it in salted and peppered flour. Brown in hot lard or drippings in an iron Dutch oven on the floor of a 500° oven. When brown on both sides reduce the heat to 350°. On top of the "turnover" strew the remaining garlic, the Japanese chile, the rest of the basil, and salt and pepper. Arrange on these the other sliced onion, the celery leaves, and on top the tomato slices. Fasten these last on with skewers stuck diagonally through the meat. Pour boiling water around the meat, put on the lid, and cook on the floor of the oven at 350° for at least 2½ hours. About every 15 or 20 minutes baste with the liquid in the pan. If this boils away add 1½ cups boiling water. When done slice down through the "turnover" and serve the thick slices wet with a little of the gravy in the pan. 6 *servings*.

## Veal Tripe Florentine (*Trippa di vitella fiorentina*)

Every now and then one of the uninitiated asks me what tripe tastes like. That is a question to which there is no really sensible answer, for tripe doesn't taste like anything except tripe, and that brings us right back to the starting place. To those who like tripe, and I am one, it is delicious in several ways, all of them paradoxical. For instance, it is somewhat peppery, yet it is mild. It has a definite texture, still it is soft. See? But whatever else one may say of tripe, it is not flat. Rather is it full of personality, a delicate feast — something worth learning to cook and eat. Tripe is just tripe, and nothing for which to apologize.

This tripe recipe is a traditional, regional Italian one, combining the sympathetic flavors of herbs and garlic. The macaroni adds to its heartiness as a main dish.

| | |
|---|---|
| 1 *pound tripe, half plain and half honeycomb* | 1 *carrot sliced* |
| | 1 *stick celery with leaves* |
| 3 *onions* | 2 *whole cloves* |

2 *tablespoons olive oil*
1 *tablespoon butter*
2 *slices raw bacon*
2 *or 3 cloves garlic minced*
1 *teaspoon wild marjoram*
  *(oregano)*
½ *cup dry sauterne wine,*
  *or ¼ cup sherry or Ma-*
  *deira*
2 *bouillon cubes*

½ *cup boiling water*
3 *tablespoons tomato*
  *sauce, or 1 tablespoon to-*
  *mato paste, or 1 large,*
  *ripe, peeled tomato cut*
  *fine*
¼ *pound Italian pasta,* tri-
  angoli *or seashells*
grated Romano or Parmesan
cheese

First be sure the tripe has been precooked by the butcher.
Wash it well and cook it in salted boiling water to cover, together with 1 of the onions, sliced, carrot, cut-up celery, and
cloves. Boil 30 minutes, then lift the tripe from the liquid,
cool, and cut with kitchen shears into "fingers" about 2
inches long and 1 inch wide. It should be tender, but if not,
cook longer until it is.

In a large, heavy saucepan or French terra-cotta casserole
heat and mix oil and butter; then add raw bacon cut in small
pieces. Fry until bacon is crisp. Add minced garlic and marjoram (oregano) and cook slowly 10 minutes; then add the
other 2 onions cut into rings and cook 10 minutes more. Put
in the well-drained tripe fingers, stir well, and cook 10 minutes. Add wine, stir well, and cook 5 minutes briskly to evap-
orate the alcohol. Meanwhile dissolve the bouillon cubes in
boiling water and add tomato sauce, paste, or tomato. Put this
mixture in with the tripe, stir well, cover, and cook slowly
1 hour. Stir well several times during the period, and when
half done taste for salt, adding some if necessary. The
bouillon cubes supply quite a bit of salt. The tripe should
now be quite tender. When ready to serve weigh out the
pasta, throw into a kettle of rapidly boiling salted water, and
cook until tender. Drain thoroughly, add to the tripe, and stir
well. Take from the fire, let stand 5 minutes, and serve with
the grated cheese. *4 servings.*

Good red wine, a green salad with cooked vegetables in it, and your dinner is before you. Eat it and sigh, like Othello:

". . . Perdition catch my soul
But I do love thee!"

## Steamed Clams Bordelaise

Steamed clams, if you have enough of them and serve them with lots of hot garlicked bread and a good green salad, with fruit and cheese for dessert, make a grand supper. The diners must be clam devotees, else they will keep wondering when you are going to take away the hors d'oeuvres and bring in the main dish! But the seasoned clam eater knows that nothing more is needed but elbow room and a go signal. From 15 to 20 clams to each diner are ample.

Live clams are used for steaming, and each clam must be tested to be sure it is alive. First, all clams with open shells must be discarded, for we know they have given up the ghost. Put all clams with closed shells into a pan of cold water. Pick up two clams, one in each hand, and rap them together. If they give out a dull thud like two rocks being knocked together they are alive; but the clam that gives out a hollow sound is dead and must be discarded. Using the live one for a tester, pick up another from the pan, rap it against the tester, and keep or discard as the occasion demands. Test all clams this way, so that only live ones remain.

30 *live clams in their shells*    3 *tablespoons olive oil*
½ *cup chopped parsley*    *black pepper*
3 *cloves garlic chopped*

Scrub the shells under cold running water with a stiff brush to remove all the sand. In a kettle with a wide bottom arrange the clams in layers. Sprinkle over the top the parsley, garlic, and olive oil. Add ½ cup water, cover tightly, and steam about 12 minutes, or until shells are partly open. Then add a generous sprinkling of black pepper

Serve the clams in individual soup dishes, with side dishes of the clam liquor in wide-mouthed glasses so that the clams, picked from their shells with fish forks, can be dipped in the broth before eating. Finally the broth is drunk. Lots of paper napkins are needed, and someplace to deposit empty shells. *2 servings.*

## Fried Potatoes with Garlic and Rosemary

One of my secret desires is to live long enough for some unparalleled mind to invent a de-caloried potato. A potato is so packed with delicacy and desirability, but also loaded with potential corpulence. Sometimes I find myself wondering whether the struggle is really worthwhile. Usually I decide it is, and we ration ourselves accordingly. But sometimes a demon possesses me, and I throw caution to the winds and fry potatoes with garlic and rosemary. I peel and peel, and fry and fry — an amount that must be dictated by a devil, not by any guardian angel of our figures. And then the combination of garlic, rosemary, and potatoes being what it is, we eat and eat — and you can guess the rest.

If you are svelte and elegant, or if you just don't care, try these. This recipe will give a nice, polite serving to 4 people. However, I must confess it doubles well, or even trebles:

| | |
|---|---|
| 3 *large raw potatoes* | *salt* |
| 4 *tablespoons olive oil* | *black pepper* |
| 3 *large cloves garlic minced* | ⅓ *Japanese chile without* |
| 2-*inch sprig rosemary or 1* | *seeds cut up* |
| *teaspoon dried* | |

Peel the potatoes, dry them well, and slice medium thin. Have the oil in an iron skillet bubbling hot and put in enough potatoes to cover the bottom. Wrap the rest in a wet towel to keep white. Scatter the garlic and the rosemary leaves, salt, pepper, and chile over the potatoes, and stir well. Cook quickly until the first batch of potatoes is well browned on both sides; then push them to one side in the pan, add another layer of potatoes, and stir well. Let cook, push over with the first pile, and proceed until all the potatoes are browned and tender. Drain all on a paper towel and serve very hot. The secret is not to put too many potatoes in at one time, and to cook them quickly. *4 servings*.

## Bordelaise Sauce for Steaks or Chops

This Bordelaise is for out-and-outers. Of course, an emasculated version of the divine sauce can be made by leaving out the garlic and using instead a small pinch of powdered garlic. Here is the unadulterated recipe. Do with it as you will:

2 *to 3 cloves chopped raw garlic*
½ *teaspoon rosemary minced*
1 *teaspoon wild marjoram (oregano)*
1 *teaspoon thyme*

2 *tablespoons butter*
1 *tablespoon olive oil*
2 *tablespoons grated Italian cheese*
⅛ *teaspoon salt*
⅛ *teaspoon cayenne pepper*

Use a mortar and pestle or a small deep bowl and a wooden muddler. In the mortar put the minced garlic and the minced herbs (pulverized if dried). Grind thoroughly with the pestle. Then add the butter and grind again until thoroughly mixed. Add oil and stir in with a spoon. Then add cheese, salt, and cayenne pepper and mix well. Spread on steak or chops that have just come from the broiler. Dip thin slices of French bread in the pan drippings, spread on them a little of the sauce, and serve with the meat.

## Garlic Dill Pickles

One spring evening years ago we visited at a country home in Oregon. When conversation had whetted our appetites to a keen edge the host and hostess served us with a supper of kippered salmon in pick-up-able slices, rye bread, cheese, beer, and these garlic dill pickles, with the garlic left in. The memory is one of the gastronomical high points of my life. The little cucumbers were delicious, and the halved cloves of garlic as crisp as the day they were born. Of course the garlic was to be eaten, not just looked at. This is how those pickles were made:

| | |
|---|---|
| *small, tender cucumbers* | *1 cup salt* |
| *1 quart cider vinegar* | *heads of fresh dill* |
| *3 quarts water* | *cloves garlic peeled* |

Wash the cucumbers and fill pint jars with them. Mix vinegar, water, and salt, and bring to a boil. In each jar among the cucumbers scatter 3 heads of dill and several garlic cloves cut in half. Cover with boiling vinegar and water. Seal jars while hot. These can be used in 2 or 3 weeks.

Well, there they are, in all their unorthodox fragrance. I hope you like them, and I hope you still continue to make the Blue Book. If not, perhaps your gustatory pleasures will make limbo supportable.

Remember, I beg, that a clove of garlic is merely one of the segments that go to make up a whole bulb of garlic.

There was once a woman who confused this matter, and in a recipe calling for a clove she put one entire bulb. I'd rather not discuss the results.

It would be hypocritical to pretend that in our house we always use garlic daintily and sparingly. Usually we are mindful of the other folks in the world and use it wisely. But now and then, circumstances permitting and the mood being mad, we cook a "Saturday night dish" and really enjoy it. Then we stay at home the next day.

Go, and do thou likewise.

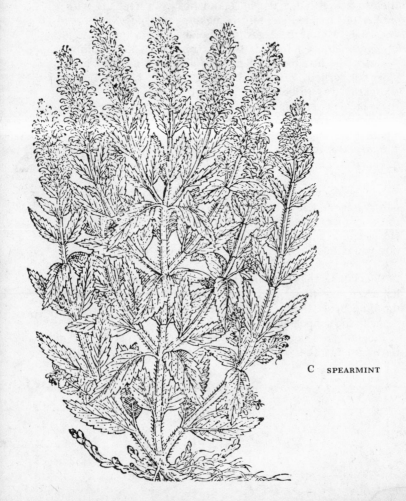

C   SPEARMINT

# ❧ FIFTEEN ❧

## Just Conceits

REMEMBER Grandmother's catchall? It might have been the closet under the stairs, or the smallest storehouse on the place. Perhaps it was only a big chest behind the front bedroom door. But every home had to have a catchall for odds and ends that were too good to throw away.

This chapter is the catchall of the book. As the writing has gone on about salads, meats, rice, and the rest, bits of information have had to be laid aside because they did not fit under the various chapter headings. Yet they are good bits, far too important to leave out entirely. So into the catchall they are going, for you to pull out and dust off when you find use for them.

D   TARRAGON

## SAUCES

First of all, here is a sheaf of recipes for sauces of various kinds. Not enough for a whole chapter, but enough to supply zest for your foods.

### English Mint Chutney Sauce

2 tablespoons dry mustard
2 tablespoons salt
1 pound sugar
2 small white onions
½ pound seeded raisins
1 pound tart apples chopped
½ pound ripe tomatoes chopped
1 dozen small red peppers seeded and chopped
good handful spearmint leaves chopped finely
2 quarts wine vinegar

Mix all these ingredients except the vinegar together well in an earthenware crock and over them pour wine vinegar (either white or red), which has been boiled and cooled. This will keep without sealing. Serve with roast lamb.

### Tarragon Sauce

1 cup mayonnaise
1 tablespoon finely minced tarragon
1 tablespoon tomato catsup
1 pimiento minced
1 green pepper minced
1 teaspoon chives minced

Mix well and serve in sauceboat. For fish or cold meats.

## Herb Mustard Sauce

4  tablespoons *mayonnaise*
2  tablespoons *prepared*
   *mustard*
1  teaspoon *minced chives*
1  teaspoon *minced chervil*

½  teaspoon *minced spear-*
   *mint, tarragon, thyme,*
   *or basil*
dash *cayenne pepper*

For artichokes, cold meats, cold vegetables.


## Vinaigrette Sauce

*red-wine vinegar*
*olive oil*
*salt*
*black pepper*
½  teaspoon *paprika*

1  teaspoon *minced shallots*
1  tablespoon *parsley*
   *chopped very finely*
1  teaspoon *basil*

Make a French dressing (pages 155–156) with 3 parts red-wine vinegar and 1 part olive oil, salt, and black pepper to taste, and add to it the paprika, shallots, parsley, and basil. Here again other herbs may be substituted for basil, according to the individual taste. For cold fowl or meats.


## Sauce for Roast Lamb

1  cup *red currant jelly*
½  teaspoon *grated orange*
   *rind*

½  teaspoon *chopped spear-*
   *mint*

Melt jelly in a double boiler, cool slightly, and to it add orange rind and spearmint. Let stand until thoroughly cool before using.

## Sweet Mustard

4 tablespoons brown sugar        ½ teaspoon chopped tarra-
3 tablespoons dry mustard        gon
tarragon vinegar (page 339)

Blend sugar and mustard. Bring vinegar to boil and add just
enough of it to make a smooth paste. Put into a jar and seal
while hot. Put away for 2 weeks, then it is ready to use. Mix
in the fresh tarragon before serving. For ham or tongue.

## Green Sauce

1 cup chopped parsley              or rosemary and oregano
½ cup chopped chervil           1 shallot minced with tops,
½ cup mixed green herbs           or ⅓ cup chopped chives
   such as basil and thyme,     1 cup mayonnaise

Mix the green herbs, add a little cold water or, preferably, a
little of the vinegar from a jar of sweet pickles. Grind the
herbs with the liquid in a mortar very thoroughly. Put
through a strainer that is fine enough to catch the pulp,
draining the green juice into the mayonnaise. For cold crab
or lobster, or cold meats.

## Herb Garnishes

With the lovely wealth of green herbs to choose from,
those with herb gardens need no longer wave only the parsley's fronds before diners' eyes. Pick tips from your other
herbs and decorate your food with imagination.

## Horehound Candy

Have you ever eaten *real* horehound candy — the dark brown kind with a bittersweet taste? The kind made from an infusion of freshly cut herbs gleaned in out-of-the-way corners? It was supposed to be used for coughs, but often it made its appearance without this time-honored excuse, and did as much good, or at least gave as much pleasure. For it is good. You can make it, if you grow a patch of silvery horehound, or if you watch the country roadsides for its flash of argent hue.

| | |
|---|---|
| *1 quart horehound leaves* | *3 cups sugar* |
| *and stems* | *a piece of butter the size of* |
| *2½ cups water* | *an egg* |

Make a strong decoction of horehound by boiling the leaves and stems in the water for ½ hour. Add sugar. Boil up, and add butter. Continue boiling until the syrup, in cold water, makes a "hard ball." Pour into a buttered shallow pan, and when cool mark into squares. Let harden, separate, and wrap each square in waxed paper.

## CHEESE

When men long ago stumbled on the secret of cheese-making, they provided themselves with a food that was a godsend to them, and besides has surely given pleasure and health to their progeny for all generations since.

We Americans were once inclined to give cheese a too-small place in our national dietary. We served it in grudging slivers with pie, shaved it tissue-thin to eat as hors d'oeuvres. But cheese as "the meat of the people" we knew not. But today we know cheese as a complete and delicious protein food. It is served often and variously, as a recognized and loved meat substitute.

Across the world today marches a parade of cheeses, each with a different face, a different character. All are good, and to the person who takes the trouble to explore among their multiplicity of tastes, rich and satisfying adventure offers itself. There is Brie, with its runny warmth of flavor; Camembert, its equally delightful cousin; Edam, salty and delicious, wearing a red coat; Swiss, pretty fine eating in spite of its hiatuses; Roquefort, nurtured in a dark, dank cave, and coming out a veritable butterfly of a cheese; Gorgonzola, the Italian half-sister of Roquefort, and thought by many to be her superior; Limburger, ablest nose-assaulter of them all, but delicious nonetheless; Romano, best for grating, and equally good for eating; Parmesan, Romano's milder compatriot; Kumminost, pale yellow and jeweled with caraway seeds; and many, many more. For the roster of cheeses is inexhaustible.

The most primitive of cheese is simple curd — which we term "cottage cheese." Our own kind, or the Italian version, called ricotta, may be made into delightful pot cheese for tea or for salad accompaniment, if herb tips are minced into it.

## Pot Cheese with Herbs

1 pound cottage cheese or ricotta
1 teaspoon minced chives
¼ teaspoon each: poppy seeds, caraway seeds, sesame seeds
salt

black pepper
paprika
2 tablespoons cream
1 teaspoon olive oil
1 small sprig each: marjoram, basil, thyme, sage

Mix all ingredients well, put into a small crock with a cover, and let stand at least 1 hour before using.

This may be served spread on Swedish flatbread as hors d'œuvres, with thin bread and butter for tea, or in balls on the plates with green salad.

## Pears and Cheese

Two kindred souls that should never be sent forth from the kitchen without each other are pears and cheese. Tuscans say knowingly that one should never tell the peasants how good pears and cheese are together, for then they will eat up all the cheese, and there will be none for the townsfolk!

So when hunger calls, or when the end of a good meal wants for a fitting finale, heap a plate with plump pale golden pears, and serve them with slices of fine cheese.

## Cheese and Wine

Cheese and wine and crusty bread — that is food. Add a plate of fruit, and know luxury that can be a whole meal. But pick the right wine, for that is important. With Camembert, Brie, Roquefort, and such soft cheeses, red Burgundy or Bordeaux is preferred; with Swiss a dry white wine. The cheeses of Italy, such as Gorgonzola, Romano, Bel Paese and such call for Chianti, either white or red, according to taste.

## TEA

How trite to say "the cup that cheers." Yet, to the seasoned tea drinker, no other beverage so lifts the fainting spirit as this golden draught. "Fragrant essence of the East," one writer calls it, and further says that "tea comforts more millions of humanity than any other stimulant on earth." It is a friendly beverage, and one that can be taken day after day without satiety.

This is an herb book, and you may wonder what herbs have to do with tea. Plenty — for an afternoon cup of tea, through the aid of herbs and such subtle seasonings, can become an exquisite liquid that banishes taste monotony.

## Rosy Tea

Into the pot with the dry tea put 1 leaf of rose geranium and 2 cloves. Add boiling water, let infuse as usual, then drain from herbs and spices.

## Minted Green Tea

Into the pot with dry green tea put 1 sprig spearmint, and infuse as usual. After 5 minutes remove the mint and serve the tea.

## Lemon Mint Tea

Into the pot with green tea put 1 small sprig spearmint and 1 of lemon verbena. Infuse and remove before serving.

## Orange Tea

No herbs here, but an extra special flavor, the secret of which must be passed on.

Into the pot when making tea grate a teaspoon of orange rind (to 6 cups of water), and infuse as usual. Strain when pouring.

## *Finnish Tea*

Now the demon Rum rears his ugly head, and sticks it into the tea pot, with commendable results. This occurs every day in Finland, so don't be afraid of it.

To each serving of hot tea add 1 teaspoon sugar, a little lemon juice, and a teaspoon of rum. Serve in glasses. Or if you are not a sweetened tea enthusiast, use just the rum.

## Tisanes

Tisane — doesn't that sound exotic? Anything with such a beautiful name should be at least ten dollars a pint. But actually tisane is nothing more than the French name for the old-fashioned drinks we call "herb teas." Yet they are valuable, for they soothe jangled nerves, American as well as Continental, and summon Morpheus in very short order. Perhaps a cup of hot water would do as well, but who wants to drink hot water when one may have a tisane?

Use green or dried herbs for these teas, and brew them not just five minutes as one does tea, but half an hour for dried herbs, fifteen minutes for green.

## *Tisane of Spearmint*

For each cup of hot water pick four sprigs spearmint. Wash them, bruise them, and infuse them for 15 minutes. Drain, serve with or without sugar as you wish.

## *Tisane of Spearmint and Lemon Balm*

Fresh herbs make this one also — 3 tips of mint and 1 of balm for each cup of water. Infused with a curl of orange and lemon peel for 15 minutes, it is a sweet and refreshing blend.

## Other Tisanes

Present-day herbalists, in common with our ancestors, recommend tisanes for their medicinal effect. A tea of lime flowers, for instance, is said to be calming. Camomile flowers are a digestive aid. Elder flowers minister to a cold, while borage flowers are very warming.

Here's a rich field for fascinating research, with material galore, for anyone in quest of a hobby! But in case you want to do it the easy way, gourmet markets these days very often offer packets of ready-mixed tisanes, labeled "herb tea." Many are imported from Switzerland.

All through this book the herbs have been in the kitchen. They do so handsomely there that it seems a shame to bring them out. But out they must come for a time, for herbs are sweet additions to daily living in every room in the house.

## *HOUSE FRAGRANCE*

An herb garden, a rose garden, and a few spices — they can be just an herb garden, a rose garden, and spices. Or they can be the means of bringing into your house the fragrance of your summer garden, and keeping it for your use and delight the whole year through.

## Rose Jars and Potpourri

Rose leaves, scented flowers, herb leaves, and blossoms, together with exotic scenting agents and fixatives from far lands, all combine to fill jars with sweet goods, and rooms with their fragrance. We can all make them if we have gardens, or even kind friends with gardens.

First to accomplish in making rose jars and potpourri is drying the flowers and herbs: Pick rose petals from scented roses on a dry morning when the sun is warm. Spread them on cardboard box covers in a warm room to dry, turning them every few hours the first day, twice the second day, once each day thereafter until they are thoroughly dry. All pretty and fragrant flowers and all herbs may also be used. Keep each kind separate for blending later.

Then, to mix the potpourri:

| | |
|---|---|
| 3 or 4 quarts dried petals of roses and other flowers | 1 teaspoon gum benzoin pounded |
| dried herbs | 1 teaspoon cloves |
| 1 grain musk | 1 teaspoon cinnamon |
| 10 drops oil of rose gera- nium | 1 teaspoon allspice |
| 4 drops oil of bergamot | ½ cup orris root |
| | 1 cup salt |
| | ½ cup brandy |

Fragrant oils and gums can be ordered from that old and beautiful pharmacy Caswell-Massey, Inc., 518 Lexington Avenue (at 48th Street), New York. Their catalogue is fascinating reading, and practical too. To obtain one, write to 320 West 13th Street, New York, New York 10014.

Match your rose-leaf bulk with a mixture of herbs, and add a quarter of the same bulk of other dried flowers. Add musk, oil of rose geranium, oil of bergamot, gum benzoin, cloves, cinnamon, and allspice. Then add orris root and salt.

Moisten with brandy, mix well, and put into jars. Cover tightly and set aside 6 months before using.

This is a representative recipe. It may be varied by using only rose leaves, or only herbs, or only rose leaves and lavender flowers. Or rose geranium, lemon verbena, and lavender make a good combination. In any case, use the spices, and the oil of any scents you wish to emphasize, such as rose geranium, lemon verbena, lavender, rosemary, jasmine, or what you will.

Make several different types of jars. Have one in each room, and open them when you wish to perfume the rooms. They will last for years, if moistened with a little brandy twice a year, and kept covered between times when not in use.

## Sweet Bags for Linens

Sweet herbs blend in endless variety for sweet bags, making one glad to open linen presses, just for a whiff of their scent. Proportions are optional. Let the herb you like best predominate, with others playing a soft accompaniment. Dry them as for potpourri, then blend, and sew into closely woven silk or muslin bags.

## Wine Vinegar

Do you have an evil time securing wine vinegars that are not too thin and acid? Why not make your own? It is no trick at all.

Buy a gallon of unpasteurized wine. This must be obtained from a winery or from a friend who is his own wine maker. Choose claret or sauterne according to whether red or white vinegar is desired. Save the "mother" from your next bottle of store vinegar and pour it into the gallon jug. Remove the cork and over the opening of the bottle tie a bit of gauze. Set the jug away in a dark, warm place, such as under the kitchen sink, and forget all about it for 4 or 5 months. It will be full of the best vinegar, rich of flavor and not too strong. If you haven't any "mother" from other vinegar to start it with, it will eventually form its own, but it takes a little longer. Just possess your soul with patience, and wait a while more. In case you are wondering what on earth a "mother" is, it is a coagulated mass of yeast and bacteria cells, which actually grows in the wine, malt, or cider liquid and chemically turns them into vinegar. It is beneficial, and not something to worry over.

## Herbal Vinegars

The whole subject of flavored vinegars is fascinating, for it is one of the best ways of using herbs in essence. Vinegar has a genius for drawing from fresh herbs all their goodness, and preserving it as wondrously sweet liquids. Today, thank Fortune, we can find on grocery shelves bottles of "Mint Vinegar," "Mixed Herb Vinegar," and the rest, as well as "Tarragon Vinegar." For apartment dwellers who have no gardens of their own, such vinegars are a wealth of flavor.

Herb vinegars are heavenly benison for green salads. They are easily made, and even more easily used.

## Tarragon Vinegar

| | |
|---|---|
| *1 pint tarragon leaves* | *2 cloves* |
| *1 pint wine vinegar, heated* | *1 clove garlic halved* |

Crush tarragon leaves slightly with the hands. Add vinegar, cloves, and garlic. Cover and let stand. After 24 hours take out the garlic, then let stand 14 days more. After that strain and press through a cloth. Bottle and cork tightly.

## Garlic Vinegar

| | |
|---|---|
| ¼ pound peeled and bruised cloves garlic | 10 peppercorns |
| 1 teaspoon salt | 1 teaspoon caraway seeds |
| 5 cloves | 1 quart hot wine vinegar |

Put garlic cloves into a jar with a cover. Add salt, and the seasonings, pounded in a mortar. Add vinegar, let stand 1 week, then strain and bottle, corking well.

## Other Herb Vinegars

Spearmint, or any other of the culinary herbs, may be put into vinegar as in Tarragon Vinegar (page 339). Or a mixture of herbs may be used. It is clever kitchen engineering to keep on hand several different kinds, so you may season with the sauce of variety.

## Herb Brandy

Those clever French chefs make herb essences with brandy that are perfect additions to gravies and soups at the moment of serving. Or a few drops scattered charily over broiled meats as they go to the table are irresistible incense.

For a mixed herb brandy:

| | |
|---|---|
| 1 cup each of several fresh herbs | 1 additional cup each of same herbs, 1 week later |
| 1 quart brandy | |

Mix and crush in the hands fresh herbs such as thyme, rosemary, marjoram, mint, and any other of the sweet herbs you may wish. On them pour brandy. Leave 1 week, then strain.

Start anew with another lot of the same herbs, and again leave the brandy on them a week. Strain, bottle in small bottles for use, keeping all tightly corked.

## Seasoned French Bread

¼ *pound butter*
½ *teaspoon paprika*

2 *tablespoons parsley finely minced*
1 *long loaf French bread*

Cream the butter, paprika, and parsley. Slice the French bread in 1½-inch-thick slices, slicing almost all the way through but leaving the slices still connected at the underside of the loaf. Spread the butter mixture between the slices. Slide the loaf into a paper bag and bake in a 350° oven until the bag begins to brown. Remove loaf from bag to hot platter, and pass, letting each person break off his or her own slice.

## Savory or Sage Biscuits

Make your chicken shortcakes with these biscuits, and know their utmost in flavor.

Follow your favorite recipe for biscuits, and with the dry ingredients sift ½ teaspoon of powdered savory or sage. Make up the biscuits as usual, bake them, then split them and top with creamed chicken. Creamed veal also may be used with equal effect.

## Curry Biscuits for Creamed Shrimp

Proceed as in preceding recipe, substituting for the herb powder 1 teaspoon curry powder. Serve with creamed shrimp or stewed lamb with thickened gravy.

If Naples had never done another thing for the world save to introduce the incomparable *pizza Napolitana,* it would still be a great and noble city for that one service to mankind. For this pizza, an oversized tart savory with anchovies, tomatoes, and seasoning, is superb food.

One of the best things about this food is that, while it is a specialty such as one might expect to find only in the finest restaurants, it is possible to make it at home. And the goodness of pizza is recompense enough for the effort of its making. Or, if you are tempted to just substitute ready-made pizza from the local pizzeria or pizza palace (*sic*), please resist. This that I offer is the original Neapolitan pizza of blessed memory. It was the parent pizza, from which descended all those multiform modern versions, some of which are good, but all too often are just "stews in an undignified position."

## *Pizza Dough*

Make a raised bread dough as follows:

| | |
|---|---|
| 2 *cups boiling water* | 1 *cake yeast, dissolved in* |
| 2 *tablespoons shortening* | ½ *cup lukewarm water* |
| 2 *tablespoons sugar* | 6 *cups unsifted flour* |
| 2½ *teaspoons salt* | |

Pour boiling water over the shortening, sugar, and salt in a large bowl without a lip. Mix well, and let stand until lukewarm. Add dissolved yeast and 5 cups of the flour, and stir until thoroughly mixed. The dough should be as soft as possible to work on the board. Turn onto a floured board, leaving the bowl clean of dough. Knead until the mixture is smooth, elastic to the touch, and has bubbles showing under the surface. Place the dough in a greased bowl, cover with a cloth, and let stand in a 70° to 80° temperature until it has doubled its bulk — about 1½ or 2 hours. Then cut through with a knife several times, and toss onto the board. Take off a piece about the size of a grapefruit, and roll and slap it out into a round the size of a pie tin and about ½ inch thick. Place in an oiled pan. Prepare all the dough in this way — it will make several rounds — and put each in a pan. Then dress their tops as follows:

## Pizza Topping

24 anchovy fillets in oil,
   each cut into 3 pieces
 1 clove garlic finely minced
contents of a No. 2½ can of
   solid-pack tomatoes,
   drained of juice, and
   picked into small pieces

1 heaping teaspoon of wild
   marjoram (oregano),
   pulverized if dried, minced
   if green
salt
black pepper

With one anchovy fillet smear the oil from the anchovies all over the tops of the rounds of dough. Then strew over them first the garlic, then the tomatoes, taking care that they are not put on solidly, but merely scattered thinly. Sprinkle with marjoram (oregano), then with salt and pepper.

Have the oven heated to 450°, and bake the pizza in it until done, about 10 to 12 minutes.

To serve, cut in wedge-shaped pieces and eat while hot as an hors d'œuvre, or with a salad. Any left over may be re-heated, if a little olive oil is sprinkled over the top to freshen it.

## Friselline (wine cookies)

These delicate anise-scented cookies are crisp and almond-studded, and are the veriest perfection with a glass of good wine for company. Wise people, emulating Anne of Austria, dip them in the wine, and realize full enjoyment. The elegant, perhaps, do otherwise.

7 *eggs*
1 *cup sugar*
2 *teaspoons brandy mixed with 1½ teaspoons anisette extract, or 4 teaspoons liqueur anisette*

6½ *cups flour (measured before sifting)*
½ *teaspoon salt*
1½ *teaspoons baking powder*
1 *cup of almonds peeled and sliced*

Beat together the eggs and sugar until they foam. Add either brandy and extract or the anisette. Sift flour, add salt and baking powder. Add these dry ingredients to egg mixture a little at a time. The dough should be of a consistency for kneading. Turn out on the board, and work the almonds into it. Work it into a shape like an overgrown cucumber, put it into an oiled pan, and bake at 350° until a toothpick or cake tester will come out clean. Remove from oven, turn out again on the board, and while it is hot cut with a sharp knife into inch-thick slices. Lay these in oiled pans and return to oven for about 3 minutes. Take out and let cool.

Keep these wine cookies in a tin box. They last well, if you can hide them from the family. Mine knows all the hiding places.

## Stuffed Eggs Deluxe

FOR EACH 2 EGGS:
1 *heaping tablespoon Roquefort cheese*
½ *teaspoon horseradish mustard*

½ *teaspoon chives or onion tops*
½ *teaspoon thyme*
*salt*
*black pepper*
*paprika*

Boil eggs hard, then peel, split lengthwise, and remove yolks. Add to yolks Roquefort cheese, mustard, chives or onion tops, thyme, and salt and pepper to taste. Blend, then fill the egg whites with the mixture. Top with a bit of paprika.

# DRINKS

Alcoholic beverages are so mixed up with antiquity that every drinking practice is steeped in unguessed tradition. For instance, when you roll glibly off your tongue a reference to "the hair of the dog that bit you," do you suspect the hoariness of the phrase? Whatever its actual origin, it is quoted in Athenaeus's "Banquet of the Learned," which proves its relative age:

> Take the hair, it well is written,
> Of the dog by whom you're bitten.
> Work off one wine by his brother,
> And one labour with another.

Along with drinks in history went herbs, for the custom of flavoring beverages with sweet herbs was once prevalent. Today nothing remains to us but the celebrated julep, frosty and fresh with mint, and those sweet and dry vermouths, which owe their flavors to herb combinations. To the drinker who cares for the flavor of herbs, however, other old-fashioned potables still will carry their savor with grace.

## Old-Fashioned Cocktail with Costmary

Follow your own recipe for old-fashioneds, but make them up before you are to serve them, and into them put 2 leaves of crushed costmary for each cocktail. Let stand in the refrigerator half an hour, then drain and serve.

## Claret Cup

*peel of 1 lemon*                    *1  quart claret*
*several tender sprigs borage*       *sugar*
*several sprigs balm*                *1  bottle seltzer water*
*5  ounces sherry wine*

Put thinly peeled lemon rind in a bowl, add herbs, cover with sherry, and bruise well with muddler or pestle. Add claret, sweeten to taste, and let stand in refrigerator several hours. Strain, add seltzer, and serve on shaved ice.

## Sauterne Cup

In a large bowl, using only 6 of the spearmint sprigs, mix:

*2  oranges sliced*              *½  cucumber sliced un-*
*juice 2 lemons*                      *peeled*
*4  cups tea infusion*           *4  tablespoons sugar*
*12  sprigs spearmint*           *6  whole strawberries*

Stand in the refrigerator 1 hour, then strain into a large glass pitcher. Sink in it 6 fresh sprigs spearmint, 6 whole strawberries with stems, and a large slice cucumber rind. Pour in enough iced sauterne to fill the pitcher. Let stand 10 minutes more in refrigerator, then strain over shaved ice and serve.

C    VALERIAN

## Lemonade with Herbs

A simple lemonade becomes intriguing when served in company with green herbs.

Make your lemonade to suit your taste. Several hours before you are to serve it, put in, together with the squeezed lemon peels, several sprigs fresh spearmint and several leaves of costmary, in a large pitcher. Let stand in refrigerator until ready to serve. Strain and serve.

## Spearmint in Water Ice

| | |
|---|---|
| 1 cup sugar | ⅛ cup lemon juice |
| ½ cup water | 2 teaspoons fresh spear- |
| 1 cup orange juice | mint chopped |

Boil sugar and water together 10 minutes, then add juices. Cool, stir in mint, and freeze. This is an ideal summer's day dessert.

# WINE IN FOOD

The first cook who tilted a wine bottle over a bubbling kettle is lost in the fogs that cover the gates of history. But his or her name, whatever it may have been, is blessed many and many times each day. For wine in food supplies that final touch of flavor that spells finished excellence. A soup for supper is a gratefully received dish. But dash that soup, before serving, with sherry, and know what true gratitude can be. Veal *en ragoût* thrills the diner. But let that veal be cooked *en ragoût* with a moistening of dry sauterne, and the diner thanks Fortune for one adventurous cook.

## Cooking Wines

To think of using a bottle of vintage wine in cookery is going to hurt the feelings of a thrifty cook and budgeteer. Nor can we blame that cook, particularly since the use of vintage wines or any very expensive wines is not necessary to good cookery. Humble wines, those which will come into our kitchens for a small price, if their flavor is good can give food as much flavor as a flagon of *Château Carbonnieux* or its fellows. Even the lees of the wine may be confidently emptied into the pot, for they carry the true taste as surely as the clear liquor from the top of the bottle.

## Which Wines for Which Foods?

Though you may safely be broad-minded about the quality of your cooking wine, you must never be wrong when choosing the kind of wine to use for any dish. That does not mean that you must master those subtle differentiations that make wine connoisseurs the envy and despair of the rest of the world. It does not mean cudgeling your brain to decide whether to use a Graves or a Bordeaux for the roast. On the contrary, it will mean only knowing whether dry or sweet, white or red, wine is called for. Actually, it is enough to suit your own taste, if you have definite preferences.

"Red wines for red meats (beef, lamb, venison), and for brown sauces; white wines for white meats (veal, pork, hare, fowl) and for white sauces" is a rule that usually holds. Since there must be exceptions or it is no good rule, do not be surprised to find recipes calling for red wine in chicken, sherry with pork, champagne with ham!

## Ham Steaks with Sherry

Lay steaks in a flat pan, sprinkle with a small amount of brown sugar, barely cover with dry sherry, and bake slowly until tender. If the sherry cooks away add a bit more.

## Onion Soup with Brandy

| | |
|---|---|
| *1 large onion per person* | *1 tablespoon cream per person* |
| *1 tablespoon butter per person* | *1 tablespoon brandy per person* |
| *1½ cups bouillon per person* | *1 slice dry toast per person* |
| *salt* | *1 tablespoon grated Parmesan cheese per person* |
| *black pepper* | |

Slice onions thin and cook for 15 minutes in melted butter, cooking slowly so that they do not brown. Add bouillon and salt and pepper to taste. Cook until onions are very tender — about ½ hour. Add cream, and at last minute brandy. Lay toast in dish, pour soup over it, sprinkle with cheese, and serve.

More wine-flavored dishes will be found in the index under that heading. If you like them, try others for yourself, and soon you will know that the addition of wine to cookery means the addition of flavor that no other ingredient can supply.

Lest you be abstemious and hesitate to introduce alcohol into your food for fear of prandial befuddlement, be assured that in nearly all cases there is nothing heady about liquors in cookery. During the process of heating or cooking, the alcohol itself is driven off, leaving nothing more intoxicating than a very delicious flavor.

Perhaps old scruples may caution you to keep the wine bottle out of the seasoning closet, for goodness' sake. But if you want only a gentle shove to become a user of wines in food, let the honored St. Paul administer the shove:

Drink no longer water, but use a little wine for thy stomach's sake, and thine own infirmities.

I Timothy V: 23

# DESSERTS

A word in praise of simple desserts suggests itself here. Meals carefully seasoned to excel in taste do not need overly sweet desserts to console their eaters. Instead, they need what a dessert is ideally conceived to be — a savory, refreshing, uncloying dish, designed more to be a harmonious ending to a delicious meal than to fill any dietary want.

Tempting ices are crowns for good repasts, or fruits in their season, with a bit of choice cheese to tie them to what has gone before. Apples blushing in beauty, served with walnuts oven-roasted in their shells, and old port wine make a fitting end to the finest dinner.

So herbs and wine and food, joined in joyous company, can assure an unending procession of delectable meals, and will cause family and guests to bless the name of the cook. Our friend Carl quotes an old adage to its marked advantage:

Hunger is also a good cook.

To you housewives who have dreamed of careers and find yourselves with nothing but "three meals a day" are rededicated the words of Euphon, a very wise old Greek comic:

A cook is fully as useful as a poet.

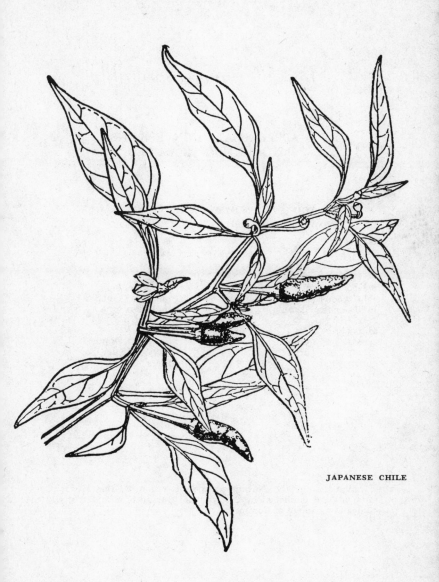

JAPANESE CHILE

# Metric Conversion Table*

## APPROXIMATE CONVERSIONS TO METRIC MEASURES

| When You Know | Multiply By | To Find |
|---|---|---|
| | WEIGHT | |
| ounces (oz.) | 28 | grams (g.) |
| pounds (lb.) | 0.45 | kilograms (kg.) |
| | VOLUME | |
| teaspoons (tsp.) | 5 | milliliters (ml.) |
| tablespoons (tbsp.) | 15 | milliliters (ml.) |
| fluid ounces (fl. oz.) | 30 | milliliters (ml.) |
| cups (c.) | 0.24 | liters (l.) |
| pints (pt.) | 0.47 | liters (l.) |
| quarts (qt.) (liquid) | 0.95 | liters (l.) (liquid) |
| (dry) | 1.1 | liters (l.) (dry) |
| gallons (gal.) | 3.8 | liters (l.) |

* Adapted from the November 1972 Revision of the Metric Conversion Card published by the National Bureau of Standards, United States Department of Commerce.

## APPROXIMATE CONVERSIONS
## FROM METRIC MEASURES

### WEIGHT

| | | |
|---|---|---|
| grams (g.) | 0.035 | ounces (oz.) |
| kilograms (kg.) | 2.2 | pounds (lb.) |

### VOLUME

| | | |
|---|---|---|
| milliliters (ml.) | 0.03 | fluid ounces (fl. oz.) |
| liters (l.) | 2.1 | pints (pt.) |
| liters (l.) (liquid) | 1.06 | quarts (qt.) (liquid) |
| (dry) | 0.91 | quarts (qt.) (dry) |
| liters (l.) | 0.26 | gallons (gal.) |

# Index